The Gender-Technology Relation

The Gender-Technology Relation

Contemporary Theory and Research

Edited by Keith Grint and Rosalind Gill

Taylor & Francis
Publishers since 1798

UK   Taylor & Francis Ltd., 4 John St., London WC1N 2ET
USA   Taylor & Francis Inc., 1900 Frost Road, Suite 101, Bristol, PA 19007

First published 1995

**A Catalogue Record for this book is available from the British
Library**

ISBN 0 7484 0160 1
ISBN 0 7484 0161 X (pbk)

**Library of Congress Cataloging-in-Publication Data are available
on request**

Typeset in 11/13pt Times by Solidus (Bristol) Limited

*Printed in Great Britain by Burgess Science Press, Basingstoke on
paper which has a specified pH value on final paper manufacture of not
less than 7.5 and is therefore 'acid free'.*

Contents

Acknowledgments

This collection has its origins in the conferences on Gender and Technology organized at the Centre for Research into Innovation, Culture and Technology (CRICT) at Brunel University. We would like to thank the Economic and Social Research Council's Programme on Information and Communication Technologies for supporting the conferences and all those who helped organize them, particularly: Donna Baston, Cynthia Cockburn, Claire Fisher, Christine Hine, Janet Low, Janet Rachel and Steve Woolgar. Rosalind Gill would also like to thank Thomas Gill and Andy Pratt for providing welcome distractions from work – in Thomas's case invariably in the wee small hours; and Keith Grint would like to thank Kris for the lego model of Marx's Mode of Production, Beki for her sense of humour, Katy for occasionally not using the phone, and Sandra for an early lesson in degenderizing car maintenance.

Introduction

The Gender-Technology Relation: Contemporary Theory and Research

Rosalind Gill and Keith Grint

What is the relationship between gender and technology? Are technologies inherently masculine? What sort of assumptions about gender go into their design, production and use? Are technologies implicated in women's oppression or could they play a part in women's liberation? Do the rapid changes we are witnessing in medical, industrial and information technologies pose threats to or offer opportunities for women? These are just some of the empirical questions which this book sets out to answer, by bringing together a selection of new articles by prominent writers in the field. Equally important to the book are a series of theoretical issues, concerning the ways in which the nature of the gender-technology relation can be understood. The collection contains articles which address one of the major theoretical debates of the 1990s: the relationship between feminism and social constructivism. Does constructivism pose a threat to, or provide a potential ally for, the feminist movement?

The last fifteen years have seen the development of an important new field of research: feminist studies of technology. Growing out of technology studies and feminist critiques of science, this work represents a significant and exciting body of research. To date, most energy has been expended by workers in this field producing detailed empirical studies of particular types of technology, for example, reproductive technologies. Whilst these have been valuable and illuminating, this focus has had two implications: firstly, there have been few attempts to examine the issues raised by *different* technologies, and secondly, theoretical understandings of the gender-technology relation remain underdeveloped. This book aims to begin to redress both these omissions. The articles address a range of different technologies, from cervical screening to telephones, and from food processors to software design. By including discussion of a wide variety of technologies and technological cultures, we hope to give some indication of both the generality and the specificity of the issues raised by particular technologies. Are the gender issues raised by computer hackers' culture the same as those in a software installation? What questions are raised by new reproductive technologies that might also be relevant to understanding domestic appliances? Whilst it is clearly crucial to study technologies in their own specific contexts of use, design and production, it is also important that we do not foreclose the possibility of constructing more wide-ranging theoretical understandings of the gender-technology relation. We no longer need to argue the case that the relations between gender and technology deserve attention; that argument has been won. Our task now is to explore the *nature* of gender-technology relations. Fifteen years on from the early discussions, it is time to take stock and to ask where work on gender and technology should be going theoretically, methodologically and politically.

In this chapter we set the scene for the debates and studies which follow, by providing an introduction to a variety of perspectives on gender and technology. We start our consideration by examining the widely held conviction that technologies are masculine. This perspective – in various guises – lies at the heart of most theoretical work on gender-technology relations, and has its origin in a set of assumptions about what counts as technical knowledge. The next three sections consider three positions on gender and technology: eco-feminism, liberal feminism, and the more historical perspective which sees technology as masculine culture. The latter perspective is discussed in some detail, as it represents (in our view) the most sophisticated attempt to theorize gender-technology relations. We raise a number of critical points in relation to the perspective, before going on to examine some of the overlaps, tensions and dilemmas raised by the nascent dialogue between this feminist perspective and social constructivism. The issues raised have significance far beyond considerations of gender and technology; at their core are disagreements about the nature of power and patriarchy, about how we should understand gendered subjectivity or identity, the role of the analyst, and the kinds of epistemological positions which operate as 'foundations' for each perspective. By the end of this chapter – and certainly by the end of the book – we hope to have shown that in attempting to make sense of the gender-technology relation, one must necessarily engage with a whole series of questions which lie at the heart of contemporary debates right across the social sciences. But whilst these questions – in their broadest sense, questions about modernism and postmodernism – are often discussed in abstract and esoteric ways, here we hope to illuminate them via engagements with what might be regarded as particular concrete phenomena – the relations between gender and technology.

Gender and Technology

The cultural association between masculinity and technology in Western societies is hard to exaggerate. It operates not only as a popular assumption – from which much sexist humour about women's 'technical incompetence' has been generated – but also as an academic 'truth'. Some analysts see it as biological in origin, others as social, but there are few who seek explicitly to challenge the idea that technology and masculinity go together. Even feminist writers, usually at the forefront of attacks on assumptions about gender, have mostly accepted the association, and, rather than challenging its existence, have sought to understand how and why this state of affairs has come about – and how it might be disrupted. Faulkner and Arnold, introducing a collection of articles on the subject, give voice to a common belief:

> To talk about women and technology in the same breath seems strange, even incongruous. Technology is powerful, remote, incomprehensible, inhuman, scientific, expensive and – above all – *male*. What does it have to do with women? (Faulkner and Arnold, 1985, p. 1, emphasis in original)

Whilst this quotation captures the tone of much feminist writing about technology, it is not the whole story. Interestingly, alongside the belief that technology is masculine, there exists in feminist writing a different argument – namely, a seemingly paradoxical appreciation that women are *not* entirely alienated from technology. Indeed, as feminist writers have argued, historically, women could be understood to have invented early technologies, and they continue to have relations to technology which are not characterized wholly by fear and alienation (Wajcman, 1992; Faulkner and Arnold, 1985). Some feminists see as a key task the 'recovery' of those female inventors and technologists who have been 'hidden from history' (Rothschild, 1983). Women's contributions to technological innovation, overlooked by male historians of the subject, are 'rescued' and accorded the respect which is rightfully theirs.

More fundamentally, feminist writers on technology have been concerned to interrogate the very nature of what counts as technical (Cockburn,

1992; Wajcman, 1991). They have shown that the technical has been defined in such a way as to exclude both those technologies which women invented and those which are primarily used by women. The link between masculinity and technology is thus an ideological link. Maureen McNeil (1987) warns that we should not accept too readily these ideological representations, but should retain a 'healthy scepticism' about the assumption that men have, and women lack, technological knowledge.

What is clear from feminist writing on technology, then, is that there is a dynamic tension between the view that technology is closely related to masculinity, and a perspective which sees this apparent association as itself ideological, based upon a narrow and specific understanding of the technical and a set of exclusions which position women outside the technical realm. Feminist analyses see-saw between these contrary views, trying to sever the link between masculinity and technology, whilst simultaneously attempting to acknowledge the force and effects of this deeply held cultural assumption. It is a difficult tension to negotiate, and mostly, as we shall show, feminist research remains within, rather than outside, the ideological problematic set by the assumption that masculinity and technology are intimately related.

Eco-Feminism

One response to the perceived link between masculinity and technology has come from eco-feminists. Writers in this tradition see technology as an example of the way in which men try to dominate and control both nature and women. From this perspective, women are seen as being essentially close to, and in tune with, nature. As Susan Griffin puts it:

> We [women] can read bodies with our hands, read the earth, find water, trace gravity's path. We know what grows and how to balance one thing against another ... and even if ... they [men] have transformed this earth, we say, the truth is, to this day, women still dream. (Griffin, 1984, p. 175)

This closeness to nature is conceived of as being rooted in biology, specifically in women's capacity to give birth. From this biological 'fact' flow a number of 'radical implications'.

> I have come to believe ... that female biology – the diffuse, intense sensuality radiating from the clitoris, breasts, uterus, vagina; the lunar cycles of menstruation; the gestation and fruition of life which

can take place in the female body – has far more radical implications than we have yet come to appreciate. (Rich, 1977, p. 39)

Women's biology, it is argued, has led to a specific way of 'knowing' and experiencing the world, based on emotions, intuition and spirituality. Eco-feminists call for a celebration of the 'female values' which allegedly result from this – pacifism and nurturance. The eco-feminist position has been most powerfully articulated in relation to military technology, which is seen as the logical conclusion of masculine technological domination. It has also been influential in critiques of medical – especially reproductive – technologies, arguing that they represent patriarchal exploitation of women's bodies.

Part of the force and the attractiveness which eco-feminist arguments seem to hold lies in their very simplicity, and the way in which they bring to the fore questions about the gender politics of technologies. Ultimately, however, the essentialism of eco-feminism, its inability to deal with change, and its reproduction of traditional ideas about femininity – albeit in celebratory terms – make it flawed as a theoretical perspective and disempowering as a political one. It might be argued that the selection of values associated with nature is highly contentious. Why should nature be associated with creativity, tranquillity and harmony when it might also be seen as destructive, dangerously unpredictable and wild? There is something ironical about the fact that eco-feminists, and radical feminists more generally, locate women's essence, their power and their virtues, in their biology – reducing them specifically to their sexual and reproductive capacities – given the central role which feminists have played in challenging the idea that biology is destiny. Cross-cultural research has shown that there is no behaviour or meaning which is universally associated with masculinity or femininity; they are socially constructed and changing categories. Moreover, the values ascribed to women by eco-feminists originate in women's subordination; precisely those characteristics which other feminists have tried to historicize and have shown to be contingent – the product of oppression – are here valorized as essentially feminine. As Lynne Segal (1987) has argued, it is difficult not to see in this the politics of despair.

Eco-feminist positions suffer from another kind of determinism, in addition to the biological determinism discussed above. In this variant, society and technology are conflated, such that it is assumed that the essentially patriarchal nature of technology can simply be read off from the patriarchal nature of society. As such there seems to be no point in actually studying any particular technology, since its patriarchal nature can be assumed in advance. Perhaps more importantly, it also leaves no space for negotiation or resistance, and the only path open to feminists is one of absolute rejection of technology – and indeed of society (Van Zoonen, 1992). Society is presumed to be made up of two discrete cultures – a male (patriarchal) one and an undervalued female one. The only principled course of action for eco-feminists is separatism – to retreat into their female culture and produce 'woman-friendly', feminine technologies and, alongside them, feminine intellectual work – 'gynocriticism' and 'gynoscience' (such as Daly, 1979).

Liberal Feminism

If for the eco-feminists technology is inherently and inevitably patriarchal, then a different view is put forward by liberal feminists. For them, technology itself is neutral; what is at issue is the different ways in which men and women are positioned in relation to it. Women are conceived of as 'lagging behind' in their understanding and use of new technologies, and indeed in the fields of science and technology more generally, as a result of the roles which they have had to take on in a sexist society. For liberal feminists women and men are seen as both equal and, at some fundamental level, the same, sharing a basic humanity and rationality. However, women's potential, it is argued, has been distorted by gender stereotyping. Women have been forced to take on particular sex roles (such as housewife and mother) which have concealed their true nature and capabilities. From this perspective, then, gender is conceived of as a system of representations, an ideology, which has been overlaid on authentic, unspoiled and equal human beings. The significance which is accorded to gender by liberal feminists varies. In some inflections its effects are seen as profound, it having spread its tentacles, through socialization processes, into women's very sense of who they are and what they can expect; in others, gender is seen purely as a set of stereotypes whose effects, it would appear, are relatively discrete and superficial; gender is seen not in terms of social structure but as 'the summation of numerous small-scale deprivations' (Walby, 1990, p. 4). According to this latter view, it is stereotyped notions of what is appropriate work for women which keep them out of such fields as engineering or computing (Swords-Isherwood, 1985).

To combat what they see as the pernicious effects of gender stereotyping on women's relationship to technologies, liberal feminists have advanced a whole series of programmes designed to help women 'catch up' – such as information campaigns to encourage women into 'non-traditional' careers, special educational or training programmes for women in science, engineering and computing, and affirmative action policies (see Cockburn, 1987,

1991, and Van Nostrand, 1993, for a critical analysis of training and equal opportunities in organizations). These initiatives have had limited success. For some, this is read as an indication that 'more imaginative and far reaching programmes of positive action are required' (Faulkner and Arnold, 1985, pp. 9–10). However, it is also possible to see the lack of social transformation brought about by these policies as resulting from the flawed theoretical perspective of liberal feminism.

One criticism that has been raised in relation to liberal feminism is that technology itself is not subjected to critical analysis (Karpf, 1987); it is thought of as 'an independent factor affecting social relations without being affected by them' (Van Zoonen, 1992, p. 14). As such, liberal feminism stands in stark contrast to much feminist writing about technologies which has argued that technologies 'bear the imprimatur of their social context' (Karpf, 1987, p. 162), that is, that they come to embody in their very design certain sets of gender relations or assumptions about gender. This view may itself be problematic. But, as we will argue later, it is not necessary to argue that technologies *embody* gender relations in order to highlight the relevance of the wider matrix of meanings ascribed to technologies for gender relations.

The 'flip side' of liberal feminism's view of technology as neutral is the tendency to see women as the problem and to demand that they overcome the effect of sex role stereotyping and adjust themselves to technology. Although, in an abstract sense, sex roles are held to be imprisoning for both men and women, in practice liberal feminists have been preoccupied with the changes which *women* will have to make, and have left masculinity unchallenged. The male is treated as the norm, and women are supposed to adopt masculine ways of relating to technology.

Liberal feminism is clearly theoretically underdeveloped. Its critique of existing social relations does not bear sustained analysis, since gender is presented both as being profoundly important (the primary division in society) and simultaneously as having had no impact on technologies or any other social products. Its idea of a true and unspoiled human nature which lies untouched behind the distortion of gender is difficult to maintain. By recognizing the importance of processes of sex-role stereotyping and socialization, liberal feminism acknowledges the influence of society on individual identities and 'seems just a step away from the idea that identity is not predetermined but socially constructed' (Van Zoonen, 1992, p. 15). The problem is that it offers no principled way of distinguishing between those aspects of identity which are deemed to be natural and authentic and those which are seen as socially constructed. Finally, its assertion that gender is the primary division in society has led to a neglect of other dimensions of power, in particular those of class and 'race', and to a tendency to ignore differences between women.

Technology as Masculine Culture

The last decade has witnessed the emergence of a powerful critique of both the liberal and the eco-feminist positions. This challenged the view that women's uneasy relationship to technology resulted from a lack of access to technical training or employment, and from the effects of sex-role stereotyping. It also rejected the idea that women's absence from the technological domain could be understood by reference to the idea that there is some essential difference between the ways in which women and men relate to the world. Instead, it argued that women's alienation from technology is a product of the historical and cultural construction of technology as masculine (Cockburn, 1983, 1985, 1992, 1993; Cockburn and Ormrod, 1993; Wajcman, 1991). Masculinity and technology are conceived of as being symbolically intertwined, such that technical competence has come to constitute an integral part of masculine gender identity, and, conversely, a particular idea of masculinity has become central to our very definition of technology. As Wajcman puts it, 'the culture of masculinity ... is largely coterminous with the culture of technology' (1991, p. 19).

Technology, from this perspective, is seen as being much more than simply artefacts or 'hardware', but also refers to the knowledge and practices which are involved in its use (MacKenzie and Wajcman, 1985). These are thought of as both expressing and consolidating relations among men:

> [Technology] fundamentally embodies a culture or a set of social relations made up of certain beliefs, desires and practices. Treating technology as a culture has enabled us to see the way in which technology is expressive of masculinity and how, in turn, men characteristically view themselves in relation to those machines. (Wajcman, 1991, p. 149)

One of the strengths of this body of work has been its attempt to locate the cultural connection between masculinity and technology historically. This has proved a valuable corrective to the ahistoricism and essentialism of some other perspectives. Women's exclusion and alienation from technology is seen as a consequence of a number of changes which occurred during the industrial revolution and the early development of capitalism in the West. Most notable among these changes was the separation of the public and private spheres and the move of manufacturing out of dwellings and into factories. This resulted in a gendered division of labour which 'laid the foundations for male dominance of technology' (Wajcman, 1991, p. 21).

For some writers the introduction of capitalism is seen as decisive in *originating* women's exclusion from the knowledge and practices which constitute technology (Griffiths, 1985). Technologies which emerged in the period of the industrial revolution – or 'capitalist technologies' – are presented as being 'more masculine' than previous technologies (Faulkner and Arnold, 1985). This view stresses the idea that the shape of contemporary relations between men and women arose as a result of the introduction of capitalism and the legislation which accompanied it, denying women property rights and educational opportunities.

In other formulations, the development of capitalism is seen as *consolidating*, rather than originating, power differences between the sexes and their relationship to technology (Cockburn, 1985; McNeil, 1987). In a subtle and sensitive analysis, Cynthia Cockburn (1985) has argued that, as capitalism developed, already existing power differences between women and men were given a *new articulation* in relation to class differences, such that women lost out both as women and as workers. The machinery that was developed for the new factories was designed by and for men, and reflected male power as well as capitalist domination. Cockburn describes how male craft workers actively resisted the entry of women into the new spheres of production, refusing them membership of unions which would have offered them the means to bargain collectively for better positions. As such, women were denied the opportunity to 'enter and defend jobs deemed skilled' (Faulkner and Arnold, 1985, p. 8), and were forced into those jobs considered unskilled and which were accorded the lowest rates of pay.

> It is the most damning indictment of skilled working class men and their unions that they excluded women from membership and prevented them from gaining competences that could have secured them a decent living. (Cockburn, 1985, p. 39)

It could be argued that there is a dialectical relationship between women and 'skill', such that women are concentrated in jobs which are deemed unskilled, and, conversely, that those occupations in which women constitute the majority of workers come to be seen as relatively less skilled than those dominated by men. 'Skill' is not some objectively identifiable quality, but rather is an ideological category, one over which women were (and continue to be) denied the rights of contestation.

The debate about the origins of the cultural association between masculinity and technology is part of a much wider set of issues concerning whether 'patriarchy' can be said to pre-date Western capitalism, and to what extent asymmetrical gender power relations are necessary to, or are part of the logic of, capitalism itself. As a whole, it can be understood as part of the engagement of feminism with Marxism, and has been particularly valuable in highlighting the (frequent) invisibility of gender divisions within Marxian accounts.

Feminist research stresses that the exclusion of women from technology is as much a feature of contemporary Western society as it was during the early development of capitalism. Women are still rarely involved in the design of technologies, which are 'shaped by male power and interests' (Wajcman, 1992). Those who argue that technology is intimately related to masculine culture point out that the effects of this are profound. For them, technologies are not neutral artefacts which would be the same whether they were produced by men or women, but rather objects which 'bear the imprimatur of their social context' (Karpf, 1987, p. 162) – including the gender relations which constitute that context. Work on the 'social shaping' of technologies has highlighted the way in which military, industrial, national and class interests shape the design of a vast number of technological artefacts. Feminists have pointed out that technologies are also shaped by interests of a deeply gendered character.

> The effect of male control of technology – and women's exclusion and alienation from it – is that the technologies produced for use by women may be highly inappropriate to women's needs, and even pernicious (e.g. the Pill) as well as embodying male ideologies of how women should live. (Karpf, 1987, p. 159)

Technologies, it is argued, are *gendered* (Cockburn, 1992). As a result of the context or culture of their production they come to embody particular assumptions about social relations, to embody 'patriarchal values' (Wajcman, 1991, p. 17). They can thus be seen as an index or sign of women's continuing oppression. More than this, however, once created, they come to constitute part of the *source* of this oppression. It is this double aspect – as both sign and source of women's oppression – which Cockburn (1992) describes as the 'circuit' of technology. Technology becomes physically implicated in the domination of women by men; it is 'constituted by, but also helps to constitute, social relations' (Karpf, 1987, p. 162).

One of the key concepts used by those who see technology as 'masculine culture' is identity. As we noted earlier, technology is seen not merely as hardware, as objects 'out there', but also as something which has important symbolic dimensions which enter into gender identity. Masculinity, it is argued, is partly constructed through notions of technical competence: 'It is evident that men identify with technology and through their identification with technology form bonds with one another' (Wajcman, 1991, p. 141). In contrast, the idea that women lack technical competence is not merely a sex stereotype but 'does indeed become part of feminine gender identity' (Wajcman, 1991, p. 155). Identity, then, seems to be posited as an important mechanism through which the seemingly natural association between masculinity and technology gets reproduced. This is given a 'performative' inflection in some accounts, such that using particular technologies is seen as 'doing gender' (West and Zimmerman, 1987). Cockburn (1992) makes this explicit, asserting that gender is 'more of a doing than a being'. From this perspective, Wajcman (1991) suggests that one reason that most of the liberal feminist programmes designed to 'encourage' women into technical spheres have failed is that women are actively resisting technology because of the implications for their feminine identities. Sherry Turkle's (1988) work on girls' and boys' uses of computers underlines this point. She argued that women use their rejection of computers to assert something about themselves as women: in rejecting computers they are *doing femininity*. To enter the field, she suggests, would be to endanger their very sense of femininity.

The notion of identity allows a way of linking discussions of large-scale social structures and historical trends with everyday, individual practices. This is summed up well by Margaret Lowe Benston:

> Male power over technology is both a product of and a reinforcement for their power in society. Even at the household level, every time a man repairs the plumbing or a sewing machine while a woman watches, a communication about her helplessness and inferiority is made. (1992, p. 37)

It is in such mundane everyday experiences, it would seem, that the association of masculinity and technology is reproduced.

The perspective that considers technology as masculine culture is far more satisfying than either the liberal or the eco-feminist accounts. The understandings of both gender and technology are sophisticated and the emphasis on the *relation* between them is central to the articles which make up this book. Nevertheless, there are a number of problems and tensions in this work which are worth discussing if we are to move forward in our theoretical understanding of the gender-technology relation.

The Essentialist Drift

The essentialism which besets radical and eco-feminist positions has proved extremely difficult to eradicate, even from the work of those authors who disavow it. The notion of a fundamental difference between men's and women's values underlies much more work in this vein. Faulkner and Arnold (1985), for example, argue that technology is 'alienating to women in the sense that the goals embodied in it are not necessarily women's goals' (p. 6). They point explicitly to military technology as an example of this disjuncture between 'women's values' and technology, and ask us to note the significance of the fact that weapons of destruction are often 'penis shaped', whilst reaffirming the need to 'take the toys from the boys' (p. 2). The notion of 'women's goals' is subjected to no critical interrogation; the idea that women as a group share specific goals and interests which, as in eco-feminist writing, are deemed to be anti-militaristic and pacifist, is implicitly accepted. Men as a group are also deemed to have their own distinctive set of interests which are not just different from, but inimical to, those of women (Karpf, 1987; Wajcman, 1991). A slightly different variant of this argument is found in Benston's claim that 'technology is a language' which does not allow women to 'say' what they want. That is, it is structured in such a way as to preclude the making of women's meanings. This argument suffers from the same problems of essentialism as Dale Spender's (1985) work on men's and women's different languages, on which it draws (see Segal, 1987; Cameron, 1985).

The problem with this work – a problem which, as we argue later, is common to much work which utilizes the notion of patriarchy – is that the relations between the key terms, 'men' or 'males', 'masculinity' and 'patriarchy', are not fully explicated. The writers draw on and move between the different terms, and different senses of the same term, inconsistently, in order to do particular discursive work. As a discourse analyst might point out, there is considerable variability in the way that these key terms are used (Potter and Wetherell, 1987), and it is this variability which allows writers in this tradition to explicitly disavow and yet implicitly draw upon essentialist accounts of the gender-technology relation.

Dilemmas of Ideology

A central feature of this perspective is the argument that technologies are not neutral but gendered, and that the masculinity of technologies will not be changed merely by the inclusion of more women in the design process.

A gendered approach to technology cannot be reduced to a view which treats technology as a set of neutral artefacts manipulated by men in their own interests. While it is the case that men dominate the scientific and technical institutions, it is perfectly plausible that there will come a time when women are more fully represented in these institutions without transforming the direction of technical development. (Wajcman, 1991, p. 25)

It would seem from this argument that technologies acquire their gendered features by dint of more than the prevalence of male actors in their design, since the presence of more women is seen as not enough to change their character fundamentally. Yet, at other times, it is precisely the domination by men of the creation of technologies which explains their gendered nature. Men are depicted as designing technologies which are 'inappropriate' or even 'pernicious' for women's use (Karpf, 1987) and 'male interests' are said to shape their eventual form. Here we see an apparent contradiction, which revolves around the terms 'men' and 'male interests'. On one hand, the gendering of technology is held to have little to do with the prevalence of actual male subjects (and the absence of female ones) per se, but is implicitly attributed to some 'bigger' structure such as 'masculinity' or 'patriarchy' which transcends individual men. On the other hand, actual embodied males are deemed to act in terms of their own 'male interests', with the implication – sometimes made explicit – that the presence of women would, in fact, make a difference – that women would design *different* technologies.

In the first version, a notion of ideology is implicitly being mobilized. Masculine or patriarchal ideology is presented as subjecting both men and women, such that involving more women in technological design would be fruitless, or at least insufficient, as a measure to generate change. In the second version, however, no notion of ideology is posited, and men are depicted as simply acting in their own (male) interests. The implication is that if women were involved in envisioning technologies, they too would be able to design artefacts in line with their own (female) interests.

There are two issues here. The first concerns the use of these two inconsistent arguments. Wajcman argues that it is 'the ideology of masculinity that has this intimate bond with technology' (1991, p. 137) and not actual embodied men, some of whom may feel no connection to technology whatsoever. She draws on Bob Connell's work to argue that 'hegemonic masculinity ... is strongly associated with aggressiveness and the capacity for violence' and with 'control of technology' (1991, p. 143). Yet, as we have seen, there are many occasions on which an entirely different stance is taken: namely that men simply act in their own sectional interests in designing technologies. To point this out is not mere pedantry, for this inconsistency goes right to the heart of this perspective, to the question of the very nature of the relationship between gender and technology.

Clearly, a notion of ideology is important. Without it we are left with the kind of essentialism espoused by the eco-feminists. But even if we take at face value the claim that it is the ideology of masculinity which has the connection with technology, a problem still remains: the nature of the relationship between the ideology of masculinity and actual human subjects is not addressed. Yet this is of utmost importance in understanding how the cultural connection between masculinity and technology is reproduced. The notion of identity seems to be posited as central, but the precise mechanism through which it works is not discussed. The issue of how the ideology of masculinity serves to perpetuate women's alienation from, and oppression by, technology remains largely untheorized. This represents a key task for the development of this perspective.

The Problem with 'Patriarchy'

The tension between essentialist accounts and those which utilize a notion of ideology is a common feature of research which rests upon the concept of patriarchy. Whilst this concept is by no means central to all work which sees technology as masculine culture, it is nevertheless invoked sufficiently to merit some attention (Faulkner and Arnold, 1985; McNeil, 1987; Wajcman, 1991, 1992).

The use of the term 'patriarchy' in social scientific writing can be traced back to Weber (1948) who used it to refer to a particular form of household organization in which the father is dominant. Since then, it has been widely developed in feminist writing and has largely lost any connotations of generational power. It is now used primarily to capture 'the depth, pervasiveness and interconnectedness of different aspects of women's subordination' (Walby, 1990, p. 4). As Cockburn (1992) puts it: 'The notion supposed the existence in all societies of some kind of normative arrangements for governing reproduction, sex and gender' (p. 42).

A major problem with much writing on patriarchy is its tendency to imply that it is a universal and transhistorical phenomenon (Rowbotham, 1981; Segal, 1987). Patriarchy is held to exist in all cultures and to have existed in most, if not all, historical periods, so to use the concept is frequently to 'invoke a generality of male domination without being able to specify historical limits, changes or differences' (Barrett, 1980, p. 14). Clearly, this is a particular problem for radical feminist writing, but accounts which take a materialistic or historical angle are not immune from difficulties. The question is: how useful is the concept of patriarchy for writers who wish to make historically and culturally grounded analyses of the gender-technology relation?

The problem for work in this vein is in theorizing the relationship between patriarchy and other forms of oppression and domination. This has been an enduring headache for feminists, particularly those located within a Marxian tradition. Zillah Eisenstein (1979), in one of the best known and most respected attempts at resolution, argues that patriarchy preceded capitalism, but 'capitalism uses patriarchy and patriarchy is defined by the needs of capital' (p. 28). Here, then, patriarchy is given a (token) analytic independence, but is then referred to solely in terms of its functions for capital. As Michele Barrett (1980) has argued, almost all materialist writing on patriarchy falls prey to this problem. As such, the theoretical value of the concept is unclear:

> It is not clear to me what is being claimed here for the concept of patriarchy. For if patriarchal relations assume the form of class relations in capitalism, then however centrally the authors may pose patriarchal relations in the subordination of women, they do not resolve the question of the effectivity of patriarchy as the determinant of women's oppression in capitalism. (Barrett, 1980, p. 17)

This theoretical problem can lead, in writing about technology, to confusion about the extent to which men's interests and the interests of capital can be conflated. Margaret Lowe Benston, for example, argues: 'The logic of ruling-class men then leads to a technology that reflects ruling-class men's experience and view of reality ... [T]his view of reality is, to a large extent, shared by other men in the society' (1992, p. 35). Here, ruling-class and working-class men are given an identity of interests, and treated as a homogeneous group whose technologies alienate and oppress women.

If the theoretical value of the notion of patriarchy seems tenuous and problematic, then there are also serious doubts about its practical use in specific analyses. As Håpnes and Sørensen (in this volume) argue, the effects of patriarchy are difficult to 'unpick' and to differentiate from other structures. They point out that a reanalysis of Thomas Edison's work would face great problems 'in differentiating between the effects of Edison as a man versus Edison as an American versus Edison as a capitalist versus Edison as a person with particular cognitive characteristics'.

To be fair, the best research in this tradition does acknowledge this problem. Wajcman (1991), for example, notes the problems of disentangling the effects of class and race from those of gender. Nevertheless, the question remains of how useful the notion of patriarchy is when it is so difficult to operationalize in research on the gender-technology relation.

The Tendency to Functionalism

The final problem we wish to consider in relation to the 'technology as masculine culture' tradition concerns what we see as its tendency towards a kind of functionalism. As we noted earlier, a central theme of this perspective concerns the symbolic dimensions of technology and the way in which they enter into gender identity, such that an involvement or non-involvement with technologies is seen as part of the practice of 'doing gender'.

This performative turn in feminist research – and in constructivist work more generally – has been very valuable in drawing attention to the fact that the meanings of technologies do not merely exist 'out there' in the public realm, but become integral to our very sense of self. However, there is a danger that, in stressing the performative aspects of the gender-technology relation, the arguments become functionalist, explaining men's and women's relationship to technology only in terms of its functions for gender identity.

Cynthia Cockburn, dismissing the view that women's lack of involvement with many technologies is attributable to fear or passivity, has argued that women may *actively resist* technology because it is stereotyped as an activity appropriate for men. For a woman to enter into the technological field, she suggests, may be to forsake her very sense of femininity. This argument, then, is similar to that of Sherry Turkle, discussed earlier. Cockburn (1993) argues:

> If an actor behaves as a man or woman within the frame of a technology study, manifesting certain authority or defence, say, that behaviour, exemplifying certain power relations, is not explainable without reference to those longer lived and widely spread patterns of culture and relationship, particularly those of class, 'race' and gender, that span between the worlds within and without the laboratory of a technology study.

It is the first part of this passage which we are interested in here. The problem is that the issue of what it means to act as a man or a woman – within the confines of a technology study or anywhere else – is answered in advance. That which should be the analytic question is, instead, built into the research as a set of assumptions. The result is that only people who have been identified independently in advance as men or women can be seen as doing masculinity or femininity respectively. Moreover, only those practices which reinforce or reproduce existing patterns of gender relations are 'noticed' analytically. Gender relations, then, are always seen to be reproduced. There is no space for challenge or change and no theoretically principled way of dealing with those occasions in which biologically female actors engage in behaviours defined as masculine (or vice versa). It is a half-hearted kind of 'performative turn' which only remarks upon the occasions when a man repairs household appliances and a woman watches (Benston, 1992), and does not even ask whether or how gender relations might be challenged by a woman doing such repairs. It presents a bleak, and sometimes tautological, picture of the gender-technology relation: 'male use of technology communicates power and control ... [T]he whole realm of technology and the communication around it reinforces ideas of women's powerlessness' (Benston, 1992, p. 41). One implication of this view is that there is a stock of stable, routine ways through which gender is 'done', which are knowable in advance and can somehow be used as an index of the practice of masculinity or femininity. As such, it only directs our attention to those practices or performances of femininity or masculinity which are familiar, and which are assumed to 'exemplify' gender power relations.

Paradoxically, this view of gender relations being maintained by a limited number of (already familiar) practices – for example, the exercise of authority or defence – may actually lead us to *underestimate* the significance and persuasiveness of gender as a relation of dominance. Discourses of gender are fluid, and sexism is far more flexible than is traditionally assumed (Massey, 1991). As work on 'unequal opportunities' in employment has shown, discriminatory practice is maintained and justified in a whole range of ways, some of which even draw upon feminist discourse (Gill, 1993). Cockburn's analyses themselves acknowledge this point, showing, for example, that the ways in which men appropriate engineering as a masculine domain are far from obvious: 'At one moment, in order to fortify their identification with physical engineering, men dismiss the intellectual world as "soft". At the next moment, however, they need to appropriate sedentary intellectual engineering work for masculinity too' (Cockburn, 1985, p. 190). As her own analysis suggests, the practice of gender is much more complex and subtle than Cockburn's phrase 'if an actor behaves as a man or woman' would seem to imply. It is precisely this kind of detailed analysis which is needed if we are to understand the entangled relationship between gender and technology.

Feminism and Constructivism

One of the most exciting developments in research on technology in recent years has been the beginning of a debate between feminists and other researchers taking a broadly constructivist position. Many of the issues discussed so far in this chapter have been taken up and dramatized in this engagement, with arguments about patriarchy, essentialism and interpretative flexibility. It is becoming clear that many feminist writers see themselves as working both within and against what they characterize as a 'mainstream' social constructivist tradition (Cockburn, 1992, 1993; Wajcman, 1991, 1992; Singleton, this volume), seeing many confluences of interest, yet also struggling to place gender relations centrally on the agenda of sociological studies of technology.

In writing from this position there is a risk of ignoring important differences between the various bodies of work which constitute the 'broad church' of constructivism. There are at least as many differences between the various strands of constructivist thought as there are between feminism and constructivism. There is also a danger of reifying the idea of a strong mainstream tradition in relation to which feminist researchers see themselves as marginal. Cockburn, for example, attributes to actor network theory (ANT) the status of dominant orthodoxy, yet it would not be difficult to make the case that ANT is as marginal as feminism to social constructivism.

However, putting aside these qualifications, it is clear that there are significant ways in which feminist constructivism, as exemplified by work on technology as masculine culture, differs from other strands of constructivism. One criticism which feminists have levelled at ANT is that it makes gender invisible (Cockburn, 1992). By focusing on the design and development phases of an artefact's life, constructivist studies often fail to see women at all. This is not necessarily attributable to chance: the research focus *keeps shifting* to 'new arenas where women are scarcely present' (Berg and Lie, 1993). Cockburn (1992) argues that 'Ironically, women's invisibility has been increased by the shift we have made from technological impact studies to social shaping studies. For a hard fact remains that, in matters of technological change, women are more impacted upon than impacting' (p. 38).

Singling out actor network research, feminists have argued that in an important sense women are simply not seen as actors at all. In order to 'see' women analytically, it is necessary to move beyond the network as normally defined (Cockburn, 1992, 1993). More fundamentally, Berg and Lie (1993) accuse constructivist researchers of treating gender as synonymous with women, and thus of believing that gender is not relevant when women are absent.

This raises an issue for both 'mainstream' and feminist constructivist research, namely, how the relevance of anything will be manifested – or can be demonstrated – in empirical analyses. This has been the subject of considerable discussion in relation to interests (Woolgar, 1981; Callon and Law, 1982). For many constructivist writers, the notion of interests should not be used as an explanatory resource unless it can be clearly demonstrated within the frame of reference of the analysis. Against this some feminists have argued that it is perfectly reasonable to impute interests to particular actors in order to explain their behaviour. The imputation of interests must be reasoned for and is always contestable but is an important part of sociological analysis (Cockburn, 1992). Transposing this debate to gender we are left with the question of whether and how gender can be deemed relevant in any given situation. Constructivist researchers argue that if gender is relevant then it will become evident to the researcher. Their argument is similar to that of ethnomethodologists and conversation analysts who claim that gender will be oriented to by participants if it is relevant as a dimension in any given situation. The category, they argue, must not be imported by the analyst, but should be allowed to emerge from the study of participants' interactional orientations; everything that is relevant to the interaction will be displayed discursively.

This faith that 'it will all come out in the (discursive) wash', however, is disputed by feminists. In an important reanalysis of a conference paper and the discussion which followed it, Deborah Cameron (1989) neatly highlights the problems with this assumption. The issue in question was a conversation analytic paper which analysed a transcript of a telephone call to the emergency services following an incident of domestic violence. Cameron (1989) points out that in this paper (written and presented by a male conversation analyst) no mention was made of gender because the parties in the telephone call showed no 'obvious' sign of orienting to it. Not only was gender not mentioned in the paper, but in the discussion following its presentation no one brought up the issue either. 'Feminists present felt constrained not to point this out; they were sensitive to possible accusations of vulgarity and bias' (Cameron, 1989, p. 16). Thus, not only was gender deemed interactionally irrelevant in the account constructed by the paper, but a transcript would reveal that it was also, apparently, interactionally irrelevant to the conference discussion. Cameron argues that this was not the case at all – in fact, women felt silenced and met separately at the conference to discuss this. Silence, like absence from networks, is itself gendered. Moreover, Cameron argues that the relevance of gender was displayed in the telephone call analysed, but that the majority of the men at the conference were simply not sensitive to it. This raises a whole set of issues about the interpretative resources which (classed, gendered, 'raced') analysts bring to bear on their research, which are not even addressed by most constructivist researchers. As Berg and Lie (1993) argue, 'the relevance of gender does not spring to one's eyes unless gender is actively used as an analytical tool'. There is a problem, however, in that, if gender is used as an analytical tool, researchers run the risk of 'black-boxing' it, of treating its meanings as self-evident and stable, producing an artificial analytic closure. This is the basis of constructivists' attack on feminist research. Diverse, flexible and contra-dictory social practices are reduced to one thing, and analytic judgments are always made in advance. 'Feminist work is boring and predictable. You always know who done it right from the start: the plot is far too flat' (Hirschauer and Mol, 1993). The question which feminist research asks, it is argued, is how pre-existing social relations are expressed in and shape technologies (Ormrod, this volume). Feminists are accused of 'selective relativism', of seeing some things as socially constructed, but not others.

> [T]he gender of individuals is taken to be constructed, but this happened a long time ago in the dark ages of early childhood. It was a once in a lifetime experience, beyond words, out of reach for ever after. We were not born a woman, but we became so and the outcome of the process is that we *are* one. (Hirschauer and Mol, 1993)

Underlying the disagreements between feminists and other constructivists are fundamentally different epistemologies. Writing about ANT, Cockburn (1993) argues:

> The problem for us was the agnosticism in the ANT school concerning 'society' – that is a social world with distinguishable, if historically changing and culturally varied, structures existing outside and prior to the interactions of the observable laboratory or actor network.

Cockburn, like many other feminist researchers, employs an ostensive definition of society – concepts such as social structure are posited as background determinants of action. In contrast, ANT works with a thorough-going performative definition in which the very things treated as determi-nants of action in most sociological accounts are understood instead as consequences: 'Society is not what holds us together, it is what is held together. Social scientists have mistaken the effect for the cause' (Latour, 1986, p. 276).

ANT professes an epistemological or radical scepticism towards traditional sociological concepts, amongst them power and gender. Power is seen as a consequence of struggle, of attempts to enrol other actors, and not as something given and 'held' by particular actors. As such it is entirely counterpoised to most feminist understandings of power, which stress enduring relations of asymmetry and oppression. Cockburn (1993) argues that a theory of power which only stresses capacity is unable to account for gender relations in which power is often experienced as domination. Taking a stance against ANT, her characterization of gender relations may seem rather crude: 'Men dominate women as a sex, exploiting and controlling women's sexuality and reproductive capacities' (Cockburn, 1992, p. 42). This is as unable as ANT to grasp the diversity and flexibility of gender relations. Nevertheless, it does highlight an important weakness in actor network research to date: a failure to consider networks temporally. A theoretical imperative not to 'black-box' should not lead to the opposite failing: an inability to see that some networks are remarkably enduring. Power may be a consequence, accomplished and re-accomplished on a moment by moment basis and always contestable, but some networks are more stable than others.

It may be, as Cockburn says, that feminists and actor network theorists are asking different questions. In technology theory the key question has been how to explain change, while for feminists it seems more urgent to explain continuity, the enduring inequalities and the fact that gender relations survive so little changed through every successive wave of technological innovation. For feminists, research on technology is not just about adding to our academic knowledge, it is also an emancipatory project. One of the questions which it asks of any theoretical or methodological approach is whether and how it can contribute to women's liberation. Since feminism and other liberation movements have for so long been wedded to realist discourses, the challenges represented by constructivism and relativism present particular dilemmas. On the one hand, such positions offer the liberatory possibilities of deconstructing categories such as woman or man and all the ideological baggage which accompanies/constitutes them; on the other hand, feminists often feel they need to hold onto these very categories for political reasons. The deconstructive feminist critic may spend her days deconstructing gender categories, but find herself at the weekend demonstrating around 'a woman's right to choose' – mobilizing around the very category which she spends her working life deconstructing. Such tensions are not limited to feminists but apply to many involved in political struggles. It is precisely this desire to deconstruct the naturalness of the oppressive dichotomies which have constituted Western knowledge since the Enlightenment, combined with the need to intervene politically in the world, which led Stuart Hall to describe himself as 'a theoretical anti-humanist, but a political humanist'. The question is whether a realist or objectivist discourse is the only one appropriate for a liberatory project or whether constructivism may itself have emancipatory possibilities.

This question is taken up in the first part of the book, which considers contemporary theoretical perspectives on the gender-technology relation. Susan Ormrod's answer is unequivocal: constructivism, she argues, is essential if we are to discuss relations of gender and technology in all their specificity and difference – and thus to be able to challenge them. The social is discursively constructed, as are our very subjectivities. Ormrod is critical of what she sees as the implicit social theory which informs many feminist critiques of technology, arguing that it is reductive and conservative in effect, and relies upon problematic dualisms such as individual and society, and male and female. Her chapter looks in detail at the problems with the notion of patriarchy, and the conception of power upon which it rests. Rather than focusing our energy on examining how pre-existing social relations of patriarchy express and shape technology, she suggests that we should explore what post-structuralist approaches have to offer feminists. By way of examples, she discusses two distinct but related approaches – one a variant of the discursive analysis associated with Foucault, the other actor network approaches. Both these approaches, she suggests, avoid the problem of 'black-boxing' and allow for dynamic and sensitive analyses of the gender-technology relation.

A contrasting perspective is taken by Keith Grint and Steve Woolgar in their chapter. They do not seek to reinstate realism, but rather to show the similarities between feminism and constructivism in their 'nervousness' about following through the radical implications of their critique of essentialism. Grint and Woolgar argue that rather than disavowing essentialism altogether, both feminism and constructivism have simply replaced technological determinism with an equally problematic social determinism. According to this, the properties of any given technology are said to derive not from its internal technical capabilities but from the circumstances and social relations involved in its development.

Grint and Woolgar discuss a number of problems with this view, arguing that they arise from a failure to acknowledge the *textual character* of technologies. Advocating a new position, which they call post-essentialism, they argue that what counts as a masculine, feminine or neutral technology lies in the interpretations that are made of it, not in the technology itself. Theirs is an unashamedly epistemologically relativist position, and the chapter devotes considerable attention to considering possible feminist objections to it. They argue that realist commitments have not served feminism well, as 'the truth' about women has often been profoundly oppressive, and they highlight the liberatory potential of post-essentialism for feminism and other emancipatory struggles.

Case Studies

In the second part of the book, we present a series of case studies, each concerned with examining the gender-technology relation. The subject matter here is diverse, taking in medical technologies (Hirsch; Singleton), domestic appliances (Chabaud-Rychter), telecommunications (Frissen) and information technologies (Tierney; Håpnes and Sørenson). What unites the chapters is the concern they share with highlighting the different ways in which gender relations are implicated in the design, marketing, under-standing and use of technologies.

Valerie Frissen's chapter offers us a historical survey of the domestica-tion of the telephone in Europe and America. Initially presented to the public as a tool for business, the telephone quickly became a medium for social communications, overwhelmingly used by women. In the days before direct dialling, women were recruited in their thousands as operators, hired for the pleasant and discreet manner associated with Victorian femininity. Frissen shows how these women – 'the voice with a smile' – played a significant part in the development of new forms of social interaction.

Turning to the contemporary scene, Frissen asks what kind of role women are playing in the new telecommunications environments. She focuses on four areas of development, examining each for its gender implications. Discussing a variety of issues such as safety and security, sociability and entertainment, work and instrumentality, and access and availability, she raises questions about developments as diverse as the growth in erotic chatlines, the uptake of cellular phones and the implications of call tracing technologies for gender relations. None of these, she argues, are either wholly liberatory or wholly oppressive for women, but they present potential for changing gender relations.

Frissen argues that gender was and remains largely invisible to those involved in the development of telephone services. In stark contrast, Danielle Chabaud-Rychter's chapter highlights the *salience* of assumptions about gender amongst those involved in the design of kitchen appliances. Drawing on research in a French company which produces food processors, Chabaud-Rychter highlights the way in which women's cooking practices are 'configured' by designers, and translated into mechanical actions. She explores in detail the process by which domestic practices are itemized, categorized and counted in order to define markets for appliances. Interestingly, however, there is a 'double language' in use by designers: on one hand, the parameters of cooking practices are established and stabilized with precise measurements; on the other hand, the practical experience of the designers is drawn on liberally to explain or defend particular innovations. This double language produces objects which are hybrid, containing, in Chabaud-Rychter's words, 'both the domestic and the industrial worlds'.

The next two chapters focus on medical technologies. Hirsch's chapter, like Chabaud-Rychter's, is concerned in part with the relationship between public and private worlds. Hirsch reports on research into how married couples make sense of the increasingly rapid developments in new reproductive technologies (NRTs). He shows how two scenarios were repeatedly evoked by the couples he interviewed to express concern about how NRTs would be used. One scenario stressed the fear that NRTs could lead to children being seen merely as commodities – one more consumer item to be bought and sold. The other scenario conjured up an image of a 'brave new world' in which NRTs were used by 'big brother' to produce a master race. Hirsch notes that an interesting feature of these scenarios is that they draw on ideas not normally associated with 'conjugal reproduction': the market (consumerism) and the state ('big brother'). He suggests that the assumed separation between public and private (with its familiar gender mappings) in Euro-American culture is neither as clear-cut nor as durable as it once seemed.

Vicky Singleton's topic is the Cervical Screening Programme (CSP) established by the British government in the 1960s. Her chapter moves between the theoretical and the empirical levels as she explores what actor network approaches have to offer as a way of understanding the different actors involved in the CSP – health professionals, feminists and women's health activists, and lay women. She is simultaneously attracted to and critical of actor network approaches, arguing that they have not yet developed ways of incorporating difference, multiplicity and instability into their narratives and analyses. But feminism, she argues, faces similar problems. She shows that whilst feminist health activists offer women a voice which has been excluded from the 'government CSP actor network', they do so at the price of 're-black-boxing' and artificially unifying the category 'woman'. Singleton argues that we need a multi-perspectival approach, and need also to develop ways of thinking about the tension between our roles as analysts and our own political commitments.

In Singleton's chapter, we see clear echoes of the theoretical concern expressed by Ormrod and by Grint and Woolgar about the problems with the notion of patriarchy. This emerges as a central concern in the book as a whole, and is also taken up by Tove Håpnes and Knut Sørensen. They are concerned about what they see as a tendency in some feminist research to treat gender categories as static and pre-given. This leads to romantic and essentialist analyses, they argue. Like Grint and Woolgar, they suggest that we have not yet developed an adequate language for describing the different kinds of masculinities displayed in the context of design or production of technologies, and nor can we say categorically what it is about the properties of a technology which makes it either feminine or masculine. Attempting to avoid these problems, their own research focuses on the culture of computer hackers. They explore the different meanings which various groups of young people attribute to hacking and to hackers, showing, for example, how girls used the notion of 'hackers' as a metaphor for everything they disliked about computer science, whilst, in contrast, the hackers themselves saw what they did as being creative and a rejection of mainstream computing.

Tierney's chapter, which concludes the book, is also concerned with questions of culture. She presents a fascinating analysis of the informal and subtle ways in which a particular group of workers within a software company – 'the lads' – were systematically privileged, so that they progressed up the career ladder much more smoothly and much faster than other colleagues. Drawing on considerable research in an Irish software installation she demonstrates how this group of young, single (or at least childless) men, were able to capitalize upon an informal, but exclusive, network, which involved playing football and poker, eating lunch and drinking together. In the absence of a standardized meaning, within the company, for what a particular job was worth (in terms of salary, status and task content), the lads' network became a powerful means of earning bonuses, getting positive appraisals and securing promotions. The informal atmosphere, the arm's-length managerial policy, and the inexplicit promotions strategy, then, worked to benefit this group of workers at the expense of others – particularly the women within the company.

Although Tierney's research is located in one particular company, her analysis offers us a way of thinking about work and technological cultures which has a far broader relevance. It is hoped that her work, together with that of the other contributors to the book, will provide an inspiration to others to tackle the difficult nexus of questions that constitute the gender-technology relation. Our collective analyses suggest that there are neither grounds for utter pessimism nor for complete optimism, but there are 'cracks' or interstices, and there are spaces for struggle and change. We need to develop a new language for talking about gender-technology relations, a language which does not rely upon simply reproducing the old, oppressive dualisms, but, equally, does not efface real differences of power, access and control in relation to technology along gender, class, 'racial' and other lines. Alongside this theoretical project, a long-standing feminist political project remains: to develop gender-technology relations which will liberate and emancipate all women and men.

References

BARRETT, M. (1980) *Women's Oppression Today: Problems in Marxist Feminist Analysis*, London, Verso.

BENSTON, M.L. (1992) 'Women's Voices/Men's Voices: Technology as Language', in KIRKUP, G. and KELLER, L.S. (Eds) *Inventing Women: Science, Technology and Gender*, Cambridge, Polity.

BERG A.J. and LIE, M. (1993) 'Do Artifacts Have Gender? Feminism and the Domestication of Technical Artifacts', paper presented at Conference on European Theoretical Perspectives on New Technology: Feminism, Constructivism and Utility, CRICT, Brunel University, 16–17 September.

BUTLER, J. (1992) 'Contingent Foundations: Feminism and the Question of "Postmodernism"', in BUTLER, J. and SCOTT, J.W. (Eds) *Feminists Theorise the Political*, London, Routledge.

BUTLER, J. and SCOTT, J.W. (Eds) (1992) *Feminists Theorise the Political*, London, Routledge.

CALLON, M. (1986) 'Some Elements of a Sociology of Translation: Domestication of the Scallops and Fishermen of St Brieuc Bay', in LAW, J. (Ed.) *Power, Action and Belief: A New Sociology of Knowledge?*, London, Routledge.

CALLON, M. and LAW, J. (1982) 'On Interests and their Transformation: Enrolment and Counter-Enrolment', *Social Studies of Science*, vol. 12, pp. 615–25.

CAMERON, D. (1985) *Feminism and Linguistic Theory*, London, Macmillan.

CAMERON, D. (1989) 'Conversation, Discourse, Conflict: A Reply to Torode', *Network*, no. 45.

COCKBURN, C. (1983) *Brothers: Male Dominance and Technological Change*, London, Pluto Press.

COCKBURN, C. (1985) *Machinery of Dominance: Women, Men and Technical Know-How*, London, Pluto Press.

COCKBURN, C. (1987) *Two Track Training: Sex Inequalities and the Youth Training Scheme*, London, Macmillan.

COCKBURN, C. (1991) *In the Way of Women*, London, Macmillan.

COCKBURN, C. (1992) 'The Circuit of Technology: Gender, Identity and Power', in SILVERSTONE, R. and HIRSCH, E. (Eds) *Consuming Technologies: Media and Information in Domestic Spaces*, London, Routledge.

COCKBURN, C. (1993) 'Feminism/Constructivism in Technology Studies: Notes on Genealogy and Recent Developments', paper presented at Conference on European Theoretical Perspectives on New Technology: Feminism, Constructivism and Utility, CRICT, Brunel University, 16–17 September.

COCKBURN, C. and ORMROD, S. (1993) *Gender and Technology in the Making*, London, Sage.

DALY, M. (1979) *Gyn/Ecology*, London, The Women's Press.

EISENSTEIN, Z. (Ed.) (1979) *Capitalist Patriarchy and the Case for Socialist Feminism*, New York, Monthly Review Press.

FAULKNER, W. and ARNOLD, E. (Eds) (1985) *Smothered by Invention*, London, Pluto Press.

FLAX, J. (1992) 'The End of Innocence', in BUTLER, J. and SCOTT, J.W. (Eds) *Feminists Theorise the Political*, London, Routledge.

FRISSEN, V. (1992) 'Trapped in Electronic Cages? Gender and the New Information Technologies in the Public and Private Domain: An Overview of Research', *Media, Culture and Society*, vol. 14, pp. 31–49.

GILL, R. (1993) 'Ideology, Gender and Popular Radio: A Discourse Analytic Approach', *Innovation*, vol. 6, pp. 323–39.

GRIFFIN, S. (1984) *Woman and Nature: The Roaring Inside Her*, London, The Women's Press.

GRIFFITHS, D. (1985) 'The Exclusion of Women from Technology', in FAULKNER, W. and ARNOLD, E. (Eds) *Smothered by Invention*, London, Pluto Press.

GRINT, K. (1991) *The Sociology of Work: An Introduction*, Cambridge, Polity.

HIRSCHAUER, S. and MOL, M. (1993) 'Beyond Embrace: Multiple Sexes at Multiple Sites', *Science, Technology and Human Values*, paper presented to Conference on European Theoretical Perspectives on New Technology: Feminism, Constructivism and Utility, CRICT, Brunel University, 16–17 September.

KARPF, A. (1987) 'Recent Feminist Approaches to Women and Technology' in MCNEIL, M. (Ed.) *Gender and Expertise*, London, Free Association Books.

KELLER, E.F. (1992) 'How Gender Matters, Or, Why It's So Hard For Us To Count Past Two', in KIRKUP, G. and KELLER, L.S. (Eds) *Inventing Women: Science, Technology and Gender*, Cambridge, Polity.

LATOUR, B. (1986) 'The Powers of Association', in LAW, J. (Ed.) *Power, Action and Belief: A New Sociology of Knowledge?*, London, Routledge and Kegan Paul.

LAW, J. (1986) 'On the Methods of Long-Distance Control: Vessels, Navigation and the Portuguese Route to India', in LAW, J. (Ed.) *Power, Action and Belief: A New Sociology of Knowledge?*, London, Routledge and Kegan Paul.

MACKENZIE, D. and WAJCMAN, J. (Eds) (1985) *The Social Shaping of Technology*, Milton Keynes, Open University Press.

MASSEY, D. (1991) 'Flexible Sexism', *Environment and Planning D: Society and Space*, vol. 9, pp. 31–57.

MAYNARD, M. (1990) 'The Re-Shaping of Sociology? Trends in the Study of Gender', *Sociology*, vol. 24, pp. 269–90.

MCNEIL, M. (1987) 'It's a Man's World', in MCNEIL, M. (Ed.) *Gender and Expertise*, London, Free Association Books.

POTTER, J. and WETHERELL, M. (1987) *Discourse and Social Psychology: Beyond Attitudes and Behaviour*, London, Sage.

RICH, A. (1977) *Of Woman Born*, London, Virago.

ROTHSCHILD, J. (Ed.) (1983) *Machina Ex Dea: Feminist Perspectives on Technology*, New York, Pergamon.

ROWBOTHAM, S. (1981) 'The Trouble with Patriarchy', in SAMUEL, R. (Ed.) *People's History and Socialist Theory*, London, Routledge and Kegan Paul.

SEGAL, L. (1987) *Is the Future Female? Troubled Thoughts on Contemporary Feminism*, London, Virago.

SINGER, L. (1992) 'Feminism and Postmodernism', in BUTLER, J. and SCOTT, J.W. (Eds)

Feminists Theorise the Political, London, Routledge.

SPENDER, D. (1985) *Man Made Language*, London, Routledge and Kegan Paul.

SWORDS-ISHERWOOD, N. (1985) 'Women in British Engineering', in FAULKNER, W. and ARNOLD, E. (Eds) *Smothered by Invention*, London, Pluto Press.

TURKLE, S. (1988) 'Computational Reticence: Why Women Fear the Intimate Machine', in KRAMARAE, C. (Ed.) *Technology and Women's Voices*, New York, Routledge and Kegan Paul.

VAN NOSTRAND, C.H. (1993) *Gender-Responsible Leadership*, London, Sage.

VAN ZOONEN, L. (1992) 'Feminist Theory and Information Technology', *Media, Culture and Society*, vol. 14, pp. 9–29.

WAJCMAN, J. (1991) *Feminism Confronts Technology*, Cambridge, Polity.

WAJCMAN, J. (1992) 'Feminist Theories of Technology', paper presented at Workshop on the Gender-Technology Relation, CRICT, Brunel University, 16–17 September.

WALBY, S. (1990) *Theorising Patriarchy*, Oxford, Blackwell.

WEBER, M. (1948) *From Max Weber*, Berkeley, CA, California University Press.

WEST, C. and ZIMMERMAN, D. (1987) 'Doing Gender', *Gender and Society*, vol. 1, pp. 125–51.

WOOLGAR, S. (1981) 'Interests and Explanation in the Social Study of Science', *Social Studies of Science*, vol. 11, pp. 365–94.

Part I

Theoretical Developments in the Gender-Technology Relation

Chapter 1

Feminist Sociology and Methodology: Leaky Black Boxes in Gender/Technology Relations

Susan Ormrod

Introduction

This chapter concerns the methodology of feminist research into gender and technology. In particular, it notes a tendency to employ a social theory which is reductive and conservative in effect. Very briefly, this tendency results from the deployment of a notion of patriarchy to explain relations of power within the social world and then to research the oppression of women that results from this explanation. In feminist research on gender and technology, for instance, this amounts to explorations of how pre-existing social relations of patriarchy express and shape technology. I shall explore two distinct but related approaches within post-structuralism which reject this notion of 'the social'.

In one of these, the social is constructed in and through discourse, meaning and representation which also construct human subjectivities. Accordingly, women are not simply oppressed by forces and practices of representation imposed upon them from outside, as it were. They are, instead, active in positioning themselves within discourses and in investing a commitment to subject positions. The discursive social world, according to this view, gives life and meaning to the individuality they (we) associate with their (our) gendered subject positions.

In the other of these, the social is seen as performed by actors, some of which may not be human, but each of which may be enrolled or 'translated' in the creation of technologies. Sometimes called actor network theory, this approach has developed specifically within technology studies and is associated with Michel Callon and Bruno Latour (Callon and Latour, 1981). It is from their early methodological statements that I draw the term 'leaky black boxes' in my title. For Callon and Latour, the phrase 'black box' refers to the analytical closure that occurs in conceiving of the social and natural worlds separately and as of a different order. In other words, it is the creation of asymmetry. It also occurs when sociologists attribute different sizes to actors, in proposing macro-actors and micro-actors. So, when society and power are described as patriarchal, gender is 'black-boxed'. By this I mean that the content and behaviour of gender relations is assumed to be common knowledge, and their meanings are stabilized and no longer need to be considered.

Both these related approaches suggest methodological issues for doing research on gender. In the first place, neither conceives of the social world as being 'out there' for us to go out and examine. The 'data' is not simply there to be collected and described. Nor, as it turns out, do gender relations remain as stable as some feminists have assumed. If gender is constructed, continually negotiated, then the 'black boxes' will leak. Moreover, the issues go further than that of how the data is to be interpreted. It also concerns the questions that can be asked and the meaning that 'respondents' will impute to those questions. In other words, much of what is said within a research interview, for example, is conditioned by the assumption that, as feminists, we will be interested in patriarchy and women's oppression.

Agency and Structure in Feminist Sociology

Rècent work on technology by feminist sociologists has accepted the actor-network approach, up to a point. However, detecting gender-blindness, voluntarism, relativism and ahistoricism, they remain highly sceptical. Cockburn, for instance, argues that there is 'an incomplete representation of the historical dimensions of power . . . [where] men as a sex dominate women as a sex' in Callon and Latour's work (Cockburn, 1992, p. 39). Wajcman argues that actor network theory ignores gender interests and that its focus has tended to be on sites where women are absent (1991, pp. 23–4). For both Cockburn and Wajcman, a feminist sociology of technology, because of its concern with gender, must engage with subjectivity and attend explicitly to the formation of identity. While the actor-network approach does indeed engage with the relations which hold a technology together, the serious omission for these feminists is its lack of attention to relations of gender. Instead, feminist sociologies of technology tend towards approaches which examine how long-standing, institutionalized and structural patterns of male power, sometimes designated as patriarchy, express and shape technology (Benston, 1988; Cockburn, 1983, 1985, 1992; Hacker, 1989, 1990; Wajcman, 1991).

The prime assumption in feminism's use of patriarchy is that men collectively exercise a force throughout society which collectively oppresses or represses women. It is an assumption which often imputes a motive force: the exercise of power in pursuit of what men perceive to be their interests. While this concept of patriarchy may be qualified by reference to class, race and sexuality, it nevertheless assumes a model of power which I believe we must contest. It conforms with a more generally held view of what power is, how it operates, and the primacy of interests. In this view, power is held and used to cause people with less power to act in accordance with those with authority, sovereignty or legitimate power. Although there is an infinite variety of accounts of its location and distribution, power is conventionally conceived in what Hindess describes as the 'capacity-outcome' model (Hindess, 1986). Patriarchy adopts the model in a particular form, locating power in male hands. Outcomes, however, are not secure and cannot be determined in advance of struggle. Interests cannot be assumed as a precondition of a stable structure, as imputed by patriarchy. Rather they are 'a function of the discursive conditions and outcomes of struggle' (Law, 1986b, p. 12).

The concept of patriarchy, which accepts the predominant concept of power as capacity which is held and wielded over others, arises through feminist acceptance of a mainstream sociology which distinguishes between the individual and society or between agency and structure. This distinction is the basis for sociology's separation from psychology and the humanities. It is also the basis for sociology's difficulties in reaching a resolution between the determinism of functionalism and structuralism, on one hand, and the voluntarism of ethnography and phenomenology on the other. Do structures or rules govern human agents and human activity? Or do human agents construct social reality? The attempt made by Giddens to synthesize this relationship in his 'structuration theory' (Giddens, 1984) fails because of its emphasis on a subjectivist assumption of knowledgeable actors making sense of the world and 'making a difference' in it (Barbalet, 1987; Habermas, 1982, p. 286; Layder, 1987). Giddens' understanding of the human agent is sociologically conventional: the agent is defined as a unitary, rational, knowledgeable, conscious, pre-given entity.[1] The social, on the other hand, is conventionally understood in sociology as a total ordered whole, demarcated from the 'natural' world. Sociology's task is to understand and represent this totality and it is deficient to the extent that it omits certain dimensions from its appointed task. Thus feminist sociology seeks to add the gender dimension into sociology's narrative account of society. In even the most sophisticated versions where gender is analysed as socially constructed, the same presumption of a pre-existing subject that constructs the world and is socially constructed, is adopted (Connell, 1987; Game and Pringle, 1983).

Ann Game convincingly argues that the individual is insufficiently problematized in sociology by simply shifting to the level of the group, class, race, or gender (1991, pp. 32–3). 'Oppressed groups' are constituted as the *objects* of sociological knowledge in a project of liberation where sociology aims to raise their consciousness as *subjects*. Sociology is at an impasse because of its premise that social determination constitutes explanation and because sociologists also want to claim simultaneously that 'human agency' is the source of change. Game points to the contradiction in asking how we sociologists can give *them* a voice (p. 30). Feminist sociologists claim to be able to represent women by virtue of being women and by having a feminist consciousness. It is this which authorizes feminist research and its rejection of traditional malestream sociology which distinguishes between researcher and researched. Yet, as Game argues, 'The very idea of representing women, even if in the form of "letting them speak", is to constitute women as object' (p. 31).

This is a discomforting argument and a challenge which must be faced up to. In accepting the defining characteristics of sociology's concern with the dualism of agency structure, feminist sociology is accepting the same conception of knowledge where consciousness corresponds to reality, the real. Approaches which divert from sociology's concern with agency structure are ruled out as not sociological, not theoretical, or not historical. Approaches which divert from feminist sociology's acceptance of (and subservience to) an agency structure dualism run the risk of being ruled out also as unfeminist.

Power and Gendered Subjectivity

Feminism might successfully theorize gender subjectivity and sidestep the unresolvable agency structure dualism by avoiding the theory of power demanded by patriarchy, which structures femininity and masculinity as opposites in a dichotomy, where women are the object of male power. Gender is spoken of in terms of two categories. The effect is to polarize and concentrate on the fixity and continuity of gender relations. There is a long history of characterizing gender in such a way, one which has also been appropriated by feminism to political effect. Indeed, it is important to document the ways in which men and women have been constituted in relation to one another, as different, complementary and unequal: the masculine superordinate; the feminine subordinate. But as Hollway argues, femininity and masculinity cannot be taken as 'fixed features located exclusively in women and men' (1984, p. 228). And it is not the case that women and men are automatically and passively inscribed into existing power relations (Pringle, 1989). If we are to understand gender differentiation in a way which can account for changes, then we must avoid an analysis which sees discourses of gender as mechanically repeating themselves (Hollway, 1984). Otherwise feminism will be unable to *successfully* challenge the dominances now being achieved in their distinctively modern form. It will be unable to make productive alliances with pro-feminist men and disassociate itself from anti-feminist women. It will simply be locked into a 'battle of the sexes'.

To talk of strategies concerning subjectivities that might replace a battle between sexual dichotomies is to introduce a way of speaking about power different from the 'capacity-outcomes' model which underpins notions of 'male power'. Rather than equating power with oppression as a negative force, power is conceived of as productive. It produces knowledges, meanings and values, and permits certain practices as opposed to others. This is a concept of power often associated with Foucault, but Clegg illustrates its antecedents in Machiavelli (Clegg, 1989). Here, power is the overall effect of strategies and is contingent to specific instances of its operation.[2]

As is well known, Foucault demonstrates the operation of power through discursive practices. These produce regimes of truth which make possible certain practices and subjectivities and exclude others. As Chris Weedon explains in a discussion of feminism and post-structuralism:

> Discourses, in Foucault's work, are ways of constituting knowledge, together with the social practices, forms of subjectivity and power relations which inhere in such knowledges and the relations between them. Discourses are more than ways of thinking and producing meaning. They constitute the 'nature' of the body, unconscious and conscious mind and the emotional life of the subjects they seek to govern. (Weedon, 1987, p. 108)

Post-structuralism posits a subject that is not pre-formed as a rational unitary being, but is produced in its social and historical forms through discursive practices and modes of signification. Rather than an agency which negotiates the social, both are jointly created together. Butler pursues this idea in arguing that gender is not a noun but a verb, an active and continuous process, a becoming (1990). In other words, gender is performative, a process of constituting the apparent stability of gender identity. Identity politics tends to assume a foundationalist reasoning relying on a viable subject who is understood to have some stable existence prior to the cultural field that she negotiates. According to Butler, the problem for much feminism is that there is often presumed to be a doer behind the deed because an agent is held to be a necessary precursor to initiating and transforming relations of power in society. Butler theorizes subjectivity as a process of signification rather than a problem of identity. The question of agency is then re-formulated as a question of *how* identity, conceived as a signifying practice, works.

To deconstruct the subject-as-agent is to understand the subject as a position within a particular discourse (Henriques *et al.*, 1984, p. 203). While displacing the individual as coherent and unitary, we must still attend to how the fragments of multiple positionings are held together. Henriques *et al.* suggest that signifying practices of subjectivity work by both offering the security of valued social identities and also providing the desire and motivation for change. This introduces an openness to subjectivity while accounting for continuity by stressing the importance attached to available subject positions within signifying practices. In other words, this analysis accounts for both predictability and change within gender relations.

Gendered subjectivity, then, is historically produced in a series of competing discourses, which make available different positions and different powers for women and men, rather than being the product of a single patriarchal ideology. Male dominance may be the end result of particular operations of power, but this is not simply imposed on women (and some other men). Rather, gender relations are a *process* involving strategies and counter-strategies of power. Present differentiations of gender may produce the dominance of a certain version of masculinity (and particular men) around certain practices of technology. But this is not simply achieved through a circulation of the same old discourses of gender dichotomy mechanically repeating themselves. Wendy Hollway uses the term 're-production' with a hyphen, in order to signify that everyday recurring practices and meanings of gender difference may maintain such relations *or* modify them (leading to changed practices) (1984, p. 227).

'The Social' as Performative

Once we recognize that masculinity and femininity are descriptions of categories that are continually constructed, negotiated and renegotiated on an everyday basis, their (so-called) constitutive attributes can be contested.

Moreover, once we recognize that there is nothing necessarily 'given' about masculinity and femininity, the way is immediately open to investigate the mundane processes by which these categories are constituted. The apparent obviousness of these categories illustrates how successful gendering processes have been.

In part this success, this obviousness, derives from what Latour describes as the tendency in sociology to use an 'ostensive' rather than a 'performative' definition of society (Latour, 1986). That is, sociology only became possible once it started with an all-embracing society that could explain various phenomena. For instance, a patriarchal society is used as an explanatory resource. The notion of power – as a possession – of a class, the City, despots, or some other social category, is unproblematic so long as society is perceived as 'overarching'. In this ostensive view, society comprises units (the family, individuals, cities etc.) which have qualities, and which engage in forms that bind them together.

In proposing a 'performative' definition of society, Latour argues that commands are not simply issued by those with power and obeyed by those with less. Instead, if a command is successful it results from the actions of a chain of agents, each of whom 'translates' it in accordance with their own projects. Power is not located somewhere else, it is composed in the here and now by 'enrolling' many actors in a social and political scheme. As Law explains,

> Latour thus rejects the idea that there is a background, determinant, social structure. Rather, what may be observed are sets of different people trying to define the nature of social structure, and then trying to persuade others to subscribe to that definition. This claim has a methodological corollary: social scientists should stop trying to determine the *nature* of the social structure that they believe generates these conflicts, and instead treat the latter as data. In other words, society should not be seen as the referent of an ostensive definition, but rather seen as being *performed* through the various efforts to define it. (Law, 1986a, pp. 17–18, emphases in original)

Callon and Latour state this as a methodological issue when they say:

> *There are* of course macro-actors and micro-actors, but the difference between them is brought about by power relations and the constructions of networks that will *elude analysis* if we presume *a priori* that macro-actors are bigger than or superior to micro-actors. (Callon and Latour, 1981, p. 280, emphases in original)

Size is thus the consequence of long struggle and the best way to understand this is to consider actors as networks where power is the effect of enrolments and translations. But for such processes to endure beyond each interaction, it is necessary to bring into play a variety of associations – 'walls and written contracts, ... uniforms and tattoos, ... names and signs' – organized into hierarchies in such a way as to seem stable (Callon and Latour, 1981, p. 284). Once stabilized, these associations no longer need to be considered and, as Callon and Latour express it, are shut away into 'black boxes'. Of course the black boxes are never completely closed and in the constant struggle the black boxes leak. Thus for Callon and Latour, 'macro-actors are micro-actors seated on top of many (leaky) black boxes'.

Callon elaborates on this methodological issue in his 'sociology of translation' (Callon, 1986). Here he is concerned to demonstrate the processes by which an actor network is built. An actor network is not a linked set of discrete elements but the outcome of particular associations of meanings and coalitions, both human and non-human. In this sense, so-called 'agency' is the product of specific actor networks. It is achieved by translating phenomena into resources, and resources into networks (Clegg, 1989, p. 204).

Translation results from discursive moves, combining people and machines, in which actors attempt to enrol each other. The concept focuses on the necessarily interpretive work out of which technology and its associated relations (including gender) are made. Translation also indicates the *inconstancy* of the actors (for instance, people, ideas, and technologies) as they are mobilized in the construction of a network. These actors are not simply diffused, but themselves undergo changes. Moreover, these changes are not simply a matter of adaptation but involve a transformation of the very understanding and content of what is translated (Bloomfield *et al.*, 1992).

The actor-network approach can be combined with the approach to the social, discussed earlier, where the social is analysed as a discursive formation active in the making of gendered identities. Cockburn has rightly identified a lack of concern with subjectivity in the actor-network approach (1992). She suggests that it results from an inattention to the way technology enters into gender identities. This requires further elaboration because we can identify the problem more substantively around the issue of agency. If 'entities' or 'agency' are the result of networks, how is it that human actors both act during the process of a network being constructed, and are considered to come into being as a product of such interactions? I think this is where ideas about the production of gendered subjectivity through discursive practices are useful. These ideas (as I outlined earlier) include the notion of investment in valued social gendered identities as well as the notion of re-producing subjectivities as positions in discourse – continuity and change, the illusion of fixity and fluidity. In this sense we can retain the important insights from post-structuralism of power as dispersed and the social as performative, without jeopardizing the political impetus of feminist projects which seek to identify patterns of inequality, or pervasiveness and continuity of gender relations.

Although gender is not highlighted in most examples of the actor-network approach, it does enable us to demonstrate the construction of gender relations as a crucial element in constructing a new technology. The approach I have just outlined allows us to examine how gender relations are enrolled within relations of technology and vice versa: to specify technology and gender as social processes where their boundaries and content are negotiated rather than pre-existing. The boundaries between what is considered to be the 'technical' and the 'social', as well as the boundaries between genders (principally masculine and feminine), are arrived at as a result of observable social processes. History is not denied by such an account, but the emphasis is firmly on the power relations at work in the emergence of gender-technology relations and in the processes of their re-production. Of course, such processes do include the enrolment of ideas which allude to tradition, natural, normal, usual, and precedent but these are used in dynamic ways at the time. It is not simply a matter of predisposing factors (or 'structures' no matter how many or complex) which crucially 'load the dice' or determine subsequent events. Their use in the construction of networks is contingent and specific. Moreover, such processes are then seen to be processes of modification rather than the simple repetition of pre-existing patterns.

The construction of a gendered actor network cannot be determined by any predisposing history but is an active process in which actors interpret and reinterpret their respective histories to effect. So a technology or an artefact is put together and put to use within the social and historical circumstances as understood by its designers and users. The durability, or 'success', of a domestic technology such as the microwave oven is seen as more likely if it can be put together as a machine capable of serious home cooking, not simply for snacks or reheating food.[3] Its makers, retailers, and users must be convinced that a particular assembly of hardware, recipes, cooking programmes, and the domestic cook will work together. This will not depend simply on the attributes of the electronic equipment: the historical and cultural attributes of food and home cooking are just as vital. Moreover, its durability depends as much on the willingness of both women and men to perceive of domestic labour such as cooking in historically acceptable ways. But its attraction for them may equally depend on their willingness to break with the past and to see potential for altering their division of domestic labour in novel ways. A more detailed account of research into the construction of the microwave oven following this approach appears in Ormrod (1994).

Methodologically then, the actor-network approach can be, and needs to be, combined with an analysis of the subjectivities of the actors involved. It is this which allows for an analysis in which history does not predetermine the technology and can be seen as a resource. It is the absence of predetermination that some critics draw attention to when they describe post-structuralism and the actor-network approach as relativist. The suggestion that there are different interpretations of something so central to patriarchy as the sexual division of domestic labour, and that there may be different future avenues, is taken as evidence for post-structuralism's moral and political compromise on the operations of power. This is to confuse methodological relativism with substantive relativism (Bowers and Iwi, 1993, p. 390). As Bowers and Iwi point out, substantive relativism would only be plausible if

> the resources to mobilise a construction of society were always and everywhere equally distributed, so that – at any moment – any construction could be possible . . . however, part of the rhetorical task of instituting one construction of society is precisely to undercut the alternatives, to make them less 'sayable'.

We return here to the asymmetric relations which are the outcome of black-boxing identified by Callon and Latour, described earlier. For a network to endure, it has to effect a stability of social relations, to make some meanings and practices (of, say, identity and technology) less likely than others. The stability in the microwave oven network is achieved, in part, by mobilizing identities which are gendered across a number of places in the network from design and manufacture to sale and use. In each of these places, individual actors are identified with the project. It is as men employed as design engineers, women employed as home economists, or cooks projected as housewives, that they are brought into the network. These conventionally socially-valued identities, while not always wholly taken up, have to be negotiated by individual men and women both in the maintenance of themselves and within the network. Gender is a crucial component in their construction as technologically or domestically competent. Because there is a limited range of socially valued gender positions, the particular network in this research shows the (temporarily) stabilized outcome of these negotiations to be the preservation of unequal relations of power for women and men.

Let us examine one example of these particular relations. For one woman in this network employed as a home economist by a microwave oven manufacturer, her identity as employee and domestic scientist was importantly combined with being 'a housewife and mother'. Her dual identity was the cause of some frustration and anger to her. She was employed, and valued, as a representative of 'the housewife' and customer, but her employers failed to recognize, both in pay and status, her contribution to the design process as much as they valued that of the male engineers. In her role she had promoted the idea of the microwave as a versatile cooking machine as opposed to a mere pie-warmer. Her own experience as homemaker led her to believe that microwave oven design needed to put the 'pleasure back into cooking' and return to women 'the skills and the pleasure that go back for generations that are in a house'. She argued for the serious cook, principally identified as a housewife, to be given due recognition by the manufacturer in the form of recipes and cookery books, built-in cooking programmes, and a test kitchen staffed by home economists. To a large extent she was successful in this project. But in recognizing that her value was as a surrogate housewife, she also recognized that she was excluded from the full design process and management status. Her employers found her dual role ambiguous and remained unsure about where to locate her organizationally.

Her identity as employee/homemaker/woman meant she was framed by competing discourses of gender and technology relations: to retain her place in this stabilized network, she had to do the work of holding these contradictions together. The post-structuralist idea that there is no coherent, unitary self is not simply the stuff of academic discourse: people are often quite acutely aware of this in their everyday presentations of themselves. To some extent they consciously invest in certain socially valued identities to help negotiate these contradictions.

The approach I am arguing for here allows the recognition of the multiple meanings of gender and technology relations without assuming *a priori* relations of gender and technology which might black-box and foreclose the analysis. The focus needs to be on how such relations are made and re-made, rather than on revealing their nature. This is why I have advocated a methodological relativism to get the analysis going. The implications of this for a feminist sociology of technology are explored below.

The Political Project of Feminism and Performativity

The place I want to start from is that of the ethical principles underlying feminism as a political project. A commitment to sexual equality provides a normative position, a standpoint epistemology, which is an important ingredient in much feminist thought. Ethics have always been implicated in debates about gender and technology and, indeed, it would be difficult to talk of gender and technology without issues of right and wrong being at the heart of the discussion. We rarely talk of gender without an ethics of equality and fairness.

However, post-structuralism is frequently criticized for not offering any normative positions (Nicholson and Fraser, 1990). If we look, for example, at Nancy Fraser's criticism of Foucault, she observes that he vacillates between two inadequate positions. In some places he excludes a normative position and the use of legitimate and illegitimate power altogether. This appears to be a principled commitment to relativity and the impossibility of normative justification. In other places, he appears to bracket the normative simply as a 'methodological strategy' (Fraser, 1989, pp. 17–54). In turn, post-structuralism, particularly Foucault, criticizes ethics themselves as an operation of power.

The adoption of an ethical stance in research is of particular interest in discussing Callon and Latour's sociology of translation. Clegg argues that their methods enable a course to be steered between moral absolutism and moral relativism. This is most significant for him in developing his analysis of power. As Clegg points out,

> Without taking sides, without reducing all action to the manifestation of some agencies' putative intentions or interests, or making it the outcrop of some structure, the approach provides an empirical sociology of power, rather than a moral philosophy. (Clegg, 1989, p. 204)

Callon and Latour's method turns on three principles which are of immediate relevance to the present discussion: agnosticism, generalized symmetry, and free association. The agnosticism required of the observer means that the sociology

> refrains from judging the way in which the actors analyse the society which surrounds them. No point of view is privileged and no interpretation is censored. The observer does not fix the identity of the implicated actors if this identity is still being negotiated. (Callon, 1986, p. 200)

The second principle, of generalized symmetry, extends agnosticism by insisting on a single repertoire to describe all the ingredients in a network, including both society and nature. This is a commitment to explain conflicting viewpoints or different substances in the same terms. This extends further to the third principle, free association, which argues against those studies that make *a priori* distinctions between nature and society because they 'start from a closed definition of the social and then use this repertoire as an explanation of nature' (Callon and Latour, 1992).

Callon and Latour employ a radical notion of power which avoids all the difficulties associated with concepts of sovereign power, 'real interests', structure-agency, determinism and voluntarism. Their re-formation of power has important implications for gender. As I have already observed, Clegg claims that it is these three principles of agnosticism, generalized symmetry, and free association which enable a course to be steered between moral absolutism and moral relativism (1989, p. 203).

This issue of moral absolutism versus moral relativism is crucial to feminism's engagement with the actor-network approach and for theorizing gendered subjectivity and relations of power as performative. There is a problem for feminist sociology, then, if we adopt an ostensive definition of society. For in doing this the aim is to identify the source of women's oppression: to know one's enemy in order to defeat him. However, this is a mistaken strategy because if feminism is concerned to identify a system of patriarchy as the determinant of power relations, then it will divert proper attention away from those instances where power is exercised and has its effects – the places where we can analyse *how* instances of dominance by men are achieved. It is in identifying 'a system of male power' as the source of women's oppression that male power becomes the overarching power against which feminism is directed. This is to reduce diverse and widespread occurrences of oppression down to one thing. To say that there is a social system credits 'translation processes with a coherence they lack' (Callon and Latour, 1981).

For the purpose of analysis, the actor-network approach suspends judgment. Callon and Latour indicate the problems of pre-judging. They argue that this is not simply a methodological mistake but a serious error of political judgment, for

> As differences are so visible, what needs to be understood is their construction, their transformations, their remarkable variety and mobility, in order to substitute a multiplicity of little local divides for 'one' great divide. We do not deny differences, we refuse to consider them as a priori and to hierarchise them once and for all. One is not born a scallop – one becomes one! (Callon and Latour, 1992)

The point here is that a moral starting point in feminism is likely to blind analysis to the very processes by which unequal gender relations are constructed. Otherwise we risk falsely restricting the object of study to gender identity and technology as given entities. While gender and technology have been constructed as macro-actors and shut away into black boxes, we must insist on opening them up for investigation where the meaning and significance of 'technology' and 'gendered identity' are reconsidered in all their variations, as they exist for the actors.

Callon and Latour also make the point in describing their approach's relation to studies of both gender and social class:

> Who would dare promote the idea that there are no differences between men and women or between the working and upper middle classes? Should these be considered as differences of kind to be expressed in different repertoires? The recognition of the historicity of differences, their irreversibilisation, their disintegration, and their proliferation passes by way of a bitter struggle against the assertion of one great ahistorical difference. (Callon and Latour, 1992)

This quote brings us to history, the second issue that arises from considering post-structuralism's potential for examining gender and technology. Performative and discursive notions of 'the social' insist upon a contingency over power and a fluidity over subjectivity. This is opposed to the notion of pre-disposed identities historically possessing more power, as mobilized by the polemics of much feminism. The question then is: 'Is it possible to have a historically and politically engaged post-structuralist feminism?' It is a question which hinges upon whether the present is to be understood as an outcome of history, the end of history. Or is the point of history to re-constitute objects and concepts such as sexuality or the human sciences within the present? This allows a variety of histories, an openness, and an indeterminacy about the future. Post-structuralist feminists would argue that it is the contestation allowed by this history that is essential to any viable political project. Any transformation of gender relations requires the post-structuralist insight that 'the individual is not a fixed or given identity, but rather a product of historically specific practices of social regulation' (Henriques *et al.*, 1984, p. 12).

To conclude, feminist sociology on technology must be able to show *how* relations of power are exercised and the *processes* by which gendered subjectivities are achieved. It must therefore attend to the range of discursive practices and the associations of (durable) materials, meanings, and subjectivities within which gender and technology are defined and differentiated. To do otherwise is to reify gender as binarism and technology as 'thing', whereas we know that they are relational, performative and subject to negotiation. While predispositions (in, for example, history, organizations, institutions, culture) may be part of those processes, they are never determining but only ever relevant in so far as they are actively enrolled as resources which help sustain a network. We must be able to attend to the particular investments men and women may have in positioning themselves within any discourse or particular network, although some will be more usual, or difficult, or readily allowed than others (Threadgold, 1990, p. 8). If we are to successfully challenge the relations of gender/technology we think are worse, unfair, wrong, then we need to be able to discuss them in all their specificity and difference.

Notes

This chapter has been developed from papers delivered to the Gender Research Seminars at UMIST and the Gender-Technology Relation Workshop at CRICT, Brunel University, and I wish to acknowledge the comments made by participants. Particular thanks are due to David Rea at the University of Swansea who has commented on earlier drafts of this chapter and contributed significantly to the chapter's development. I also wish to acknowledge the financial support of the ESRC in funding the project from which these ideas have been developed.

1   This is as valid of Giddens' structuration as it is of other sociologies. In Parsons' structural-functionalism, people play 'roles' within a social system. Marxism uses the concepts of false consciousness and alienation to describe the effects of capitalist means of production on the 'species-being'.
2   Foucault would not reject or deny structures such as those we might describe as patriarchy. The important point, however, is that these are 'conduits', a means for channelling power rather than originating it (Foucault, 1977, p. 326). They cannot be seen as existing ostensively prior to the operation of power.
3   These ideas have been developed during a research project on domestic technologies funded by the ESRC and conducted jointly with Cynthia Cockburn in the Centre for Research in Gender, Ethnicity, and Social Change, at City University, London, between 1990 and 1992. The project is reported in full in Cockburn and Ormrod (1993). This chapter explores a different theoretical approach and represents a personal view.

References

BARBALET, J. M. (1987) 'Power, Structural Resources and Agency', *Current Perspectives in Social Theory*, 8, pp. 1–24.
BENSTON, M.L. (1988) 'Women's Voices/Men's Voices: Technology as Language', in

KRAMARAE, C. (Ed.) *Technology and Women's Voices*, London, Routledge and Kegan Paul.

BLOOMFIELD, B., COOMBS, R., COOPER, D. and REA, D. (1992) 'Machines and Manoeuvres: Responsibility Accounting and the Construction of Hospital Information Systems', *Accounting, Management and Information Technology*, vol. 2, no. 4, pp. 197–219.

BOWERS, J. and IWI, K. (1993) 'The Discursive Construction of Society', *Discourse and Society*, vol. 4, no. 3, pp. 357–93.

BUTLER, J. (1990) *Gender Trouble: Feminism and the Subversion of Identity*, London, Routledge.

CALLON, M. (1986) 'Some Elements of a Sociology of Translation: Domestication of the Scallops and the Fishermen of St Brieuc Bay', in LAW, J. (Ed.) *Power, Action and Belief: A New Sociology of Knowledge?*, London, Routledge and Kegan Paul.

CALLON, M. and LATOUR, B. (1981) 'Unscrewing the Big Leviathan: How Actors Macro-Structure Reality and Sociologists Help Them To Do So', in KNORR-CETINA, K. and CICOUREL, A. (Eds) *Advances in Social Theory and Methodology: Toward an Integration of Micro and Macro Sociologies*, London, Routledge.

CALLON, M. and LATOUR, B. (1992) 'Don't Throw Out the Baby with the Bath School! – A Reply to Collins and Yearley', in PICKERING, A. (Ed.) *Science as Practice and Culture*, Chicago and London, University of Chicago Press.

CLEGG, S. (1989) *Frameworks of Power*, London, Sage.

COCKBURN, C. (1983) *Brothers: Male Dominance and Technological Change*, London, Pluto Press.

COCKBURN, C. (1985) *Machinery of Dominance: Women, Men and Technical Know-How*, London, Pluto Press.

COCKBURN, C. (1992) 'The Circuit of Technology: Gender, Identity and Power', in SILVERSTONE, R. and HIRSCH, E. (Eds) *Consuming Technologies: Media and Information in Domestic Spaces*, London, Routledge.

COCKBURN, C. and ORMROD, S. (1993) *Gender and Technology in the Making*, London, Sage.

CONNELL, R. W. (1987) *Gender and Power*, Cambridge, Polity.

FOUCAULT, M. (1977) *Discipline and Punish*, Harmondsworth: Penguin.

FRASER, N. (1989) *Unruly Practices: Power, Discourse and Gender in Contemporary Social Theory*, Cambridge, Polity.

GAME, A. (1991) *Undoing the Social: Towards a Deconstructive Sociology*, Milton Keynes, Open University Press.

GAME, A. and PRINGLE, R. (1983) *Gender at Work*, London, George Allen and Unwin.

GIDDENS, A. (1984) *Constitution of Society*, Cambridge, Polity.

HABERMAS, J. (1982) *Philosophical-Political Profiles*, translated by John Viertel, Cambridge, Mass., MIT Press.

HACKER, S. (1989) *Pleasure, Power and Technology*, Boston, Unwin Hyman.

HACKER, S. (1990) 'The Eye of the Beholder: An Essay on Technology and Eroticism', in HACKER, S., SMITH, D.E. and TURNER, S.M. (Eds) *'Doing It The Hard Way': Investigations of Gender and Technology*, Boston and London, Unwin Hyman.

HENRIQUES, J., HOLLWAY, W., URWIN, C., VENN, C. and WALKERDINE, V. (1984) *Changing the Subject: Psychology, Social Regulation and Subjectivity*, London, Methuen.

HINDESS, B. (1986) '"Interests" in Political Analysis', in LAW, J. (Ed.) *Power, Action and Belief*, London, Routledge and Kegan Paul.

HOLLWAY, W. (1984) 'Gender Difference and the Production of Subjectivity', in HENRIQUES, J. *et al.* (Eds) *Changing the Subject: Psychology, Social Regulation and Subjectivity*, London, Methuen.

LATOUR, B. (1986) 'The Powers of Association', in LAW, J. (Ed.) *Power, Action and Belief*, London, Routledge and Kegan Paul.

LAW, J. (1986a) 'Editor's Introduction: Power/Knowledge and the Dissolution of the Sociology of Knowledge', in LAW, J. (Ed.) *Power, Action and Belief: A New Sociology of Knowledge?*, London, Routledge and Kegan Paul.

LAW, J. (Ed.) (1986b) *Power, Action and Belief: A New Sociology of Knowledge?*, London, Routledge and Kegan Paul.

LAYDER, D. (1987) 'Key Issues in Structuration Theory', *Current Perspectives in Social Theory*, 8, pp. 25–46.

NICHOLSON, L. and FRASER, N. (1990) 'Social Criticism without Philosophy: An Encounter between Feminism and Postmodernism', in NICHOLSON, L. (Ed.) *Feminism/Postmodernism*, London, Routledge.

ORMROD, S. (1994) '"Let's Nuke the Dinner": Discursive Practices of Gender in the Creation of a New Cooking Process', in COCKBURN, C. and FURST-DILIC, R. (Eds) *Bringing Technology Home: Gender and Technology in a Changing Europe*, Buckingham, Open University Press.

PRINGLE, R. (1989) 'Bureaucracy, Rationality and Sexuality: The Case of Secretaries', in HEARN, J., SHEPPARD, D.L., TANCRED-SHERIFF, P. and BURRELL, G. (Eds) *The Sexuality of Organization*, London, Sage.

THREADGOLD, T. (1990) 'Introduction', in THREADGOLD, T. and CRANNY-FRANCIS, A. (Eds) *Feminine, Masculine and Representation*, Sydney, Allen and Unwin.

WAJCMAN, J. (1991) *Feminism Confronts Technology*, Cambridge, Polity.

WEEDON, C. (1987) *Feminist Practice and Poststructuralist Theory*, Oxford, Blackwell.

Chapter 2

On Some Failures of Nerve in Constructivist and Feminist Analyses of Technology

Keith Grint and Steve Woolgar

Introduction

The shared promise of many recent feminist and constructivist approaches to the social study of technology is the development of radical alternatives to traditional understandings of technology. Frequently, both approaches take issue with the spectre of technological determinism. As has been shown elsewhere (Grint and Woolgar, forthcoming, chapter 1), however, 'techno-logical determinist' has become a rather vague term, yielding many different interpretations. In addition, even though one is now hard pressed to find anyone admitting to the label, it turns out that many of the critiques of 'technological determinism' themselves retain key elements of the condition. As a result, the target of criticism is both varied and diffuse, and many of the critiques compromise their avowed radicalism. A central aim of this chapter is to explore the extent and implications of these problems in some recent constructivist and feminist perspectives on technology.

The assessment of different theoretical perspectives on technology is more than just idle speculation; they can have profound consequences for the practical policies which we adopt. For example, if technology is inherently and essentially masculine, it follows that the interests of women are best served by abandoning such technology and developing an alternative feminine technology. If, on the other hand, we consider technology to be gender-neutral then its deployment and use is the crucial arena for change: more women into engineering is one such policy implication of this approach. Between these two polarities lie different versions of the social shaping or political technology approach (see Grint and Woolgar, forth-coming, chapter 1) which, for reasons discussed below, we term 'anti-essentialist'. Within anti-essentialism, technology is never neutral, but is actively imbued with power of one sort or another, patriarchal and capitalist power being the two leading contenders in recent literature. In one feminist application, anti-essentialism disputes both the assumption that the effects of technology are determined by their allegedly patriarchal origins and that patterns of gendered inequality can be resolved simply by widening access. Instead, a broad-based, and necessarily lengthy, strategy is pursued in which the politicized technologies are subverted by increasing the proportion of women in technological occupations and by redesigning technologies to embody values other than those which perpetuate patriarchy.[1]

It is clear, then, that the theoretical perspectives adopted in this debate are bound up with practical and policy consequences; one cannot pretend to assess theory from some pure vantage point. Consequently, it is important to assess the extent to which these avowedly anti-technological determinist arguments realize their radical promise, and to assess the implications of this for policy. For example, although in the approach mentioned above technologies are portrayed as political, and as socially constructed, they are still treated as having objective 'effects'. In this sense, even such politically motivated critiques of technology tend to adopt what we characterize as technicist and essentialist elements.[2] Here we argue that this is tantamount to a significant failure of nerve. We suggest that anti-essentialist arguments need to be taken to a more radical (post-essentialist) conclusion and we consider the implications of this for the relationship between gender and technology. In brief, this means subjecting the notion that technology has politics built into it (capitalist, patriarchal or whatever) to the same anti-essentialist critique that is currently used to deny the eco-feminist position that existing technology is inherently patriarchal.

We begin by outlining the basis for the claim that even 'constructivist' and 'social shaping' approaches are insufficiently sensitive to the demands of an appropriately radical critique of technology. We then suggest that the same problems can be found in some feminist approaches to technology. We illustrate this argument using the particular case of reproductive technolo-gies.[3] This leads us to reflect on some implications of our own critical stance. Finally, we assess the significance of our argument for certain moral and political dilemmas.

Technological Determinism, Essentialism and Anti-Essentialism

For clarity we shall distinguish two main kinds of approach to technology. Firstly, a traditional approach is based on an acceptance of one or other statement of the technical capabilities of technology.[4] In this perspective technical capacity is viewed as inherent to the technology (artefact or system). For this reason we refer to this perspective as *essentialist*: technical attributes derive from the internal characteristics of the technology. Moreover, these internal characteristics are (often) supposed to have resulted from the application of scientific method or from the linear extrapolation and/or development of previous technologies. This first perspective has been roundly criticized on several counts, most notably that it limits its discussion of 'the social' dimension to the effects of technological capacity.

The second approach we shall call *anti-essentialist*. This approach encompasses a broad church of perspectives, including 'social shaping' (e.g. MacKenzie, 1990), 'constructivist', 'social construction of technology' (e.g. Bijker *et al.*, 1987; Bijker and Law, 1992) and what we call 'designer technology' (e.g. Winner, 1980). These otherwise different approaches share the view that technological artefacts do not possess capacities in virtue of extrapolation from previous technical states of affairs; but rather that the nature, form and capacity of a technology is the upshot of various antecedent circumstances involved in its development (mainly taken to include design, manufacture and production). These antecedent circumstances are said to be 'built into' and/or 'embodied in' the final product; the resulting technology is 'congealed social relations' or 'society made durable'. Differences between anti-essentialists turn on the specific choice of antecedent circumstances – between, for example, 'social interests', the 'solutions sought by relevant social groups', and 'social structure and the distribution of power'. Although anti-essentialism is characterized by some heated disputes between, for example, 'social constructivists' and their critics,[5] all parties share the aim of specifying the effects of these circumstances upon technological capacity.

Clearly, the anti-essentialist move has enormous policy implications for technology design, development and use. It is therefore important to note from the outset that three key features of the anti-essentialist approach threaten to compromise its radical potential. The first is the ambivalence associated with the idea of antecedent circumstances being 'built in'. The second is the difficulty in specifying the nature of these 'antecedent circumstances'. The third stems from the view that technologies, albeit those at the end of a cycle of embodying antecedent circumstances – the final stabilized technological products – are still capable of having effects. In the rest of this section we show how these three features of anti-essentialist argument effectively carry forward elements of the essentialism which they purport to criticize. We subsequently consider their occurrence in explicitly feminist approaches to the problem.

The Metaphor of Building-In/Embodiment

The first disadvantage of the metaphor of embodying or having antecedent circumstances 'built in' is that it implies the possibility that a technology can be neutral until such times as political or social values are ascribed or attributed to it. The problem here is that this view distinguishes between 'the object in itself', an objective and apolitical phenomenon, and the subsequent (?) upshot of social and political overlay. The assumption is that objective accounts of a technology are what are left when the evaluative aspects are stripped away from the essential object. By contrast, the argument of the more thoroughgoing 'constitutive' variants of anti-essentialism is that it makes no sense to suppose that such an apolitical object could exist independent of evaluative aspects; it exists only in and through our descriptions and practices, and hence is never available in a raw, untainted state. This is not an ontological claim – that nothing exists outside of our construction of it – but rather an insistence on the thoroughness with which the technical is intertwined with the social.

The persistence of essentialism is evident also in formulations of anti-essentialism which speak in terms of the technology having politics *attached* to it. Again the implication is that values, politics and the rest are in principle separable from the social relationships that generate them.[6] A more careful attempt to express the sentiments of thoroughgoing anti-essentialism might be to say that technology has politics (or whatever) *inscribed* in it in the very process of its construction, deployment and consumption. Yet even this variant carries essentialist overtones – what, we might ask, is the 'it' into which politics are being inscribed? In varying degrees, the same problem arises in other formulations: technology has been variously said 'to be affected by' 'social factors', or to have these 'social factors' 'built into' or 'embodied by' it. As we discuss later, it is just this persistence of essentialism in and through our continued reliance upon realist language conventions which we need to attempt to exorcize. For present purposes our preference is for the term 'constitutive' to denote that variant of social constructivism which speaks of technical phenomena being constituted (rather than merely shaped, affected etc.) by social process.[7]

Specifying Antecedent Circumstances

A further problem with the embodiment metaphor is that its usage often presupposes the unproblematic character of what exactly is being built in. That is, attributes like interests and political values are assumed to be straightforwardly available to the analyst. The problem here is that this ignores the active interpretive work that goes into rendering motives as, say, social interests (Woolgar, 1981). In other words, the initial description and specification of antecedent circumstances, let alone their explication as causes of the design and shaping of technology, is part and parcel of the reading and interpretation of technologies.

Of course, some of the more sophisticated writing in this area recognizes the difficulty of treating features such as motive, interest, values and so on, as objectively available explanations. For example, Van Zoonen comes close to this when she points out that 'gender can be thought of as a particular discourse ... a set of overlapping and often contradictory cultural descriptions and prescriptions ... not as a fixed property of individuals but as part of the ongoing disciplining process by which subjects are constituted' (1992, p. 20). The implication is that we should at least be extremely cautious in saying that technologies 'are gendered' precisely on account of the interpretive flexibility of the precept. Although Van Zoonen begins to develop this, she still tends to reserve a realm of 'non-discursive elements' (p. 26) and to talk of the way in which (in this case, new information and communication) technologies do not in themselves exclude women; instead, women are excluded by certain forms of discourse which she conceives of as 'surrounding' the technology. Since our own assessment is that the discourse constitutes the object, our concern here is that the implied division between discourse and object once again suggests the possibility of a discourse-free (neutral) technology.

Having Effects

A similar difficulty presents itself in respect to the aspect of anti-essentialist arguments which unproblematically accept that technologies can have effects. Much anti-essentialist argument is pitched as a critique of technological determinism. However, it turns out that this is not a denial of determinism *tout court*. The ensuing argument stresses instead that the effects of technologies are complex; that its uses are unpredictable; and that, in particular, these effects do not stem from the inherent technical characteristics of the technology in question. This form of anti-essentialism turns out to be an attempt to supplant technical determinism with social and political determinisms; it is the politics built into a technology which become the origin of 'effects'. The object of critique is *technological* determinism – not technological *determinism*. For example, in Winner's (1980) account, it is the bridge designer's politics which prevent blacks having access to Jones Beach, not the mere fact of the material construction.

The difficulty here is that the analyst's own pretensions to causality – sustained in and through the conventions of her adequate accounting practice – reinforce the supposition that the technology possesses intrinsic objective properties. This follows from what Coulter (1989) would call the situated grammar of language use. To say, for example, that 'Chernobyl caused pollution' is to imply the existence of a definite entity which has properties capable of causing some effect. of course, the mere utterance of this sentiment does not establish the objectivity of 'Chernobyl' in any final sense. The point is that for practical purposes – in this case, those to do with offering a hearably sensible description of a state of affairs – the use of the term 'Chernobyl' can stand as a causal antecedent for any of an indefinite number of actual objective characteristics. Again, we are not trying to advance a philosophical claim on behalf of ontological relativism, merely attempting to draw attention to the central significance of the conventions of language use as deployed in anti-essentialist accounting practice.[8] To the extent that constructivists are unwilling or unable to critique such important and all-pervasive conventions of their language use, they implicitly buy into significant features of essentialism.

Technological Determinism and Textual Determinism

All this is to suggest that while anti-essentialist approaches help problematize the idea that we can ever have a neutral technology, they remain committed to a form of essentialism. This is particularly evident, for example, when a political design argument of the kind offered by Winner concludes that political values are actually built into the artefact. The difficulty here is that a thoroughgoing critique of essentialism would insist that values (in this case 'politics') are imputed to an artefact in the course of their apprehension, description and use – which of course includes imputations at the hand of the historian of science and/or technology. Unfortunately, the political design critique of essentialism ends up merely replacing one form of essentialism (that technologies are actually neutral) with another (that technologies are actually political).

We have seen that the metaphor of technologies having circumstances 'built into' them and the causal formulation of technologies 'having effects' both smuggle crucial aspects of essentialism into purportedly anti-essentialist arguments. In the following sections we consider the extent to which this also characterizes some recent feminist analyses of technology and discuss the implications for policy. Before doing so, however, it is important to note that the problems we have outlined in anti-essentialist critiques stem from a more general failure to acknowledge the textual character of technologies. The problem with the extent to which technologies do or do not contain inherent characteristics, and the related difficulty of ascertaining how these characteristics impinge upon users and consumers, can be understood as part of the more general problem of the nature of texts. Do texts possess intrinsic meanings, and do these meanings then have effects upon readers (for example, by causing a particular interpretation)? Or do such meanings only arise in and through the active interpretive work performed by the reader? Technological determinism is a particular instance of the more general issue of textual determinism. The anti-essentialists attempt to move away from the former essentialist answer and yet, as we have suggested, inevitably retain features of essentialism sustained through the unproblematized use of linguistic conventions of representation.

The constitutive variant of anti-essentialism achieves the most distance from essentialism. It takes the view that technology is neither neutral nor political in and of itself; that whatever it appears to be lies in our interpretive engagement with it. To ask whether, for example, an artefact is (that is, physically embodies the properties of) male or female or neutral is to miss the point; not only are these properties themselves socially constructed and therefore flexible, but the important question is how certain artefacts come to be *interpreted* (and this may well be disputed) as neutral or male or female.

We see that anti-essentialist attempts to move away from the essentialist position are fraught with an ambivalence which arises from inattention to the discursive and textual character of language.[9] Thus, for example, when arguing a form of anti-determinism that suggests that new technologies do not necessarily cause social change, it is insufficient to say that the causes are unpredictable and multiple. This view still imbues the technology with the capability of having an effect. Nor is it good enough to say that the effects are unclear if we are still willing to specify the (actual) nature and characteristics of the technology. For it is in and through our very attempts at describing a technology that we implicate its possible involvement in action, its possible and potential effects. This follows a basic feature of the conventional character of language: objects described in language are never merely and automatically just objects; they are always and already implicated in action and effect.

With this critique of anti-essentialism in mind, we now examine the extent to which the same problems recur in some recent feminist arguments about technology.

Feminism and Technology

The tradition of associating technology and science – allegedly the twin arenas of reason and logic – with men goes back at least as far as the Enlightenment. This intellectual movement appeared, in its own terms at least, to throw light on all manner of irrationalities and unreasoning, but in terms of reflexive enlightenment on the role of patriarchy it appears to have been a miserable failure. Even if Voltaire worked with Madame du Châtelet, and Diderot with Sophie Holland, even if the French Salon itself was the invention of the Marquise de Rambouillet in 1623 and was intended for women as well as men to facilitate intellectual exchange, the Enlightenment was never a vehicle for sexual equality (Anderson and Zinsser, 1990). Instead, women became associated with reflecting nature, and displaying emotion, with irrationality and subjectivity; men with their opposites: controlling and exploiting nature, reason, logic and objectivity (McNeil, 1987; Harding, 1986). In revolutionary France a short-term consequence of the 'forced separation' between women and rationality was the banishing of women from the public institutions of power; a long-term consequence throughout the world has been the virtual monopolization of science and technology by men.

While many feminists have explicitly rejected this opposition between rationality and women, one variant has emerged, sometimes labelled eco-feminism, which celebrates rather than denigrates these allegedly innate differences. A development of this approach has been one which is consistent with the notion of political technology but uses this as a fundamentalist stepping stone to women's liberation from 'male' technology. Since, in this view, all technologies are carriers of their designers' intentions, it follows that many technologies are male (Cooley, 1968, pp. 42–4) and this becomes manifest in the cultural attributes associated with working in, or studying, engineering (cf. Sørenson, 1992). As Hacker notes from her interviews with men from an engineering faculty: 'Status accrued to the masculine world of speed, sophistication, and abstraction rather than the feminine world of nature and people' (Hacker, 1989, pp. 35–6). This is often represented in its most dangerous manifestation in the military technology of war. There are various explanations for why military technology is considered as male, and why men are taken as inherently violent towards women and each other. For

Easlea (1983) it stems from male 'womb envy'. His narrative of the nuclear bomb programme describes the scheme as flowing from the excitement of 'conception' through the laborious hours of labour up until the 'birth', manifest in the aptly named 'Little Boy' dropped on Hiroshima, and celebrated by the physicists at Los Alamos in a manner very much akin to the constructive success of birth rather than the destructive terror of death.

Nuclear technology is a useful example to illustrate some fundamental differences in approach to technology. Whereas a traditional approach might concede that the design and deployment of nuclear weapons has 'political dimensions', it would probably balk at assumptions that nuclear technology per se was inherently masculine and thus, for (some) women at least, in need of replacement. Yet eco-feminism could point both to the immense power derived from nuclear sources and the prerequisite control over, and exploitation of, nature that this implied. Hence, what could be regarded as an inherently aggressive technology could not be harnessed for constructive purposes but must be interred and replaced by 'softer' renewable green technologies such as wind and wave power. An alternative, but still essentialist, account nominates a particular form of political organization, rather than masculinity, as the essential feature of nuclear power. Thus Winner argues that 'the atom bomb is an inherently political artefact. As long as it exists at all, its lethal properties demand that it be controlled by a centralized, rigidly hierarchical chain of command' (1980, as reprinted 1985, p. 32). Here it is the politics of the bomb that have effects upon society.

Whether these effects are necessarily masculine or hierarchically non-gendered is, for our purposes, largely beside the point. It may well be that the controllers of the bomb provide accounts of its technical capacity which are used to persuade the public at large that a 'rigid hierarchical chain of command' is essential. However, this does not entitle the claim that the technology, in and through itself, demands such an organizational form nor that such a form is masculine in structure. If some women's organizations themselves develop 'a rigid hierarchical chain of command' does this mean they are doing so because they too are coerced by a political technology or by a masculine technology? In either case this poses problems in trying to explain some counter-examples. For instance, some religious orders of Christians are both female and hierarchical. Of course, one might then want to consider the patriarchal culture of Christianity – but this is a cultural argument, not one grounded in the capacities and effects of technologies.

A further difficulty with the essentialist framework of eco-feminism, and one that also problematizes many of the psychoanalytic accounts, is that they tend to ground their arguments in notions of masculinity and femininity which are simultaneously inherent and permanent. Thus, whatever forms of action are deployed by men and women are ultimately derived from the 'natural' nature of each sex. But as Wajcman argues,

> The first thing that must be said is that the values being ascribed to women originate in the historical subordination of women.... It is important to see how women came to value nurturance and how nurturance, associated with motherhood, came to be culturally defined as feminine within male-dominated culture.... Secondly, the idea of 'nature' is itself culturally constructed. Conceptions of the 'natural' have changed radically throughout human history. (Wajcman, 1991, p. 9)

The implications of this account are particularly significant for those seeking to develop what might be called feminist technologies. If what count as feminine and masculine are cultural attributes, subject to challenge and change, then replacing 'masculine' technologies with 'feminine' technologies begs the question of what precisely (and who decides what) is to count as 'feminine technology'. Are all feminists the same? Unless they are, changes to the technology will not resolve the problem of asymmetric control over the technology. Would we expect the deployment and consumption of technologies in households without men to be perfectly equal between their female members? Again, this does not mean that any 'residual' inequalities would undermine the quest to construct a culture in which technology was not interpreted and deployed by men against women, but it does imply that essentialist accounts of women – and men – remain deeply problematic.

Two further examples will suffice to illustrate this point. According to Roberts (1979), the replacement of the light, single-handed sickle by the heavy, double-handed scythe was crucial in the decline of women's agricultural employment during the industrial revolution. Since the new technology (the scythe) was more efficient, but required strength and skill beyond the capacity of women, the technology was crucial in the assertion of a male monopoly over crop cutting – one of the most highly paid jobs. Was the technology designed with this in mind? Or, whatever the designers' intention, was the objective effect of the technology to masculinize crop cutting? Unfortunately, the intentions of the designer seem to be lost in time;[10] but whatever they were we might want to remain sceptical of such determinist accounts on at least two counts. Firstly, if the new technology did require greater strength and skill, one might expect to see fewer women rather than none at all after its introduction – assuming that although most women are physically weaker than men, some women are stronger than some men.[11] Secondly, as late as 1921 there were male-only farm gangs cutting crops which still retained sickles (*Guardian*, 20 May 1991). What does this imply? That the 'inherently' male scythe was also too heavy for men? Or that only a female sickle would have allowed women to remain as crop cutters? Clearly, neither of these alternatives makes sense of the persistence of the sickle in male-only agricultural gangs. We are thus led to seek explanations which, for example, concentrate on the patriarchal culture (legal restraints on female labour and the interests of male agricultural labourers) within which such technologies existed. The battle for access to relatively lucrative farming jobs was not won as a direct result of a specifically male technology but through the successful deployment of accounts of the technology that purported to 'prove' its necessarily male requirements, and through the recruitment of allies, such as the law banning women from gang labour. The re-adoption of the sickle did not facilitate the return of women to crop cutting; if the essentialist models of technology are correct then it should have done.

The second, similar, example relates to the British Post Office in the 1930s. There were, at the time, no urban postwomen, nor any full-time postwomen anywhere. They were not recruited as full-timers nor in urban areas, officially because they could not physically carry the normal load. However, women were employed as part-time rural deliverers – with the same carrying requirements! – not, as you might think, because of the atypically strong physique of rural women, nor even because of the atypically weak physique of rural men, but because, as one manager admitted, 'no man can be obtained to perform the work' (*Post Office Records*, 6033, 1930). In terms of technology, it seems, even the British Post Office was subject to the rigours of relativism.[12]

Having considered the incidence of problems with anti-essentialism in feminism in general terms, we now look in more detail at the specific example of reproductive technologies.

Reproducing Technology?

If the eccentricities of technical arguments concerning the reproduction of paid labour and the mail (male?) system are relatively easy to subvert, has the 'advance' of science and technology in the reproduction of humans been less contingent? After all, the public/private split does imply that these most intimate technologies are deployed in the one area where women are supposed to prevail.

Many accounts of technical change in domestic work (Cowan, 1983; Berg, 1991) and paid labour (Cockburn, 1983, 1985) seem to suggest that the development of technology has done little if anything to roll back patriarchal control at work. Of course, if the essentialism of the eco-feminist position is accurate then we would not expect technologies developed and deployed by men to do anything but reinforce patriarchal control. This is nicely captured in the debate concerning what Firestone (1970) called 'the tyranny of reproduction'. Firestone's essentialist position, which locks inequality to women's reproductive biology, posits technology as the solution, particularly manifest in in-vitro fertilization. But if patriarchy controls women through the different reproductive functions, and if the technology is either inherently masculine or even just controlled by men, then the search for a technical fix is unlikely to be successful. Under these circumstances only technology designed, deployed and consumed by women, or at least wrested from male control, will offer sexual equality. It is clear from the work of Corea *et al.* (1985) that the adoption of an essentialist position does not, in and of itself, generate the adoption of similar strategies. While Firestone's essentialism relates to the essentialism of biology, the essentialism of Corea *et al.* is rooted in the essential masculinity of technology. Hence, according to Klein (1985), the 'technical fix' to patriarchy for Firestone is the 'living laboratory'. Not only does male control over, and exploitation of, women as 'living laboratories' ensure the continuation of patriarchy – rather than its ultimate demise as Firestone hoped – but the links between patriarchy and 'science' may ultimately lead to reproductive techniques that no longer require the participation of women, or configure women's role as professional breeders in what Corea has called the 'reproductive brothel'.[13]

Neither the biological essentialism of Firestone nor the technological essentialism of Corea *et al.* adequately grasps the way knowledge constitutes the objects of our concern. Thus, what Firestone considers to be the determinism of biology seems incapable of explaining why those who actually have children are necessarily involved in their upbringing, nor why women who do not have children are constrained by similar patriarchal constraints. On the other hand, if reproductive technologies reflect their patriarchal origins, why do different societies appear to use technologies construed to be identical in radically different ways? Why, for example, do contraceptive policies and practices differ so much between catholic and non-catholic societies? If such technologies are inherently patriarchal they should have the same 'effects' upon women. Perhaps an old 'Popperian' question is worth asking: what would it take to persuade essentialists to give up their thesis that technology is inherently gendered? Could they ever be persuaded that gendering occurs in and through the interpretation of the technology?

The dilemmas surrounding reproductive technologies, and the question of their political colouration, is illustrated by the case of amniocentesis, a method of establishing the genetic make-up of embryos and a test particularly associated with assessing foetal abnormalities, especially Down's Syndrome. This technology can be interpreted in several different ways. It may be regarded as a method of social engineering through which the diagnosis of foetal abnormalities leads directly to the termination of the pregnancy. As Farrant (1985) argues, the test may not increase women's choice since its provision can appear conditional on termination in cases where abnormalities are considered likely. Here the technology is read as masculine and political. Alternatively, the medical profession regards the test as potentially dangerous to the foetus anyway, such that there is little point in providing a test if an abnormality will not lead to a termination. The dilemma here is twofold. On the one hand, such tests are relatively expensive in resources and this highlights the politics of all health in terms of the choices to be made about the provision of services: does health spending reflect a 'rational' distribution of resources (whatever this might mean) or the interests of powerful lobbies inside the health service? On the other hand, is the technology being used to increase or decrease the choices open to women? Why, in other words, should women be encouraged to opt for terminations just because their child is likely to be born with some kind of abnormality? Why, on the other hand, should they be encouraged not to have the termination? The more extreme scenario constructed around such technologies would envisage them being used to facilitate the possibility of choosing the sex of a child – and terminating a foetus of the 'wrong' sex. Rowland (1992) certainly has this in mind in her denunciation of 'living laboratories' – though it once again hinges on a view of women as passive victims of male technology.

As Wajcman (1991, p. 62) suggests, reproductive technologies do still *seem* to carry certain 'effects', such that:

> the technologies redefine what counts as illness. 'Infertility' now becomes not a biological state to which the woman must adapt her life, but a medical condition – a problem capable of technological intervention. The very existence of the technologies changes the situation even if the woman does not use them. Her 'infertility' is now treatable, and she must in a sense actively decide not to be treated. In this way the technologies strengthen the maternal functions of all women, and reinforce the internalization of that role for each woman.

Reproductive technologies thus *seem* to have the capacity, in and through themselves, to redefine what counts as illness or good health. It is clear, however, that the existence of these technologies does not in itself lead to all women having to redefine their infertility (or even fertility) as a treatable condition, an illness. Consider, for example, the technology of amniocentesis. Without the funding to pay for it, the staff to use it, and the culture that legitimates its use – as either a liberational or social engineering tool – amniocentesis is unlikely to have any effect upon women. What the technology is, and what the capacity of the technology is, are not things that can be assessed in the abstract.

Just as what counts as an illness is socially constructed, so too can we argue that what counts as the capacity and 'effect' of a technology is socially structured; both are consequently contingent and open to renegotiation. Condoms may have been designed to prevent unwanted pregnancies (and this may well be in the interests of both the sexes involved), but the development of AIDS has facilitated their redefinition as a method of avoiding HIV. Or, to return to amniocentesis, the use of ultrasound scanning, to locate the position of the foetus prior to the withdrawal of amniotic fluid through a syringe, has its origins in Naval sonar research. It might still be argued that this merely confirms the links between male aggression, manifest in military technology, and male control over the process of reproduction; that either the patriarchal origins or contemporary patriarchal use of the technology necessarily prevents it being used for the benefit of women. But if women's choice is increased as a result, then neither the technology's origins nor current deployment prevent any potential renegotiation of the capacity and potential of the technology. Indeed, to focus wholly on the militaristic origins, and to assert that technology necessarily carries its essential masculinity with it, diverts attention away from the interpretive acts and practices which operate to maintain patriarchal control over technology.

Overview

In discussing essentialist and anti-essentialist perspectives we find a multitude of overlapping positions. Although we concur with the move away from essentialism, it is not clear that anti-essentialism as discussed here has moved very far. The difficulty seems to be in sustaining a (post-essentialist) position which remains deeply critical of all kind of essentialist notions, whether they relate to humans or non-humans: whether men and women have inherently and objectively different natures and interests or whether technology has inherent and objective capacities. That there are feminist approaches which are compatible with both essentialism and anti-essentialism is a manifestation of the flexible nature of feminism as much as anything.

However, in the debate about patriarchy, the crucial point is not that we reject the policy implications of these diverse accounts but that we remain sceptical of the theoretical premises from which policies may flow.

For example, a perspective which asserts that the problem for women (in the area of technology) is that (almost) all forms of technology are essentially masculine implies a requirement for a feminine technology. But since what counts as masculine and feminine is culturally and historically variable it is not clear what such an alternative would look like. The counter to this tends to focus on a technology which does indeed appear invariant in space and time; military technology, or just weapons, for example, have always been masculine. Yet knives, for instance, have been used for a whole variety of purposes other than wounding or killing others. There is also considerable evidence that women would – if 'masculine regulations', or at least a powerful masculine culture, would allow them – become involved in all forms of military endeavour from the infantry through to flying combat aircraft in war (Dixon, 1976; Shields, 1988; Moskos, 1990; Wheelwright, 1992). For the post-essentialist, what counts as a feminine technology lies in the interpretation, not in the technology itself – since our apprehension of what the technology is requires that very interpretive effort. This is not to say that technology constructed by women *and* consensually defined as feminine would be irrelevant to the undermining of patriarchy. If the significance of technology lies in the interpretation, not the technology, then a radically feminist interpretation might well have some influence in the policy arena. For example, if a computer, destined for use in schools, was defined as 'girl-friendly', this might well dissuade boys from attempting to monopolize it and provide greater opportunities for girls to acquire high levels of computer literacy. Let us grasp the devil's advocate by the tail and paint this girl-friendly computer pink. The point is that potential changes in use now appear to result from a different apprehension of the computer's gender, rather than from an intrinsically 'female computer'. Does painting something pink make the technology feminine, or does it make our apprehension of its 'appropriate' gender one associated with femininity?

The anti-essentialist liberal feminist approach might not be concerned with computer colours since the problem is not deemed to lie in the technology but in the unequal opportunities which deter girls and women from engaging with computers. As Kreinberg and Stage recount, with regard to US examples:

> The biggest barriers to women taking advantage of the computer revolution are the myths and stereotypes about technology that are well established in children's minds at a very early age ... Changes

must take place in schools and outside of schools so that women will
have equal access to computer technology. (1983, p. 28)

Thus, we are more likely to see support for female pupils/students expressed
in a variety of ways: advertising campaigns, more resources, stronger
targeting of female pupils/students, 'awareness' campaigns and, perhaps,
some provision for girl/women-only computer and IT courses. Since this
form of approach does not attribute any particular gender or gender-related
capabilities to the technology, the constructivist might have some theoretical
empathy with this kind of approach; but liberal models do tend to assume that
the technology is neutral, that is, beyond the interpretive construction of the
user. In effect, for the liberal, technology cannot be the problem, and it is far
more likely that the problem lies in women's 'failure' to realize their own
potential.[14] It may or may not be coincidental that the great majority of such
policies appear, at least so far, to have been abject failures. It is precisely
because this perspective refuses to countenance the possibility that what we
take to be the same technology is apprehended in radically different ways by
different people that it will, in all probability, continue to fail. If the problem
is that we see technology differently then no amount of lens cleaning will
help – we need to recognize that people are using different lenses rather than
assume that some people are wearing smudged glasses.

One might want to question here just how non-essentialist and liberal
such a perspective really is. If the essentialist model is one where the
'essence' of a phenomenon explains its behaviour or action then although the
liberal model rejects the idea that technology is distorted through its male
origins it nevertheless implies that all humans, regardless of sex, have an
essence. Admittedly, in the case of women, this essence is distorted through
the gendered inequalities that persist, but once equal opportunities are
deployed then the true and equal essence of men and women will prevail. In
effect both liberal feminist and eco-feminist positions have at their heart a
similar essentialist position.

Deus ex Machina or *Machina ex Dea*? – The Politics and Gender of Technology

The term *deus ex machina* is drawn from the world of theatre (appropriately
enough, an arena replete with rhetoric, performance, persuasive accounts,
irony and the rest) and describes a mechanical device from which, when
drawn up over or on the stage, an actress or actor in the role of a goddess or
god was deposited, usually to unravel a complicated plot. The symbolic

nature of a divine spirit being encased within a machine represents a typical response by many people to technology itself, indeed, the Enlightenment was, and modernism is, very much a movement bound tightly to the idea of freedom through reason, a reason often manifest as technology.[15]

It seems that it is not easy for anti-essentialism to throw off this imagery. For the most part anti-essentialism takes issue with the *identity* of the god (or whatever entity) in the machine, rather than questioning the very idea that there is 'something' 'in there' in the first place. Anti-essentialists are busy trying to replace the god of technical rationality with the god of social and political interests; or, in the case of (some) feminists, with the god of gender bias.[16] But theirs is still fundamentally a religious endeavour: this god rather than that one. By contrast, post-essentialism asks what it would take to challenge the existence of (any) god. It aspires to reject the essentialist notion of gods or goddesses in machines. The appearance of a deity within the machinery has to be understood as more akin to a mirror of human hopes and fears than anything. Post-essentialism is hard work: it is a position to which we aspire rather than one we can claim to have yet attained. One of the main reasons for the difficulty is that we are, of course, prisoners of the conventions of language and representation which display, reaffirm and sustain the basic premises of essentialism: that entities of all kinds, but most visibly and consequentially technical artefacts and technological systems, possess characteristics and capacities, and are capable of 'effects'. This seems to be a fundamental property of the objectivist language game in which we are all embroiled. It follows that a radical move away from essentialism, attempted but (we have shown) failed by many anti-essentialists, requires nothing short of a major reworking of the categories and conventions of conventional language use (cf. Haraway, 1991 chapter 8). Attempts to expose 'the actual' politics, social interests, gender biases etc. are liberating and inspiring. And certainly they are an improvement on nasty old traditionalist treatments of the topic. But in the end they are merely moves within the same essentialist language game.[17] The especially dangerous temptation is to get wound up in disputes about whether one or another category of antecedent circumstances is the more appropriate essence of the machine.

The fact of our enmeshment in the language game of essentialism, and our suffocation within its base premises, is evident from the linguistic contortions and convolutions necessary even to create a small amount of breathing space. We have already pointed out how the metaphor of 'embodiment', although intended as a way of generating a fresh apprehension of familiar (technical) objects, still implies a definite independently available object. Similarly, we showed how causal features in stories about the 'effects' of a technology imply a definitive object, the explanans. We spoke with approval of the more determined efforts of the 'constitutive' wing of anti-essentialism to escape this form of discussion. But even in this case we saw the difficulty of adequately formulating the necessary language. It is better to say that technologies are constituted rather than merely shaped or constructed; that antecedent circumstances are inscribed in, rather than merely informing, design; that users are configured, not just enrolled; and so on. But all the juggling of language involved in these efforts comes to seem so precious. By this route, do we end up putting 'scare quotes' around everything?[18] Or should our alternative strategy require us instead to explore new forms of writing and reflexivity, to invent new monsters and marginal beings which might displace standard units of analysis and transcend conventional categories and distinctions?[19]

The problem, then, with, feminism, constructivism and other forms of anti-essentialism is that they are insufficiently anti-essentialist. Anti-essentialism fails to transcend essentialism in the way that post-essentialism aspires to. Anti-essentialists seem unable or unwilling to take the (difficult) step towards post-essentialism which will turn their limited insinuations of antecedent circumstances into a truly radical critique of technology. Our tripartite division is between post-essentialism, essentialism and anti-essentialism: the good, the bad and the nervous. What accounts for this failure of nerve on the part of anti-essentialism?

One obvious answer is that post-essentialism (and in the context of disputes for the political and moral high ground, post-just-about-everything-else) is regarded as simply beyond the pale. It is viewed as an extreme form of relativism which represents a distraction from the urgent demands of political action. We have already cast doubt, in general terms, on the presumption that recommendations for political action have a coherent basis in anti-essentialism. We now consider some specific objections to epistemological relativism as it has been aligned with 'constructivist' perspectives. Our point is that the failings identified in constructivism arise, not because it goes epistemologically 'over the top', but precisely because it equivocates in its efforts to escape essentialism.

For feminists like Keller (1988) (and for other anti-essentialists like Kling (1992) and Winner) 'excessive' relativism implies a rejection of the possibility of establishing 'the truth' about technology or science or anything else. They might claim that in a discussion about bicycle tyres (Pinch and Bijker, 1989), this is all well and good: such debates can throw critical light on historical processes with little fear of moral or ethical contention. But when it comes to an issue like patriarchy, they would say, relativism is the fount of moral compromise. Kirkup and Keller (1992) put the point forcefully:

epistemological relativism ... suggests that there are as many truths
as individual people and that no single truth has any claim to be
better than any other ... As a position it runs counter not only to the
aims of science, but to those of feminism of the 1970s and '80s.
Feminism as a theory, and a political movement, claims that there are
'facts' and 'realities' about the position of women, such as rape,
domestic violence and unequal pay that are a key to understanding
sexual oppression, and that these have been hidden or distorted ...
science and feminism have similar agendas in that they are both
concerned to remedy distortion and move closer towards a more
accurate description of how things are. (1992, p. 10)

There are three issues here. First, whether knowledge reflects or constructs
the truth; on this issue we have made clear our preference for the latter
position and will not rehearse the arguments again. Second, whether the
denial of a single reflective and objective truth hides the 'realities' of
women's position. The irony here is that constructivists are precisely
concerned to support alternative truth claims rather than necessarily siding
with prevailing ones. What constructivists might add to the debate here
would be a critical analysis of patriarchal claims to 'truth' – without
automatically supporting the claims of feminists to be in possession of the
alternative but truly 'real' truth. After all, do all feminists claim to support
the same interpretation of patriarchy? If, not, then, under a realist approach,
we are still left with having to assert that some feminists are in possession
of the truth and others not. If, as has frequently happened, we are accused of
siding with the powerful in such disputes, then presumably we would be
guilty of siding with the powerful feminists against the weak feminists so that
we are still no nearer 'the truth'.

The related assertion, that constructivism surrounds itself with contend-
ing claims to truth between which it has no means of discriminating is,
however, misinformed. The constructivist does not assert that all claims have
equal status but, instead, asks which claims attract the most significant
support and why this is so. Take the example of domestic violence (by men
on women). Kirkup and Keller's essentialist view is that feminism, like
'science', is (and should be) intent on uncovering 'the truth' about domestic
violence, a truth allegedly hidden from view by patriarchal distortion. This
approach implies that research can 'discover' the truth and that this discovery
will lead, eventually at least, to mechanisms which prevent it. The charge
against constructivism is that its denial of objective truth allows its adherents
either to sit on the fence and procrastinate about truth claims while women
are battered or, worse, that it actually sanctions violence by accepting the

proposition that 'the truth' is that form of discourse which is the one most successfully deployed at the time. The latter charge is simply wrong: assessing the strength of a truth claim through an analysis of its social construction is not equivalent to supporting that claim.

The former charge is more complex. Constructivism does leave one bereft of the certainties that might propel a political fanatic or religious fundamentalist; for these people the truth is self-evident and the line of action follows directly from such truth. For the constructivist there may, of course, be a pragmatic legitimation of action – doubts about truth claims are fine for the university seminar but too dangerous for the real world. Does this mean there is a clear limit to the application of Kant's injunction *Sapere Aude* (dare to know)? Acquiescence to the politics of the 'real world' – to which we are enjoined by critics of relativism – implies not just a pragmatic boundary but an epistemological, and ultimately political, flaw. Certainly Kling (1992) and Winner (1993) have attacked constructivists for being politically naive and implicitly conservative.

Elam (1994) develops one form of liberal defence on behalf of (rather than in support of) relativism, using Rorty's (1989) distinction between a liberal 'ironicist' and a liberal 'metaphysician'. The ironicist accepts truth as contingent and refuses to privilege her or his own position over that of others – since this privileging is both dubious and potentially humiliating for those who believe otherwise. Liberal metaphysicians, and we can include Kling and Winner here, strive to coerce 'ironicists' into taking sides on moral issues – and castigate them for refusing to do so. According to Elam, ironicists argue that taking sides involves inflicting cruelty on the 'other' side for refusing to accede to one's own opinion. In Elam's words, 'because we can only ever know *differently* and never *better* than anyone else, we are never justified in thrusting our knowledge upon others' (1994; p. 104, emphasis in original). Elam concludes with a liberal (though ultimately sceptical) defence of the ironicist's 'freedom to speak' and a positive evaluation of its utility in the face of those 'metaphysicians' who claim to have seen the truth and who demand that the rest of us follow suit (or risk, at best, the charge of not being politically correct). However, Elam, like Kirkup and Keller (1992), still persists in assuming that constructivism remains a neutral – or perhaps uncommitted and hence untrustworthy – voyeur at the scene of a crime. In Orwellian terms, because constructivists remain sceptical of truth claims, all truth claims are equal. For anti-constructivists the result is that constructivists, albeit by default, allow the strong to remain strong and the weak to suffer. But why should constructivists not engage in political debate and action? The recognition of contingency in truth claims does not necessarily lead to self-inflicted inaction but merely to (more) reflexive action.

Rorty's concern to avoid humiliating others may be a fine ironicist's strategy in the seminar room; after all, humiliating students is hardly the best way to encourage participation. But how far does this strategy hold? What happens when the ironicist's potential target is not a student who needs encouraging but a man accused of assaulting a woman? Is this the point where constructivists' scepticism buttresses the violence of the strong against the weak? That a woman's claim to have been assaulted by a man can be considered as a construction of the truth is not the equivalent of relegating such claims to the land of fiction: a construction is not a lie; it is the way we construct narratives, not the way we deliberately set out to deceive. The point here is, why do the claims of such women tend to be overridden in a society steeped in patriarchal values? The recognition that the truth is socially constructed facilitates rather than debilitates those who are relatively weak in society. The issue is not that constructivists undertake a self-denying ordinance to keep out of political or social controversies but that their engagement is grounded in a different appreciation of the construction of the world. Thus, in this example, women who claim to have been battered can utilize, and be supported by, constructivist deconstructions of patriarchal power in the home. For instance, the recognition of violence against women as something which society should not accept is not something that is undermined by the argument that society and its morality is socially constructed; it merely means that the sanction against violence derives from some form of social agreement and is not derived through either the instructions of a god or the distillation of moral behaviour through scientific assessment of human nature. Of course, this also means that morality is contingent in time and space – as indeed cultural historians and anthropologists are constantly reminding us. In effect, then, constructivism does not debar its adherents from supporting battered women against battering men, but it does provide a different kind of resource and it does require a reflexive monitoring of language and practice which realists and fundamentalists ignore.

Is the contingency of this approach valuable to such women? That is, what can constructivists offer that non-constructivists cannot? First, a recognition that the ability of men to batter their female partners does not depend upon distorting 'the truth', hiding reality from their partners or society. If the reality which prevails in courts is patriarchal and not objective, and if the quest for objective reality is pointless, then the strategy should be one in which the counter-claim to the truth is sculpted to appeal to the jury and where the patriarchal concept of truth is deconstructed such that doubt falls upon the attacker's story and not the victim's story. Indeed, this is precisely what already happens in many court cases: the jury is frequently given two very different versions of the truth and asked to decide which one is most believable. In effect, the judicial system is premised upon conflicting truth claims. However, this does not mean that patriarchy always wins – though it might explain why men frequently avoid conviction for alleged attacks upon women. Do we ever really know precisely what happened in any particular trial or do we simply have to side with the defence or the prosecution and assume that one account is the most likely – the most persuasive construction of the truth? That several people have recently been released from prison in the UK, and had their convictions quashed, suggests that even persuasive constructions of the truth are contingent.

We might take this one stage further to clarify the position by altering the case in hand. In the case of abortion it is relatively easy to argue that one does not have to be manifestly overjoyed by every abortion to reject anti-abortionists' claims which are grounded in an appeal to 'the truth' as revealed by god.[20] Similarly, one does not have to choose between being pro-feminist and anti-feminist with regard to the technologizing of the reproductive process. For those concerned to wrest 'the truth' from the obscurantist hands of men, the political or moral line to be followed can be derived from the 'truth' about the issue. Since men control technology, and intervention by men with technology – for example, in-vitro fertilization – must be 'truly' another attempt to control women. The policy for feminists, then, is to reject all such technologies. But there are several markedly divergent lines of feminist thought and policy in this area, so which one is closer to the truth – and is this proximity to veracity the correct criterion for action? It should be clear that those policies grounded in notions of 'truth' are potentially far more authoritarian than those which hold what counts as the truth to be a contingent issue.[21]

In sum, recognizing the contingent nature of the 'truth' need not immobilize the constructivist; but it may deter her or him from undertaking self-righteous action in pursuit of something which realists would claim is the truth. Thus, it is more likely to encourage scepticism than fanaticism, and more likely to encourage liberalism than fascism or communism. It is more likely to remain unimpressed by claims that women are indeed witches and should be burnt at the stake; its adherents are less likely to be found in the ranks of the faithful, engaged in a holy war for the truth against all unbelievers. It is not the kind of philosophy to start revolutions in pursuit of utopia; it is the kind which remains unconvinced that burning people is the best way to save their souls or that there is only one road to heaven and those not going in the right direction are going the wrong way and, for their own benefit, should be cleansed of their errors.

In pointing out the essentialist elements of much anti-essentialism, we have shown how feminism and constructivism are inconsistent, fail to be renewing and lack audacity.[22] In many respects, however, the same charge could be made about our own argument: in order to specify the faults of anti-essentialism we have had to specify its 'essential' features; our articulation of the failings entailed in reliance upon the realist language game has itself been couched within the terms of that game. What is the consequence of this observation? One interpretation is that it simply casts doubt on the force of our criticism. We have hardly progressed much beyond the use of conventions which support and reaffirm essentialism; ours is an argument well within the 'tu quoque' tradition (Ashmore, 1989). More interesting, however, is the sense in which this observation reinforces the argument we advance (but, admittedly, fail to exemplify). Adopting a post-essentialist mode seems to entail doing away with or at least taking issue with the critical attitude. But the other important corollary of essentialism is that it is seen as providing a necessary condition for political import. In other words, criticism can be taken as a token of the 'political' motivations of its perpetrators, whereas non-criticism is all too easily identified with a lack of politics. This raises an important issue. It makes us realize that realist conventions not only confine us to parameters of essentialist argument, but also commit us to a particular form of politics. The question is, then, whether and to what extent an exploration of alternative forms of post-essentialism can define an alternative form of politically relevant inquiry.

Conclusion

So where does this leave our machined deity? Is it a god or a goddess? Does it matter anyway? We have suggested, against both essentialism and anti-essentialism, that the gender of a technology does not lie encased in the fabric of the material. It is instead the temporary contingent upshot of on-going interpretation by designers, sellers and users. The politics and values of technology, in this perspective, result from the gaze of the human; they do not lie in the gauze of the machine. This does not mean that the machine is neutral. Since what it is, what its capacities are and what it represents are social constructions not objective reflections, the machine always appears (to steal a phrase from Lévi-Strauss) cooked and never raw. Descriptions of, and practices with, technology – the methods by which we come to know technology – necessarily embody social and political values, but these do not lie within the hard creases or soft folds of the machine. Thus, where a goddess or devil appears in machine form it is us who construct this form. The 'truth' of the nuclear bomb appears to combine two diametrically opposite 'truths': it is inescapably a political device, even a masculine machine, destined to first terrorize and then obliterate the entire human race – it is the god of war; or it is a neutral amalgam of chemicals and metals destined to eliminate the threat of world war – the deity designed to protect the human species. What the thing actually is, even what its exact capabilities and effects are, is not something that any kind of detached, objective or realist analysis seems capable of constructing. What it is depends on who is describing it; it is not that every account of it is equal – evidently, the eco-feminist account is not powerful enough to persuade political leaders completely to abandon the technology. But this is precisely why post-essentialism can provide resources for those seeking to change the world rather than just account for it. If Foucault is right that truth and power are intimately intertwined, those seeking to change the world might try strategies to recruit powerful allies rather than assuming that the quest for revealing 'the truth' will, in and through itself, lead to dramatic changes in levels and forms of social inequality. If the deity in the machine is male, if technology in a patriarchal society is essentially masculine, then no amount of reiteration of this point will alter 'reality' – would men really let power slip so easily from their grasp? On the other hand, if the gendered significance of a technology lies in the interpretive framework within which it is constructed, then there is a possibility of deconstructing and subsequently reconstructing the technology. As Prometheus found to his cost, even male gods with magical technologies to empower men can find themselves powerless. But whether the deity in the machine is a god or a goddess or just an actress or actor depends crucially on the active construction achieved by the audience rather than the assembly of wood, wire and flesh on the stage.

Notes

1   A recent review of this field, by Wajcman (1991), is a good example of this kind of theoretical approach. Wajcman adopts an overtly anti-essentialist model and stresses the socially and culturally constructed nature of gender, with its implication that what counts as a patriarchal technology is a social, not an objective, phenomenon.

2   We return, at the end of this chapter, to a critical evaluation of the assumption, often implicit in 'political' critiques of technology, that some form of essentialist (objectivist) account is a necessary basis for political (and policy) action (cf. Elam, 1994; Woolgar, 1992, 1993). In brief, the problem with this assumption is that it entails unexplicated preconceptions of the nature and identity of the relevant audiences, and of their motivations and reading practices.

3   A different version of this chapter appears in *Science, Technology and Human Values*, 12, 3.

4   This view accepts that there may be disagreements and ambiguities as to what

precisely that technical capacity is, but holds *de facto* to the view that some objective view of technical capacity is in principle available.

5 For example, in a recent article, Winner (1993) makes much of the particular differences in antecedent circumstances selected by his approach and by members of what he calls 'social constructivism'.

6 The same problem occurs in some symbolic interactionist accounts of language which, bizarrely, speak of items as having meaning 'attached to them' (Oh, excuse me my meaning has just fallen off).

7 Similar equivocation over the realist basis of purportedly anti-essentialist arguments has been identified in the 'labeling theory' (Pollner, 1978) and 'social problems' (Woolgar and Pawluch, 1985) literatures.

8 It follows from our observation that practical argument conventionally entails realist auspices, that it is difficult for ontological agnosticism – when couched within these conventions – to make itself heard. For similar reasons, constructivist arguments are often decried for their (allegedly) absurd (ontological) implications, usually through appeal to the brute facts of material objects and/or death. See Ashmore *et al.* (1993).

9 We discuss below some implications of this point for our own attempt to move away from essentialism.

10 This means, of course, that no historian has (yet) done the constructivist work to (re)constitute these intentions. See Stanley (1992) for some artefacts designed by women that have been 'rediscovered'.

11 That strength is an attribute which can be enhanced through practices which are themselves gendered is not something we wish to go into here.

12 In considering objections to our analysis, it is evident that a whole series of auxiliary hypotheses can be mobilized to protect the central essentialist argument. It could be said, for example, that few scythes were in fact available to the sickle-wielding gangs of 1921, or that, in employing women part-time, Post Office managers were alert to the inherently tiring prospects of making them carry loads full-time. It seems our charges of inconsistency can thus always be countered by the invocation of other antecedent circumstances which keep the basic essentialist characterization of the technology intact. This is a reflection of the conventional view that there is always more room for debate about antecedent circumstances than about the inherent properties of a technology.

13 See Margaret Atwood's *The Handmaid's Tale* for a fictional account of this scenario.

14 See Cockburn (1991) and Kvande and Rasmussen (1986) on women's 'failure' in organizations.

15 Perhaps the most bizarre instantiation of this developed in (what was) the Soviet Union under Stalin when Alexei Gastev, then head of the influential Central Institute of Labour, designed and constructed a 'social engineering machine'. This machine, never completed but composed of any array of pulleys, wire and levers, was destined to make society, and therefore the Soviet People, ever more rational. Ultimately, it should have turned out perfectly rational humans and one social engineering machine was to be installed in every major population centre across the entire Soviet Union (*Pandora's Box*, Channel 4, 11 June 1992). Here, truly, was a deity in machine form – albeit one that failed.

16 Rothschild (1983) coined the phrase *dea ex machina* to suggest not just that language is gendered but that women's role in the construction, development and

deployment of technology is all but invisible and this has led to a particular relationship between people and technology. On both counts we would agree, though she does not go on to question whether the technology itself is gendered through the language or whether the language merely reflects the gender allegedly inherent in the technology.

17   As feminists have long since charged, language is not neutral in this scene nor, as (some) other anti-essentialists argue, is language a mere carrier of meaning: language may be gendered but it is also the means by which meanings are constructed rather than reflected.

18   Or should that read 'putting scare quotes around "everything"'?

19   Some moves in this direction can be found in explorations in reflexivity (Ashmore, 1989; Woolgar, 1988); the creation of hopeful monsters (Law, 1991); cyborgs (Haraway, 1991) and quasi-objects (Latour, 1993).

20   See Elam's (1994) reconstruction of Geertz (1984).

21   The apparent moral equivocation in (some versions of) constructivism is discussed in more detail in Grint and Woolgar (forthcoming, chapter 6).

22   We are especially grateful to comments from Marianne de Laet for inspiring this section of the paper.

References

ANDERSON, B.S. and ZINSSER, J.P. (1990) *A History of their Own: Women in Europe from Prehistory to the Present*, Harmondsworth, Penguin.

ASHMORE, M. (1989) *The Reflexive Thesis: Wrighting Sociology of Scientific Knowledge*, Chicago, University of Chicago Press.

ASHMORE, M., EDWARDS, D. and POTTER, J. (1993) Death and Furniture: An Analysis of Bottom Line Arguments against Relativism', Department of Social Sciences, Loughborough University.

BERG, A.J. (1991) 'He, She and I.T. – Designing the Technological House of the Future', IFIM Paper no. 12/91, Trondheim: Institute for Social Research in Industry, Trondheim.

BIJKER, W.E. and LAW, J. (Eds) (1992) *Shaping Technology/Building Society*, Cambridge, Mass., MIT.

BIJKER, W.E., HUGHES, T.P. and PINCH, T.J. (Eds) (1987) *The Social Construction of Technological Systems*, Cambridge, Mass., MIT Press.

COCKBURN, C. (1983) *Brothers: Male Dominance and Technological Change*, London, Pluto Press.

COCKBURN, C. (1985) *Machinery of Dominance: Women, Men and Technical Know-How*, London, Pluto Press.

COCKBURN, C. (1991) *In the Way of Women*, London, Macmillan.

COOLEY, M. (1968) *Architect or Bee?*, Slough, Langley Technical Services.

COREA, G. *et al.* (1985) *Man-Made Women: How New Reproductive Technologies Affect Women*, London, Hutchinson.

COULTER, J. (1989) *Mind in Action*, Cambridge, Polity.

COWAN, R.S. (1983) *More Work for Mother*, New York, Basic Books.

DIXON, N.F. (1976) *On the Psychology of Military Incompetence*, London, Futura.

EASLEA, B. (1983) *Fathering the Unthinkable: Masculinity, Scientists and the Nuclear Arms Race*, London, Pluto Press.

ELAM, M. (1994) 'Anti anticonstructivism or Laying the Fears of a Langdon Winner to Rest', *Science, Technology and Human Values*, vol. 19, no. 1, pp. 101–6.

FARRANT, W. (1985) 'Who's for Amniocentesis? The Politics of Prenatal Screening', in HOMANS, H. (Ed.) *The Sexual Politics of Reproduction*, Aldershot, Gower.

FIRESTONE, S. (1970) *The Dialectic of Sex*, New York, William Morrow.

GEERTZ, C. (1984) *The Interpretation of Cultures*, London, Sage.

GRINT, K. and WOOLGAR, S. (forthcoming) *Deus ex Machina: Technology, Work and Society*, Cambridge, Polity.

HACKER, S. (1989) *Pleasure, Power and Technology*, London, Unwin.

HARAWAY, D.J. (1991) *Simians, Cyborgs and Women: The Reinvention of Nature*, New York, Routledge.

HARDING, J. (Ed.) (1986) *Perspectives on Gender and Science*, Brighton, Falmer.

HIRSCHAUER, S. and MOL, A. (1993) 'Beyond Embrace: Multiple Sexes at Multiple Sites', paper presented to Conference on European Theoretical Perspectives on New Technology: Feminism, Constructivism and Utility, CRICT, Brunel University, 16–17 September.

KELLER, E.F. (1988) 'Feminist Perspectives on Science Studies', *Science, Technology and Human Values*, vol. 13, pp. 235–49.

KIRKUP, G. and KELLER, L.S. (1992) The Nature of Science and technology', in KIRKUP, G. and KELLER, L.S. (Eds) *Inventing Women: Science, Technology and Gender*, Cambridge, Polity.

KLEIN, R. (1985) 'What's "New" about the "New" Reproductive Technologies?', in COREA, G. *et al.* Man-Made Women. London, Hutchinson.

KLING, R. (1992) 'Audiences, Narratives and Human Values in Social Studies of Technology', *Science, Technology and Human Values*, vol. 17, no. 3, pp. 349–65.

KREINBERG, N. and STAGE, E.K. (1983) 'EQUALS in Computer Technology', in Zimmerman, J. (Ed.) *The Technological Woman: Interfacing with Tomorrow*, New York, Praeger Publishers.

KVANDE, E. and RASMUSSEN, B. (1986) 'Who Lacks Courage – the Organizations or the Women?', NOTAT Paper No. 5, Trondheim, Institute for Social Research in Industry.

LAET, M. DE (1993) Discussant's Remarks: Workshop on European Theoretical Perspectives on New Technology: Feminism, Constructivism and Utility, CRICT, Brunel University, 16–17 September.

LATOUR, B. (1993) *We Have Never Been Modern*, Hemel Hempstead, Harvester Wheatsheaf.

LAW, J. (Ed.) (1991) *A Sociology of Monsters: Essays on Power, Technology and Domination*, London, Routledge.

MACKENZIE, D. (1990) *Inventing Accuracy: A Historical Sociology of Missile Guidance*, Cambridge, Mass, MIT Press.

MCNEIL, M. (Ed.) (1987) *Gender and Expertise*, London, Free Association Books.

MOSKOS, C. (1990) 'Army Women', *Atlantic Monthly*, August.

PINCH, T.J. and BIJKER, W.E. (1989) 'The Social Construction of Facts and Artefacts: Or How the Sociology of Science and the Sociology of Technology Might Benefit Each Other', in BIJKER, W.E., HUGHES, T.P. and PINCH, T.J. (Eds) *The Social Construction of Technological Systems*, Cambridge, Mass., MIT Press.

POLLNER, M. (1978) 'Constitutive and Mundane Versions of Labeling Theory', *Human Sciences*, 31, pp. 285–304.

PRINS, B. (1993) 'The Ethics of Hybrid Subjects: Feminist Constructivism According to Donna Haraway', paper presented to Conference on European Theoretical Perspectives on New Technology: Feminism, Constructivism and Utility, CRICT, Brunel University, 16–17 September.

ROBERTS, M. (1979) 'Sickles and Scythes', *History Workshop Journal*, no. 7, pp. 3–28.

RORTY, R. (1989) *Contingency, Irony and Solidarity*, Cambridge, Cambridge University Press.

ROTHSCHILD, J. (1983) *Machina Ex Dea*, Oxford, Pergamon Press.

ROWLAND, R. (1992) *Living Laboratories: Women and Reproductive Technologies*, London, Lime Tree.

SHEILDS, P.M. (1988) 'Sex Roles in the Military', in MOSKOS, C. AND WOOD, F.R. (Eds) *The Military:More Than Just a Job?* Oxford, Pergamon-Brassey.

SØRENSEN, K.H. (1992) 'Towards a Feminized Technology? Gendered Values in the Construction of Technology', *Social Studies of Science*, 22, pp. 5–31.

STANLEY, A. (1992) *Mothers of Invention*, New Jersey, Scarecrow Press.

TURKLE, S. and PAPERT, S. (1990) 'Epistemological Pluralism: Styles and Voices within the Computer Culture', *Signs: Journal of Women in Culture and Society*, vol. 16, no. 1.

VAN ZOONEN, L. (1992) 'Feminist Theory and Information Technology', *Media, Culture and Society*, vol. 14, no. 1, pp. 9–30.

WAJCMAN, J. (1991) *Feminism Confronts Technology*, Cambridge, Polity.

WHEELWRIGHT, J. (1992) '"A Brother in Arms, a Sister in Peace": Contemporary Issues of Gender and Military Technology', in KIRKUP, G. and KELLER, L.S. (Eds) *Inventing Women*, Cambridge, Polity.

WINNER, L. (1980) 'Do Artifacts Have Politics?, *Daedalus*, vol. 109, no. 1, pp. 121–36. Reprinted in MACKENZIE, D. and WAJCMAN, J. (Eds) (1985) *The Social Shaping of Technology*, Milton Keynes, Open University Press.

WINNER, L. (1993) 'Upon Opening the Black Box and Finding It Empty: Social Constructivism and the Philosophy of Technology', *Science, Technology and Human Values*, vol. 18, no. 3, pp. 362–78.

WOOLGAR, S. (1981) 'Interests and Explanation in the Social Study of Science', *Social Studies of Science*, **11**, pp. 365–94.

WOOLGAR, S. (Ed.) (1988) *Knowledge and Reflexivity: New Frontiers in the Sociology of Knowledge*, London, Sage.

WOOLGAR, S. (1992) 'Who/What Is This For? – Utility and Value as Textual Accomplishments', paper presented to 4S/EASST conference, Gothenburg, 12–15 August.

WOOLGAR, S. (1993) 'What's at Stake in the Sociology of Technology?', *Science, Technology and Human Values*, vol. 18, no. 4, pp. 523–9.

WOOLGAR, S. and PAWLUCH, D. (1985) 'Ontological Gerrymandering: The Anatomy of Social Problems Explanations', *Social Problems*, 32, pp. 214–27.

Part II

Case Studies of the Gender-Technology Relation

Chapter 3

Gender is Calling: Some Reflections on Past, Present and Future Uses of the Telephone

Valerie Frissen

Introduction

In communication studies until recently the social uses and implications of the telephone have been strikingly neglected, in spite of the crucial role the telephone must have played in some major changes in the industrialized countries. In particular, the uses of the telephone in everyday life have received little attention from either communication researchers or applied researchers in telecommunications. Relative to other communication media, the telephone is often taken for granted. Consequently, little is known about the ways in which the telephone is implemented and used in everyday life.

Recent research (e.g., Fischer, 1988, 1992; Martin, 1991; Moyal, 1992; Rakow, 1988, 1992) has shown that residential telephone usage tends to be remarkably gendered. Women might be characterized as heavy users of the telephone (Adler, 1993; Claisse and Rowe, 1992; Dordick and LaRose, 1992; Maddox, 1977). What is even more interesting is that there seems to be a 'dynamic, feminine culture of the telephone' (Moyal, 1992). The Australian researcher, Moyal, observed an extensive and intensive telephone traffic between women, particularly between family members and between close women friends. According to Moyal, this results in a social support system that has vital consequences for the nation. In Australia, people often live far apart, and the telephone is used by women to overcome separation because of distance. In this respect women's telephone communication is crucial to create and maintain a system of social relations. Moyal refers to this as the 'telephone neighbourhood'.

According to Rakow, telephone use can be conceptualized as 'gender work' (social practices that create and sustain individuals as women and men) and 'gendered work' (productive activity assigned to women) (1992, p. 1). On the one hand, the ways men and women use the telephone underline and reinforce cultural constructions of masculinity and femininity. On the other hand, the uses of the telephone by women can be labelled gender work, because the objective is to build a network of social relations and in that way women 'hold together the fabric of community'.

In spite of the crucial role the telephone seems to play in women's everyday life (on which I shall speak in greater detail in the following sections), the uses women make of the telephone are not taken very seriously. Jokes about women gossiping on the telephone are familiar to everyone. Even the telephone industry itself had a blind spot for women's uses of the telephone. The American and Canadian industries (see Fischer, 1992; Martin, 1991) promoted the telephone mainly for business purposes. Domestic telephone use, particularly for sociability reasons, was not only weakly promoted, but even disapproved of. Social calls were labelled 'idle talk', 'frivolous and unnecessary'. Although many people, particularly women, used the telephone mainly for sociability reasons, it took the industry about twenty years to realize that sociability was a goal worthy of being advertised and marketed.

We are now witnessing a new phase in the innovation process of telephony. All kinds of new services and applications are being, or will soon be, introduced in the domestic sphere. The discourses accompanying these innovations again show a striking absence of attention to gender differences. It goes without saying that the potential uses of new telephone services will be heavily influenced by the uses of the 'plain old telephone'. Nevertheless, gender is still almost never taken into account by either researchers or professionals in the field of telecommunications.

In this chapter I shall formulate some preliminary ideas about the gendered uses of some new services and applications in the field of telephony. By taking the gendered uses of the 'plain old telephone' as a starting point, I shall try to assess the potential of the 'new telephone' from a gender perspective.

A question underlying my interest in this issue is whether the telephone is used as a 'space-adjusting technology': in what ways do men and women use the telephone to arrange and to rearrange their geographical and social space? What is the role of the telephone in reshaping definitions of social space, such as the traditional division between a public and a private sphere? In the next section I shall first describe the gendered uses of the *old* telephone from this point of view.

The 'Plain Old Telephone'

Recently, a small wave of papers, articles and books has been published in which, after a long period of striking neglect of this subject, the relation between gender and the telephone is analysed. Several publications have documented the early history of the telephone and in doing so have paid more (Maddox, 1977; Martin, 1991) or less (Fischer, 1992) attention to the way gender relations enter into this history. Looking at the social history of the telephone from a gender perspective, two issues spring to attention. First, in the USA, Canada and Europe, Bell's invention created a new field of employment for women as telephone operators. Second, by heavily using the telephone as an instrument in social traffic, women users influenced the unwilling telephone industry to accept sociability as an important use for the telephone, worthy of being marketed as such.

Both issues are relevant to gaining insight into how the telephone functions as a space-adjusting technology. Furthermore, some interesting parallels can be drawn between the early history of telephony and some more recent innovations. In what follows I shall try to demonstrate this.

The 'Voice with a Smile'

In setting up a telephone system, the industry faced a paradox (Martin, 1991). The early telephone system could not work without operators functioning as mediators between users of the system. At the same time, these operators represented an obstacle: users wanted to have private conversations, but they could be listened to by the operator. The telephone system was a public space, but at the same time a space used for private interactions. Particularly since we are speaking here about the Victorian era, moral regulation of this paradoxical situation was considered necessary. Communication by telephone, it was argued, should not undermine the public image of the telephone companies, and therefore it was seen as necessary to develop an etiquette for telephone behaviour. In this process the role and behaviour of the operator were considered crucial.

These considerations led to the almost complete feminization of the job of telephone operator. The perfect operator should have certain qualities and moral values that could serve as an example to potential users and subscribers. In the starting period of the telephone, the industry used boys for this job, particularly because boys were supposed to have some technical know-how that was considered useful for the job, for example, to do minor repairs. However, according to some of the company managers at that time, very soon telephone companies started to employ mainly women as operators, because boys appeared to be the wrong choice: 'they were noisy, rude, impatient and talked back to subscribers, played tricks with wires and on one another' (Martin, 1991, p. 55; see also Maddox, 1977). Women were considered more suited for the job, precisely because of the qualities and virtues that were highly esteemed in women of the Victorian era.[1] They were more patient, had softer and more musical voices, were never rude and always discreet and, not least, their work was very cheap. Already in the 1880s nearly all of the telephone operators were women, often from the middle classes, and mostly young, because they were expected to leave when they got married (Maddox, 1977).

Reading these social histories of the telephone, what becomes clear is that the female operator had become very important for the telephone industry. According to Martin, company managers did not hesitate to admit that female operators were instrumental in the growth of the telephone industry. The specific 'feminine' qualities of operators were exploited by the industry in several ways. The telephone system was promoted by using images of their employees: they were pictured as the 'voice with a smile'. By developing a moral standard for telephone communications through their female workers, the companies tried to attract new subscribers and to improve their corporate image at the same time. The work of an operator was not only to make the right connections, but also to keep subscribers informed, for example on time, weather, transport schedules and election results (Maddox, 1977, p. 268), and to deal with the questions and problems of the public. It is, therefore, fair to conclude that these women played an important role not only in the diffusion of the telephone system, but also in the development of a new pattern of social interactions. Communication by telephone must have been rather revolutionary for people who were not used to it and it seems logical that the 'voice with a smile' made it much easier to get accustomed to this new form of communication.

The central role of operators in interactions by telephone is even more evident if we look at the role of the operator in rural areas. The social history of the telephone reveals that well into the twentieth century, operators in small rural communities had a high social status, and a certain degree of power, because these women often knew everything that was going on in the village. Particularly in the early stage of the telephone system, when party lines were still common, the operator was the focal point in a communication system that bound the rural community together. All information passed through one person. The party line system made it possible for subscribers sharing the same line to listen in on each other's communications. This, again, resulted in a strong regulation of telephone behaviour in which the operator was crucial: subscribers were supposed to use the phone only for serious matters and for a limited time span. To use the telephone just for chatting was disapproved of. In the old days, in many rural communities particularly, women had the reputation that they misused this important means of communication for idle purposes.

Although in some areas (such as the community Rakow describes in her study) remains of the system of party lines have survived until the 1980s, overall this system has now been replaced by private lines. This development parallels some paradoxical social changes. On the one hand, geographical and social space has been considerably expanded outside the borders of local communities, a process in which the telephone played an important role (De Sola Pool, 1977). On the other hand, communication is now much more limited to individual, private households. The introduction of a system of private lines in this respect mirrors the process of withdrawal to the smaller social space of the domestic, and the resulting, more rigid, separation between public and private spheres.

A remarkable recent development in telecommunications – more specifically in the field of audiotext – is the introduction of partylines and chatlines and the possibility of conference calls. As a consequence of these new telephone services we can see a renaissance of the job of the telephone operator. These modern operators again function as a knot between individual callers: they direct callers to group interactions or individual conversations on separate lines. At the same time, they have to guard, to a certain extent, the standards of conversation and try to prevent abuse of these services. Here a parallel can be drawn between the early history of telephony and a recent 'innovation'. It might be interesting to study this renaissance of the telephone operator from a gender perspective: are the assumptions about the necessary 'feminine qualities' of operators, for example, still valid?

The work of telephone operators – now and in the past – can be seen as a crucial link in the process of implementation of telephone services: operators represent a 'human touch', and in that respect make the transition to new ways of communicating, and the adjustment to new social spaces, easier. Gender enters into this process, because the image of the 'ideal operator' leans heavily on specific cultural constructions of femininity.

Early Uses of the Telephone

As I have already pointed out in the introduction, one of the more striking findings of the historical research on the early uses of the telephone is the amazing discrepancy between the intentions of the telephone industry and the actual uses of the telephone in everyday life. Residential telephone use was only weakly promoted by the industry, and considered to be of minor importance in comparison with the preferred business uses. Furthermore, when the industry did actually market the telephone for domestic use, very specific uses of this new technology were advocated.

Martin reports that many early subscribers were businessmen who had their offices connected to their homes. As a result, the telephone companies issued prescriptions for how to use the telephone: during the day it had to be used in an instrumental way for business or housekeeping matters, such as ordering things or making social arrangements. Only in the evenings was 'chatting' or 'visiting' by telephone permitted, although this should be restricted in any case. Promotion and marketing campaigns were mainly aimed at men. Women were only addressed in these campaigns as managers of the household. Even in this case, the American and Canadian industry promoted a particular use of the telephone: the housewife should use it for ordering things and services, which would save her much time and energy (Fischer, 1992; Martin, 1991).

This approach, however, was not very successful: not only was this early form of 'teleshopping' not popular at all among women, but – against all prescriptions – women cultivated their own social uses of the telephone. Firstly, they used the phone for lengthy conversations with friends and relatives. Secondly, they used it for making social arrangements; in rural areas women often used the phone to help them with the community activities they were involved in. By predominantly using the telephone as an instrument in social traffic, in the end women users influenced the unwilling telephone industry into accepting sociability as an unexpected but interesting marketing strategy. Only then was the telephone advertised as a means of social and psychological support ('reach out and touch') as well. This appeared to be a profitable strategy: until now the main part of residential telephoning has served sociability purposes.

Looking at recent developments in telecommunications, what strikes me is that in the promotion of new services, sociability again seems not to be advocated very strongly. In the discourses surrounding the implementation of 'teleservices', it is particularly instrumental uses of the telephone (such as teleworking, teleshopping, telebanking, tele-education or even telepolling), that receive a lot of attention. Looking at the audiotext market, however, what becomes very clear is that the most popular services (in this case chatlines, partylines and erotic lines) again particularly serve sociability purposes.

The telephone undoubtedly played an important role in processes of modernization. The telephone was embedded in wider social processes and related to rearrangements of geographical and social space, such as the development of suburbs and the separation of a public and private sphere (De Sola Pool, 1977, 1983). This can partly explain why particularly women used the phone for sociability reasons. As their social position became more isolated, they sought ways to overcome this isolation. However, there are other explanations for women's telephone use, explanations that take not only their social position but also their cultural practices into account. In the next section I shall deal with this in greater detail.

The Telephone in Everyday Life

Apart from the transition from party lines to private lines and some minor changes in appearance, the telephone as an artefact has not really developed since its introduction and diffusion in the early twentieth century. It has become an indissoluble part of everyday life, which is very much taken for granted. This perhaps explains the lack of attention from researchers to the social and cultural implications of the telephone. Particularly compared to other media, such as the television, which has conquered the consumer market in a comparatively absolute way, it is amazing how little we know about the role of the telephone in everyday life.

Recently, expected new developments in the field of telecommunications have caused some researchers to realize that insight into the uses of the plain old telephone in everyday life is needed to predict the success or failure of new telephone services on the residential market. This has led to some cross-cultural research on the social uses of the telephone in France, the USA and Germany (Adler, 1993; Claisse and Rowe, 1992; Dordick and LaRose, 1992; Lange, 1991).

The results of these studies indicate that nowadays the telephone is still particularly used for social and emotional reasons, in other words to create and maintain a psychological neighbourhood. Most conversations by telephone are with relatives, friends and acquaintances (for example in Germany 60 per cent, and in France as much as 80 per cent of all household telephone traffic). What is also evident in these studies is that gender is still an important factor in explaining differences in telephone use. Women are the heavy telephone users: in the French study women telephone twice as much as men. This finding is remarkably stable: whether these women are old or young, working or not working, have children or not, they still telephone twice as much as their male counterparts. Furthermore, women often function as 'operators' in the household: in France in 80 per cent of cases women are responsible for answering the telephone. In the American study

60 per cent of the 'telephone decision makers' are women. Another remarkable finding in the French study is that women use the phone mainly to make relational calls. When they make functional calls, these calls often serve a collective interest. On the other hand, for men the functional uses dominate, and this functional telephone traffic serves mainly personal interests. These results show that in modern telephone traffic, gender differences are still very significant.

Ann Moyal's research in Australia (1992) and Lana Rakow's study in a small rural community in the USA (1992) describe the gendered uses of the telephone in everyday life in greater detail. Australian women attach great importance to the telephone, to sustain relationships with family and friends and to contribute substantially to all kinds of community activities. Moyal refers to this 'deeply rooted dynamic feminine culture of the telephone' as a telephone neighbourhood. Her findings show, for instance, regular and intensive telephone contacts between mothers and daughters, highly valued by her respondents. Furthermore, she reports an increase in telephone interactions between close women friends, who often call each other for support or emotional and intellectual stimulus. These telephone contacts have become more important, because nowadays more women are living alone and more have responsibilities as single parents. The telephone, according to Moyal, is particularly important for maintaining and enhancing these key feminine links (p. 58). This finding is valid for almost all women, undifferentiated by education, social environment or age. The telephone, furthermore, appears to be crucial for the social responsibilities women have: they use the phone to maintain social networks in the family, neighbourhood or community, or to do volunteer social work.

The popular negative image of women 'gossiping' on the phone and 'tying up' the lines, according to Moyal, ignores the fact that this specific information flow represents a 'critical social support system, that underlies family, community and national development' (p. 67). It is a form of hidden work, which is very much taken for granted. Here the concept of telephone use as 'gendered work' as introduced by Rakow is useful. Technologies obviously are not neutral, they do not function outside the social relations and cultural practices of the people using them. Technologies such as the telephone are shaping and shaped by social processes. Traditionally, it is considered to be women's work to put time and energy into the maintenance of close social relationships. Women's uses of the telephone appear to be strongly interwoven with these responsibilities and with their traditional strong position in the private domain. Women use the telephone mainly for maintaining social relations, for care-giving, for community responsibilities and for business work that enters the private sphere.

This social shaping process also influences the ways men and women experience the telephone. Rakow, for instance, describes how women in Prospect (the community she studied) often made calls for their husbands: not only calls related to business or farm work, but also social calls to family members, such as the husbands' mothers. She reports that men often show a certain degree of reluctance and shyness in telephone contacts. The telephone is identified by men and women as a part of women's sphere, with all the positive and negative connotations involved. For women, telephone use can be very satisfying, because it 'contributes substantially to [their] sense of autonomy, security, participation and well-being' (Moyal, 1992, p. 67). On the other hand, it can be experienced as very demanding and time-consuming as well. This notion of telephone use as 'gendered work' – productive activity assigned to women – is well expressed in a comment made by one of Rakow's respondents: 'It's supposed to be part of our job' (Rakow, 1992, p. 55).

According to Rakow, telephone use can also be conceptualized as 'gender work'. Women's uses of the telephone are embedded in a set of ideas, values, beliefs and practices, expressing what it means to be a man or a woman. The telephone, in other words, is also part of a cultural shaping process; it is part of the discourses in which gender identities are constructed. This can be illustrated by looking at some of the notions about women's talk connected to their use of the telephone. Women's talk has no high social prestige: it is mostly described in rather negative terms such as 'chatting', 'visiting' or 'gossiping', and is often considered to be idle and a waste of time. Women are supposed to small-talk mainly about silly subjects concerning the private sphere. All these familiar negative connotations related to women's talk and women's sphere are also recognizable in discourses surrounding women's uses of the telephone. This is also expressed in the feelings of guilt women themselves show when they are 'tying up the lines' and in the regulations and restrictions that fathers and husbands impose on women's use of the telephone.

Thus, the telephone can be seen as a mirror of social arrangements, such as gender relations, and as a reflection of cultural notions and practices related to these arrangements. The telephone, in this respect, is socially and culturally *shaped*. But the telephone is not merely shaped by, but can also be seen as, an active agent in the *shaping* of socio-cultural arrangements.

According to Rakow, the telephone has altered the shape of women's geographical and social space, by broadening the boundaries of the private sphere. Through the telephone, problems of isolation or restricted mobility can be overcome more easily. The telephone, furthermore, is important because it offers women a sense of safety and security, and in this respect limits feelings of restriction of space.

Rakow describes how the rural community she studied has gradually changed because the men left it behind to make money elsewhere. As a result, women now run most community businesses and do most of the volunteer activities in the local community. This has led to an expansion of women's space: the community has, more and more, become a part of their domain, and in this process the telephone played and plays an important role. However, this space-adjustment has not given women substantial influence in the public domain, because the public sphere of power has moved away with the men, beyond the limits of the community. 'The boundaries of the private have merely been shifted, rather than transcended ... the telephone did not bring women closer to the world of power and decision-making but rather took power and decision-making farther away', Rakow concludes (1992, p. 79).

Having considered the telephone as part of a socio-cultural shaping process, it is fair to conclude that gender is a constitutive part of this process. It might be interesting to take this as a starting point to assess the potential uses of new telephone services. What can be said about the use of the 'new telephone' from a gender perspective? What is the significance of some of the recent developments in telecommunications, if we take the social history of the telephone into account?

The New Telephone

Recently, major changes have been taking place in the field of tele-communications. These changes may strongly affect the character of the 'plain old telephone'. The telephone is changing from a shared household appliance, which is very much taken for granted, into a highly personalized communication medium (Dordick and LaRose, 1992). Users are supplied with an endless range of services, appliances and technological possibilities which enable them to create a 'telecommunication environment' that is completely adjusted to their personal situation and needs.

In this section I shall try to assess the potential of some of these telephone-related developments from a gender perspective. I shall concentrate here on four patterns of uses of the 'new telephone' which might be interesting to analyse from a gender perspective: the use of the new telephone for sociability and entertainment reasons, for safety and security reasons, for instrumental or functional reasons and, finally, the use of the telephone for reasons of access and availability.

Sociability and Entertainment

As the social history of the telephone has shown, women are heavy users of the telephone and they use it particularly to 'socialize': to create a social and psychological neighbourhood of relatives, friends and acquaintances. Women particularly like to use the phone for long and intimate chats, while men tend to use the phone more for instrumental reasons.

A striking development in telecommunications that is relevant here is the explosive growth of the audiotext market. Audiotext can be described as a mass medium that delivers audio entertainment and information programming to the home (LaRose *et al.*, 1993). In the USA these services are known as 800- and 900-number services, while in the Netherlands they are known as 06-numbers. The 'adult entertainment' services are especially interesting from a gender perspective. A substantial proportion of these services – particularly in Holland – have an erotic content, and are therefore also known as 'pink traffic'. Another remarkable development here is the growth of partylines and chatlines. In Holland, sex services and chatlines account for almost 80 per cent of the total traffic (Bouwman and Slaa, 1992).

Audiotext offers callers not only ready-made information, but also the possibility of interacting with other people. In this respect, sociability reasons can be important for using these services. However, a distinctive feature of these interactive services is their anonymity, which sets them very much apart from the plain old telephone, and its use by women: women use the phone particularly for intimate contacts with people they know. Not surprisingly, one of the characteristics of the average Dutch 06-user is that he is male (Bouwman and Slaa, 1992). This can evidently be explained by pointing to the predominance of erotic messages in Dutch audiotext, messages which are primarily aimed at a male audience. In the USA, where sex lines are not that widespread, the use of adult entertainment audiotext services is more equal in terms of gender. However, although similar percentages of men and women used these numbers, men were more likely to be repeat callers. Another remarkable finding here was that women used the toll-free 800 numbers more often; many of these services are related to household management (purchasing products, service information, etc.) (LaRose *et al.*, 1993).

Little is known yet about the specific uses of partylines and chatlines. My impression, based on popular literature, is that women use these interactive lines more often compared to other adult entertainment lines, but they are not as popular among women as they are among men. This can probably be explained as a result of the anonymity of the interactions. Perhaps interactions with strangers are more often experienced as threatening by women. Furthermore, anonymous interactions might be experienced as contrary to one's gender identity; it might not be considered appropriate for women to have social relations with strangers.

Safety and Security

Some recent innovations might be particularly relevant for women, because they have the potential to increase the safety and security of users. Women are more likely to be victims of harassment by telephone, and a possible weapon against this is Caller-ID. The issue of Caller-ID is rather complicated, because it raises all kinds of questions regarding privacy and the reversion of the power balance between caller and 'callee' (see for instance Katz, 1990). Automatic number identification (ANI) or Caller-ID implies the possibility of revealing the telephone number of the person who is calling. For women this might have a positive impact, because it will probably reduce anonymous, obscene and threatening calls.

A more frivolous comment on Caller-ID which is also interesting from a gender perspective, though from a quite different angle, is the following reaction quoted by Katz (1990): 'No more calling from the local tavern and telling your spouse you're still at the office' and another quote: 'Caller-ID means, fellow seekers of domestic tranquillity, that you know damn well the number flashing is . . . that smashing blonde you met at the last business-card exchange and cocktail wing-ding. You acknowledge this incoming torpedo and you're a dead man' (p. 407). An interesting question is how these possibly conflicting gender interests might influence the acceptance of new services such as Caller-ID.

Another innovation in telecommunications that is supposed to increase the safety of women (and is sometimes marketed as such) is mobile telephony. Rakow and Navarro (1993) studied why women use the cellular telephone. They report that husbands often bought these telephones for their wives, because they were concerned about their safety: in this way they wanted to protect their wives when they were alone in their cars. Surprisingly these women often used the cellular phone for quite different purposes: to keep in touch with their children and to manage the household from a distance. This use of the new telephone is particularly relevant to gain insight into the question of how modern women manage to 'commute' between public and private spaces and what role technology plays in this process.

Instrumentality and Functionality

The social history of the residential telephone has shown that instrumental or functional uses have been rather overestimated by the industry. In their early marketing strategies the telephone companies advocated the use of the telephone as a tool for the management of the household: for instance to save time by ordering goods or services. As described earlier, this approach was not very successful. In spite of this historical lesson, discourses surrounding new developments in telecommunications again put a strong emphasis on comparable instrumental uses, such as teleshopping, telebanking, tele-education or teleworking. These specific services are supposed to have a great potential. Findings from research on the French Minitel (one of the very few successful experiments with videotext), a system that offers comparable services, however, show that services with an entertainment or social function are particularly popular.

This does not imply that instrumental uses of the new telephone are irrelevant. New telephone services and appliances are sometimes promoted by pointing to the possibility of combining domestic and work responsibilities. This is particularly clear in the discourse about teleworking. The suggestion is that teleworking has an emancipatory potential because men and women can share work and caring responsibilities more equally. Research shows that teleworking households use the phone significantly more and have significantly more new appliances, such as modems, fax machines and mobile phones, and that they have more special features and services (Dordick and LaRose, 1992).

French research (Claisse and Rowe, 1992) has shown that working women tend to have a double telephone activity, corresponding with their double activities in working and private life. Heavy telephone use for business purposes does not decrease their private and relational telephone use, especially because women tend to have a responsibility as family 'operator' as well: they answer all family calls. Against this background, working women, particularly when they are teleworking, can be seen as an interesting target group for the telecommunications industry. However, working women do not seem to have been discovered yet as a promising new market, which is probably the result of the familiar blind spot that the industry has when it comes to gender.

The question of how the new telephone functions for teleworking purposes, and how this is experienced from a gender perspective, remains to be answered. Nevertheless, this is an interesting research focus, because teleworking has the potential to disrupt traditional boundaries between the public and private spheres, and this must have some impact on gender relations. Whether this impact is emancipatory remains to be seen.

> *Access and Availability*

A prominent issue in the promotion and marketing of new telephone services is the possibility of being reached always and everywhere. With respect to answering machines, this strategy seems to have been rather successful. For example, in the USA 39 per cent of the population have an answering machine, particularly in small households of young couples and starting-out singles (Dordick and LaRose, 1992). Paradoxically, people often use this device not to be available to anyone, but to select between wanted and unwanted calls or to protect privacy. It might be revealing to study gender differences in the use of the answering machine. Women apparently often function as operators in the household, which possibly has an impact on their use and experience of this device. Who, for instance, is responsible for answering the people who left messages on the machine?

Another strongly promoted new development is mobile telephony. Although the business market is crucial in the marketing strategies of the telecommunications companies, the residential market is recently also receiving some attention. Rakow and Navarro (1993) report some new marketing strategies involving women, such as the 'supermom approach': campaigns aiming at women 'juggling' a career and family (p. 149). Their study of a small group of women users of cellular telephones shows that this approach appears to have a reason to exist. In spite of the intentions of husbands, who bought these phones for their wives in order to protect them, these women actually used their cellular phones primarily for personal and family reasons and to manage their domestic responsibilities from a distance. Almost every respondent expressed the desire to be available to her children. The cellular phone gives these women the opportunity to practice what the authors call 'remote mothering'. A finding which is very similar to the findings of the French research, described earlier, is that women tend to have double activities, which are mirrored in their uses of the telephone. Rakow and Navarro conclude that 'women who are trying to bridge the space and time gap between the domestic and work worlds [are] working "parallel shifts" rather than what has been described as the "double shift"' (p. 153).

Not surprisingly, in a Swedish study (Malm and Link, 1993) the combination of household and professional activities of working women is seen as an interesting marketing angle: the authors conclude their report by stating that women are probably a very promising market for private usage of mobile telephony (p. 47).

Discussion

According to Rakow and Navarro (1993) the cellular phone can be seen as an extension of the public world when used by men: they take the public into their personal lives. When it is used by women, the boundaries of the private world are extended: women take their personal lives with them wherever they go. With this conclusion they follow the same line of argument that Rakow (1992) used to analyse the gendered uses of the plain old telephone in a small local community.

This argument underlines a potential effect of the new telephone, which is relevant if the telephone is conceptualized as a space-adjusting technology. New telephone services have the potential to blur the traditional boundaries between public and private spheres: the 'new' telephone is no longer attached to the domestic and the household, but more and more taken out of the home by individual members of the household. This implies that public and private uses cannot easily be separated any more.

What are the consequences of this rearrangement of social space, particularly from a gender perspective? In my view this is a very important research question, which has not yet received much attention. The public/private distinction is not only an arrangement of social space and social relations, but also a cultural construction, in which notions about gender identities are solidly anchored. The telephone is a product of these social arrangements and cultural constructions and is in turn influencing the direction and form these developments will take.

Note

1. At least in Britain an exception was made for night telephonists, who were originally male only. I would like to thank Keith Grint for bringing this exception to my attention, and for pointing out that in effect this night/day division of labour can be seen as yet another example of the gendered nature of telephone work.

References

ADLER, J. (1993) 'Telephoning in Germany: Callers, Rituals, Contents and Functions', *Telecommunications Policy*, May/June, pp. 281–96.

BOUWMAN, H. and SLAA, P. (1992) 'Audiotex Services, in the Netherlands', paper presented to the workshop on Telematics for the Mass Market, Vienna.

CLAISSE, G. and ROWE, F. (1992) 'Vers une sociométrie stratégique du téléphone', paper presented at the 9th International Conference of the International Telecommunications Society, Nice, 14–17 June.

DORDICK, H. and LaROSE, R. (1992) 'The Telephone in Daily Life: A Study of Personal Telephone Use', Department of Radio-Television-Film, Temple University, Philadelphia and Department of Telecommunication, Michigan State University, East Lansing.

FISCHER, C. (1988) 'Gender and the Residential Telephone 1890–1940: Technologies of Sociability', *Sociological Forum*, 3, pp. 211–34.

FISCHER, C. (1992) *America Calling: A Social History of the Telephone to 1940*, Berkeley, University of California Press.

FRISSEN, V. (1992) 'Trapped in Electronic Cages? Gender and New Information Technologies in the Public and Private Domain: An Overview of Research', *Media, Culture and Society*, vol. 14, no. 1, pp. 31–50.

KATZ, J. (1990) 'Caller-ID, Privacy and Social Processes', *Telecommunications Policy*, October, pp. 372–411.

LANGE, U. (1991) 'The Berlin Telephone Study: An Overview', in MOYAL, A. (Ed.) *Research on the Domestic Telephone*, Melbourne: CIRCIT.

LaROSE, R., GLASCOCK, J., DORDICK, H. and JUN, Y. (1993) 'Understanding the Audiotex User in the United States', paper presented to the ICA Conference, Washington, D.C.

MADDOX, B. (1977) 'Women and the Switchboard', in POOL, I. DE SOLA (Ed.) *The Social Impact of the Telephone*, Cambridge, Mass., MIT Press.

MALM, A.T. and LINK, F. (1993) 'The Residential Market for Mobile Telephony: A Study of User Patterns and Preferences in Sweden', *Communications and Strategies*, **12**, 4, pp. 31–50.

MARTIN, M. (1991) *'Hello Central?': Gender, Technology and Culture in the Formation of Telephone Systems*, Montreal, McGill-Queen's University Press.

MOYAL, A. (1992) 'The Gendered Use of the Telephone: An Australian Case Study', *Media, Culture and Society*, 14, pp. 51–72.

POOL, I. DE SOLA (Ed.) (1977) *The Social Impact of the Television*, Cambridge, Mass., MIT Press.

POOL, I. DE SOLA (1983) *Forecasting the Telephone*, Norwood, Ablex.

RAKOW, L. (1988) 'Women and the Telephone: The Gendering of a Communication Technology', in KRAMARAE, C. (Ed.) *Technology and Women's Voices: Keeping in Touch*, New York, Routledge, pp. 207–28.

RAKOW, L. (1992) *Gender on the Line: Women, the Telephone and Community Life*, Urbana, Chicago, University of Illinois Press.

RAKOW, L. and NAVARRO, V. (1993) 'Remote Mothering and the Parallel Shift: Women Meet the Cellular Telephone', *Critical Studies in Mass Communication*, vol. 10, no. 2, pp. 144–57.

Chapter 4

The Configuration of Domestic Practices in the Designing of Household Appliances

Danielle Chabaud-Rychter

The subject of this chapter is the relations that the designers of household appliances establish with domestic practices in the course of their work. Two aspects of these relations will be examined here. The first is the configuration of women's cooking practices by the innovator for their transmutation into the mechanical actions of kitchen appliances; the second, the innovator's design for the use of the machines by the actors of the domestic world and the inscription of this use in the shapes and the properties of these technical objects.

This study is the outcome of research on the processes of the design, production, distribution and use of kitchen appliances.[1] The fieldwork consists of following, as it unfolds, the full trajectory of these technical objects. The part discussed here concerns the innovation phase and was conducted in a French company that produces and markets small household appliances. The company comprises several industrial plants, each specializing in the production of certain appliances, and a central structure which includes the commercial and marketing departments. The research focuses on food processors, but also includes incursions into the field of coffee machines (manufactured at the same plant).

The food processor is an electric appliance designed to perform a number of different food preparation tasks mechanically. It consists of a cylindrical bowl inside which rotate interchangeable blades. Its basic functions are to cut up, that is chop, mince, slice or grate the food introduced into the bowl through a funnel in its lid. Each operation is performed with a different kind of blade accessory. The main approach to innovation has been, and still is, to add new functions by adding new accessories and varying their speed of rotation. All the functions operate on the same principle, invented in the early 1960s, of a blade spinning inside a bowl. Different kinds of accessories of a variety of shapes and sizes can now be fitted into the bowl, and, depending on the model, the food processor can thus also be made to knead dough, beat egg whites, whip cream, make mayonnaise, or extract fruit or vegetable juices. Yet more functions can be obtained by changing the size and shape of the bowl, from the very small bowl used for chopping chives and garlic, to the tall, narrow bowl of the blender for making soups, sauces and milkshakes.

The definition of the functions is modelled on the different acts involved in food preparation. The performance of these functions by the processor is a transposition of the activities performed by women in their kitchens with manual utensils (knives, spoons, graters, vegetable mills), or electric appliances operating on other principles (beaters, mincers). The food processor is defined by the designer as a useful machine which affords the advantage of performing a variety of what are considered to be fastidious tasks at least as well as women with their traditional instruments, and with a substantial saving of time and effort. The machine can only be sold if its usefulness is recognized by the women who prepare their meals at home.

In order to design new processors with new functions or combinations of functions, the cooking practices of women must be known, and in particular their food preparation activities. Then, to be able to transform these activities into the mechanical action of a food processor, this initial information must be translated into technical language, that is, into parameters and measurements. It is these cognitive activities of the innovator that we will first attempt to analyse here.

Knowledge of Cooking Practices: From Inventory to Statistical Generalization

It is essentially the responsibility of Marketing to produce the knowledge about women's practices. To begin with, an inventory of cooking practices and the methods of food preparation involved must be established. The marketing men draw up this inventory, in part, on the basis of their own everyday experience as consumers of soups, grated carrots, or mince, and as observers of the women in their family at work in the kitchen, and (sometimes) of their own cooking activities. They also conduct or commission surveys in which women will be asked, for instance, to describe recipes and how they make them. Or, in a more directly operational approach, the women will be presented with a description or mock-up of an idea for a new accessory and asked if they see a use for it and whether they would buy it. In this way, by combining methods deriving from common sense – to which the other actors participating in the conception of the food processor also have recourse – with more formalized survey methods, Marketing produces a descriptive inventory of food preparation practices.

The designer must be able to attribute the practices he is seeking to transform into the actions of a machine to a large number of women, that is to a number large enough to be able to constitute a market (or segment thereof). He thus needs knowledge of a statistical order, which will give him the means to generalize his description of practices. For this, individual cases that have been observed or reported in the surveys must be reduced to categories of practices. The construction of categories presupposes the definition of the distinctive characteristics of each type of food preparation activity and of its boundaries. For example, the act of grating is separated into two operations ('shredding' and 'grating') which appear identical but are distinguished by their results: in the first, the food comes out in strands; in the second, it comes out in the form of powder or fine particles. The next step of the operation consists of classifying the individual activities into the categories. Of course, Marketing does not categorize and classify from scratch. A culinary culture exists which bears its own categorizations, and cookbooks have long offered glossaries with definitions of food preparation operations. Consequently, any inventory will already comprise implicit operations of categorization and classification. However, these operations become explicit when Marketing conducts studies of the cooking practices of women in different countries with a view to internationalizing the company's food processor market. For instance, a preliminary study was carried out in two European countries to test the market for a combined product that would provide a food processor and sauce-maker on a single base. An electric sauce-maker, which consists of a small non-stick saucepan set on a hot plate and fitted with slowly rotating blades, is used for sauces and dessert creams (such as custard) which need to be stirred while heating. The first step in the study was to compile an inventory of all the kinds of sauces and dessert creams, with their rates of frequency, made by women in the two countries. Then the preparations were classified into two categories – those justifying the use of a sauce-maker (that is, those requiring simultaneous heating and stirring), and all the others. Finally, a third category was established for preparations for which both the processor and the sauce-maker could be used, which would justify the existence of the proposed model itself. Into this final category went all the sauces using chopped garlic, onion or chives or minced meat, as well as pastries with creamy fillings or desserts combining beaten egg whites and custard.

In a statistical procedure, generalization presupposes a count of the individual cases in each category, on the one hand, and the representativity of the sample, on the other. Marketing conducts its quantitative surveys on small samples which rarely exceed 100 individuals. The sample populations are selected among the social categories forming the company's clientele for the kind of product being tested in the survey. Their representativity is based more on intuition and an accumulated knowledge of the market than on statistical methods. The results from these samples are then generalized, with a few formal precautions in the writing of the survey report. Other studies, described as qualitative, and conducted with very small groups of up to a dozen women, are also used to produce generalizations. This can be the case for surveys designed to test the chances of success of a product new to a particular market. In one example, about ten women in the target country, recruited from potential customers, were given a machine to take home for two weeks, with a programme for its use, after which they were asked to discuss the machine, its use, and their recipes at a group meeting.[2] In the survey report, it was stated explicitly that 'the information collected cannot be used for statistical extrapolation'. Nonetheless, the writer generalized his results to the female population of the country, and the recommendations at the end of the report relied on this generalization. The generalization here drew on what was already known from belonging to a society and to a culture. It relied on the fact that the survey results were not surprising, but were in accordance with this incorporated knowledge.

The marketing department, which must detect needs and define markets for the products, thus uses different methods to generalize the individual practices observed and described in the surveys. The design engineers and technicians must also transform individual actions into actions that are generalizable to all women, for they are designing appliances for industrial production, which, even if it cannot be qualified as mass production, still implies a certain standardization of the products. Even when the planned range comprises a number of different models, the basic functions will be identical, as will be most of the components, and the different models will be assembled on the same production line with the variations from one model to another kept to a strict minimum. In order to carry out this task, these actors, too, must have knowledge of food preparation practices, but their form of knowledge is different to that used by Marketing.

Formalization of Cooking Practices

Finding a mechanical equivalent to a manual activity used in the transformation of foods presupposes establishing a stable interpretation of that activity and its results. The empirical experience of food transformation is transcribed in recipes which are transmitted to women; this is one form of stabilization on which food processor designers base their work. For example, to beat up egg whites, an implement is needed which will introduce air into the whites by lifting them up and breaking them, the movement must be rapid, and the whites must not be beaten for too long or they will lose their stiffness; if the stiffness is to be maintained for any length of time, adding a pinch of sugar while beating will help. This operational mode, or recipe, is the result of accumulated empirical experience, and it owes its stability to tradition. In order to design a machine that will execute this task, more detailed information is required: for instance, the speed of the beating and when to stop must be determined. This can be done by conducting empirical experiments in the laboratory and introducing parameters of measurement. A large part of the innovation process is carried out in this way, but the trend (perhaps a recent one) is for the designer to substitute scientific objectivization and stabilization for the traditional stabilization. Thus, at the plant research centre, the different modes of transformation of foodstuffs are translated into the language of physics and chemistry. Here, by way of example, is an analysis of 'the evolution of the characteristics of beaten egg whites during formation of the foam':

> When the duration of the beating is increased for a given speed of rotation:
> * the number of air bubbles increases, their size decreases, and they squeeze up against one another;
> * proliferation (increase in volume) and stability are inversely proportional: proliferation increases (linear rise); stability decreases.
>
> Why do proliferation and stability occur in an inverse relationship?
>
> When proliferation is high, the fact that the bubbles squeeze up against each other increases the flow of liquid from their walls. The thickness and resistance of the walls diminish, resulting in the collapse of the material.
>
> The operational conditions which will yield an optimal proliferation-stability relation must thus be sought.
>
> Beyond a certain duration of beating for a given speed of rotation:
> * the proliferation decreases.

Proteins at the air/water interface appear to coagulate. These proteins would thus not be absorbed correctly, causing the liquid walls of the air bubbles to rupture under the effect of the whipping.

Egg whites are thus sensitive to excess beating.

By referring to an established scientific corpus and using its language to describe what happens when egg whites are beaten, the designer substitutes a formalization for a description whose reference is tradition (Thévenot, 1985; Boltanski and Thévenot, 1987). This change of regime, to use the terminology of Boltanski and Thévenot, opens the way to another mode of innovation, one that is no longer derived from the observation of cooking practices, but, instead, from the scientific knowledge of the transformation of foodstuffs. Thus, in the case of carrots, knowledge of the kinetics of oxidation (which depends, among other factors, on the surface exposed to the air and the thickness of the pieces), rather than the habits and tastes of the consumers, could serve to define the calibre and shape of the grated food. This does not mean that the innovator does not keep in mind the usefulness of the innovation for the cook and the consumer, but that this usefulness is a new one, one which they will have to discover.[3]

When the project of a new food processor is launched, Marketing and the R&D engineers and technicians define the criteria of performance for each of the planned functions. It is the marketing department which, within the design group, acts as spokesperson for the consumers of grated, minced or puréed foods as well as for the women who prepare them. They thus determine the optimal performance for the machine, taking into account the desired sale price, and the engineers and technicians have the task of designing a machine which will meet these criteria. One can imagine that these criteria are the object of negotiations between these two sets of actors throughout the design process, but this is not of immediate interest to us. What concerns us here is that, in order to set the objectives for the machine, a process is undertaken to translate the operations of food preparation, and particularly the results of these operations, that is the state of the food after it has been processed, into measurable terms. In the schedule of functional specifications, a central document in the design process which provides the basis for testing the proposed technical solutions and the successive prototypes, criteria for evaluating the results of each new function of the processor are defined; these permit the performance of the machine and the acceptable limits of this performance to be measured.

For example, for the function defined as 'making batter from basic ingredients':

first criterion of evaluation: quantities processed in a given length of time:
unit of measurement: litres/second;
level of performance for crêpe batter: minimum 0.4 litres in 15 seconds, maximum 0.8 litres in 15 seconds;
acceptable limits: ± 10% of the stipulated duration.

second criterion of evaluation: homogeneity:
unit of measurement: percentage of the preparation;
performance level: 0% lumps (unmixed flour).

The schedule of specifications translates domestic practices into the language of measurement, thus transposing them into the industrial sphere: the results of food preparation practices become the results of the operations of the food processor. The document only expresses requirements concerning the results and, theoretically, gives no stipulations on methods, thus leaving open the search for technical solutions, that is, the operations by which the processor will achieve the results. The language of measurement is necessary to this search at two levels. Firstly, because innovation is a collective process in which actors with different skills (marketing executives, engineers and technicians from Research and Development, quality control technicians, industrial designers, etc.) have to work on the same object, these actors need instruments that will unify the representations of this object. The schedule of specifications, which is circulated among all the actors, is undoubtedly one of the most powerful of these instruments, particularly because it uses a language of measurement which establishes the description of the expected performance of the machine. Secondly, expressing the requirements in terms of measurement makes it possible to verify, by means of tests which are themselves measurable, whether the technical solution that has been found meets these requirements, and it also guides later reproduction on the assembly line. It is one of the conditions of the standardization of the product.

However, establishing criteria for measuring the results of food preparation operations is no simple matter. In certain cases, a way of attributing numerical values may not have been found, yet the characteristics of the processed food have to be evaluated. This means that other means of measurement must be found. Visual tests are developed. For instance, the consistency of mayonnaise is judged by seeing whether a spoon placed on the surface will leave an imprint. The smoothness of soup mixtures and fruit juices can be measured by filtering them through increasingly fine sieves and weighing the residues. Minced meat, on the other hand, does not lend itself to measurement. While there certainly are criteria for evaluation (the meat particles must be of the same calibre and neither too big nor reduced to a mush), these still leave a wide margin of judgment. In this case, the test technician will ask his laboratory colleagues – who have all worked on food processors – to evaluate the results. He appeals to their experience and competence to back up, reinforce or possibly question his own judgment. For functions that have already been produced, comparisons with earlier models or competitor products, which are thus raised to the rank of standards, provide another means of evaluation.

Not only is it not possible to measure all aspects of the results, but mere measurement does not divulge everything the innovator needs to know. Even when measuring is possible and reliable (for example, for the smoothness of soup mixtures), the technicians in the test laboratory or at Quality Control call in volunteers to evaluate the results visually and (if the product is not raw meat) to taste as well. In this case, the volunteer testers are not consulted as experts on food processors, but as consumers. A further step is taken towards the domestic world when women production and clerical workers are called upon for in-house 'client' tests, and yet another when Marketing recruits women from the general public. The food processed by the robot thus shifts progressively from the domain of technical expertise to that of domestic expertise. The results measured in the industrial world must be validated in the domestic world.

Designing Use

The innovator must not only design a technical object that fulfils certain functions; the object must be usable. A fair part of the innovator's activity thus consists of working on the use of the processor, in both senses of the term: that is, on the features that make it usable, such as the controls, the handles, and the assembly of the various accessories, and on the actions – the sequences of gestures and conceptualizations – that the women users will have to go through in order to make it work. Here, then, is the woman user, rather than the consumer of the foods prepared by the processor, who is at the centre of the designer's work. Use includes setting up the machine for the first time, the relation to the instructions, mounting the accessories, and executing the various functions, as well as dismantling, cleaning and storing it all. The designer's initial aim is to conceive a use which is simple, effective, pleasant and safe. Then he turns to issues of style, as expressed, for example, in the controversies and choices regarding the controls: a knob to be turned means an analogy with older machines has been chosen, and use is inscribed in the framework of habits; the choice of buttons to be pressed, or, even better, just lightly touched, inscribes use in the trend to modernity.

Working on use, as Madeleine Akrich has shown, means distributing skills, responsibilities and actions between the user, the technical object, and possibly other actors such as installers and the after-sales services.[4] In the case of the food processor, this distribution varies with each device or function and its design. For example, the safety device, which complies with French and international standards, prescribes a determined operational mode for the user: she must fit the bowl on its base, put on the lid and lock it in place before being able to start the machine. Responsibility for the safety of the user is delegated, here, to the machine.[5] Another example is the processor case, which contains the motor and mechanical parts: this is closed with special screws for which screwdrivers are not commercially available. Women users, as well as their do-it-yourselfer spouses, are forbidden entry, and the technical capacity, in this instance, is conferred exclusively on the after-sales service. The design of the slicer disk accessory allows the user to set the thickness of the slices at her choice: here the manual dexterity she would exercise with a knife is transferred to the machine. On the other hand, the speed control button accords her the mental and sensory process involved in relating the materials to be treated to the type of treatment (mincing, grating, mixing) and the speed of the blades, a process that needs to be learnt. This control button exists on the so-called 'electronic' models, whereas on the others, only two speeds are made available, which reduces the scope of the skill required. And so it goes on. Each time a feature of the processor relating to use is transformed, this modifies, to a greater or lesser degree, the distribution of the skills and actions between the woman user and the machine. These are not unintended consequences. The intent to modify this distribution is present throughout the work of the designers: their overall objective is to increase the automation of the processors, and thus the share of activities taken on by the machine.[6] As we will see later, this intent is just as apparent in their meticulous working on connections and adjustments between the action of the user and the action of the machine.

Designing use is also to design the affordance of the object. We use this term here in the definition given by Donald A. Norman:

> the term *affordance* refers to the perceived and actual properties of the thing, primarily those fundamental properties that determine just how the thing could possibly be used. A chair affords ('is for') support and, therefore, affords sitting. A chair can also be carried. Glass is for seeing through and for breaking .... Affordances provide strong clues to the operations of things. Plates are for pushing. Knobs are for turning. Slots are for inserting things into.

> Balls are for throwing or for bouncing. When affordances are taken advantage of, the user knows what to do just by looking: no picture, label or instructions is required. Complex things may require explanation, but simple things should not. (Norman, 1990, p. 9)

The object must express, by its visible features, what it is for and how it is to be used. Affordance is information on use, written into the shape of things, the object guiding the action of the user. One of the main problems with food processors is the large number of accessories; as we have seen, practically each function requires a different accessory, some can even have several accessories (such as the different grating disks for each calibre of grated food) and for others, the bowl may also need to be changed. The innovator's work on affordance has two objectives: to make the function of each accessory visibly identifiable, and to guide assembly by the shape of the different parts that need to fit together. The disks provided for grating are immediately identifiable because they reproduce the sharp-edged openings already present on hand graters. They are thus identified by analogy with objects that have long been integrated into women's cooking practices. For the same reason, it is immediately clear that the cutting edges of the openings must come into contact with the carrots being pushed down the funnel, and thus which way the disk needs to face when mounted. On the other hand, there is nothing in the shape of the undulated plastic disk to show that it is meant for beating up egg whites. The motion and the action it evokes have nothing to do with those of a fork, hand whisk or electric beater.

The procedures for assembling the bowls and the various accessories, some of which comprise several parts, need to be learnt by following the instructional material. However, the parts can be given a shape that will help limit the learning process to the first use. The actions needed for assembly essentially involve fitting male into female parts. The processor base comprises a vertical shaft (which transmits the motion of the motor), and the bowl has a funnel in the middle so that it can be fitted over this shaft; the blades are mounted, as in a propeller, on a central axis consisting of two concentric tubes: the outer tube, which is grasped when the accessory is to be placed in position, covers the funnel in the bowl, and the inner tube fits over the shaft. Each shape has a clear function and serves to guide the order of assembly so that the user does not have to memorize it; she only needs to assemble the machine once, following the instructions, after which the shape of each part will remind her of the order of the operations. Here, as Norman has shown, the innovator undertakes to distribute knowledge, or information, between the machine and the user: the shapes which inform her of the function of the accessories and how to use them also bear a large part of the know-how necessary for use. In this case, the know-how does not need to be interiorized by the user, who finds it again each time she looks at and handles the object.

When the innovator works on use, one of his objectives is to make it comfortable, that is, simple, pleasant, and effortless. The comfort of use is strongly linked to the affordances of the object inasmuch as these save the user questioning, thinking, looking up the instructions, getting involved in trial-and-error sequences of actions, or memorizing procedures. In part, comfort is an effect of well-conceived affordances. Some aspects, however, are independent of these. For example, the physical effort required when handling the processor, the noise it makes when running, or the efficiency and the comfort of the handles, lids and all the parts that need to be assembled and taken apart, all these are elements that enter into the ease of use and that are worked on by the designer.

Working on Use

Affordance and comfort designate the properties of the object to be perceived and interpreted within the framework of the action of use that the user undertakes, or is about to undertake. In order to work on these properties, the various actors in the design group thus place themselves within this framework of action. They do this when they handle objects – competitor processors, company products, mock-ups provided by the industrial designer or functional prototypes – in the course of their work and particularly during their group meetings. There, the objects pass from hand to hand, each actor simulating use, or testing the ergonomics. The finest details are examined and tested. For example, a control knob is tested for its movement, its prehension, the strength needed to turn it, the catches at its various positions, how it is set into the casing (whether it must be flush with the surface, or protrude fully or partially). All the senses are brought into play: the aim is to feel and to experience, with their own hands, the surfaces and volumes and the efforts entailed, and to listen to the noises.[7] When handling the objects, the designers put themselves in the position of women users, they go through the gestures involved in use, experience, test and mimic it, in short, have recourse to their own bodies and their own judgments of how well the object is adapted to its use.[8] It is on the basis of this experience of use that the designers construct the properties of the object that constitute its affordance.

When they work on use, the designers bring into play a complex approach in which their own practical experience, representations of users, and the properties of the processor expressed in terms of measurement are all linked together. The following extract from the transcription of a meeting between engineers and Marketing will enable us to see how the actors make this linkage. Under discussion was the design of the indicator light on a coffee machine (also manufactured at the same plant).[9]

> Engineer, Project Manager (E1): So we're going to discuss visibility at a certain distance, we're also going to talk about the angle with regard to the coffee machine, or rather to the indicator light: the light must be visible within a cone of vision of 120 degrees, which makes that 60 degrees relative to the median axis. The problem of the brightness of the light ... it hasn't been defined yet.
>
> Marketing executive, Product Manager for coffee machines (M1): No, but wait ... how does your cone go? Like this or like that?
>
> E1: A cone is like this.
>
> M1: Can you draw that for me, with the eye and then the /
>
> Marketing Director (M2): Your 120 degrees seem too little to me, personally I would have said 180. Because if the machine is facing this way, I must be able to see ...
>
> Director of the coffee machine division (E2) (*laughs*)
>
> M2: Well, it's along this piece of furniture, and I'm at this end, I must be able to see it!
>
> E2: You're designing a special piece of furniture there just for the coffee-maker.
>
> M2: What?
>
> E2: You're putting it in the middle of ...
>
> M2: No, it's like that in my house, it's uh ...
>
> E2 (drawing on the board): Here you have the cone ... there you have the source of radiation, and here's the radiation cone.
>
> M1: And where's my head?
>
> E1: Your head can be here, say /
>
> M1: No, I don't agree with that ... what I suggest is that there be a, uh, if you like ... (*goes to the table where several models of coffee machines have been set out and chooses one*) because, OK, you have the product, imagine that this is it, you have very few people who're going to be looking at it from here, eh, you've got a lot of people who're going to be looking from there. And if you make a cone, I don't know how your cone goes, if it's like this, it's OK, if your cone's like that, it's no good.
>
> ...
>
> M2: In fact it's not a right circular cone that we should take ... it should be an ellipse.

E1: OK, we'll keep that in mind, we'll check the (*inaudible*)

M1: That will have to be visible under normal conditions of use by a dwarf and then by someone who's 6 feet tall ... when he's one inch away from the product.

M2 (at the board): ... if my coffee machine is there on some piece of furniture and my room is this shape, in my opinion nothing justifies the 120 degrees, it has to be figured like that, it's 180 degrees. We can write 120 degrees, but the right way is 180 degrees. If we say 120 degrees, we're playing with I don't know what, but it doesn't come out of a reliable study, if you ask me.

M1: But that depends if you want to see it when you're moving around the room.

M2: Obviously I want to see it when I'm moving around my room! It's there to tell me that it's on, or to remind me that it's on; wherever I am, I must see it, except when I'm down flat on my stomach, as Gerard [M1] was saying, or when I'm on the ceiling, because I'm hardly ever there. But in my horizontal moving about ... it's not something like that, in other words, it's an ellipse.

M1: Yes but in your car you see nothing if you're outside the car, it's the same thing, we have to stay within the limits of reasonable use.

M2: Yes. Well that's what I'm saying, when I'm walking around that room I must be able to see it from everywhere, so my eyes are at a certain height, as you were saying, so there's no point in having a cone with a very wide angle from the floor up.

M1: Yes there is, because you're going to get very close up to the product at some point.

M2: ... having a very wide angle ... it can have an axis (*drawing*) ... on a vertical plane it can be like that, it's not ... and it goes up like that, as wide as possible so that even a guy who's 6 foot will still see it even from close up ... and on the other plane, there must be 180 degrees.

M1: There you are, that's what Marketing says! (*laughs*)

. . .

E1: Well, we used the X [earlier model] as an example, and, sorry, the angle is 120 degrees (*inaudible*)

M2: And why do we take it that our X is the answer to what we're looking for here? We didn't ask that question!

M1: Take the P—s [competitor brand], for example, Pascal [E1], they have small buttons that stick out, and well you can see them

from far away, and from just about any angle. We set it in, we
made that mistake of setting the button inside the product at a
place where it isn't seen.

E1: We added the observation [to the schedule of specifications] that
the important criteria for . . . at the level of the performance level,
it's really the position of the light on the machine. If it's really set
flush at one place, we're obviously going to reduce the angle of
vision. If it's in the middle of the machine, like on the T
[competitor appliance], then it's visible /

M2: . . . at 180 degrees /

E1: . . . at almost 180 degrees.

What was being discussed was a property of the machine perceived by
the user. The engineer in charge of the project proposed a measurement for
the field of visibility of the indicator light. The two marketing executives
immediately confronted this measurement with the practical experience of
the user. M2 referred to his personal experience, that is, where his coffee
machine is kept and how he moves around in his own kitchen; from this he
drew conclusions, generalized to all kitchens, on the angle of visibility of the
light on a horizontal plane, which he expressed as a measurement (180
degrees). M1 continued this reference to practical experience, extending it to
that of a variety of users of all sizes. He imagined them facing the machine
and moving towards it, and focused on the visibility of the light on a vertical
plane. M1 and M2, working collectively, confronted and composed their two
approaches; they arrived at a complete definition of the field of visibility and
suggested a new measurement for it. The discussion then switched to making
a light that would offer this field of vision, comparing machines, known to
all the group, whose lights were good or bad from this point of view.

During the discussion, M1 and M2 configured practical experience with
the aim of making it relevant to the problem of designing an indicator light.
This work consisted of selecting and describing the relevant characteristics
of users, of their environment and their actions, and only these, and in getting
them accepted as such by the other actors. Thus, the features retained were:
the size of the users (no other feature was taken into account, except perhaps
age inasmuch as children were implicitly excluded from the category of
users); the movements of the users all around the room in which the machine
is kept; the shape of the room, the position of the furniture holding up the
machine, and the position of the machine on this piece of furniture; the
movement of a very tall person towards the machine; and 'normal conditions
of use', a category that links a 'normal' state of the environment and a
'normal' reasoning of the actor. Whether M1 and M2 used their personal

experience or imagined that of other actors, they retained only these relevant features. Each one individually configured practical experience and then they pursued this work collectively, in a discussion, thus rendering it 'visible'. The aim of this work was to define the angles from which the light must be able to be seen.

The actors participating in the discussion were engaged in a second kind of work which enabled them to shift from practical experience, used to define the field of perception of the signal, to the design of the property needing to be perceived, that is, the radiation of light corresponding to the field of perception considered. This work consisted in defining, in terms of measurement and elementary optical notions, the property of the light: to radiate at an angle of 180 degrees on a horizontal plane and at an angle that could be less open towards the ground on a vertical plane. The work on measurement was not completed. In fact, the language of measurement was used essentially, here, to construct a sufficiently precise representation of the property of the light for the different actors to understand it and agree on it. From a formal point of view, this representation was neither complete, nor entirely correct (for example, light radiating at an angle of 180 degrees, that is, along a straight line, cannot generate an ellipse); nonetheless, it was sufficient for Marketing and the engineers to reach agreement. It was the engineer in charge of the project who, after the meeting, would complete the definition of measurement for the schedule of specifications.

The progression of this sequence reveals that the work of conceiving use is done in a repeated to-ing and fro-ing between the property of the object and the perception of this property. The passage from one to the other was marked by a change in language: the ordinary language of practical experience for discussing what the user perceived, and the language of measurement when the property of the technical object was the issue.

Conclusion

The designing of household appliances is a hybrid activity mingling domestic practical experience and industrial formalization. To accomplish their work, the innovators bring the domestic world into the company. However, it is only in a reconstructed form rendering them relevant to the company that domestic actors and practices are brought in. Domestic practices are itemized, categorized and counted in order to define markets for the appliances. The results of cooking practices are parametered and stabilized by measurements in order to be transformed into performances of the machines. The practical experience of the users and of the designers themselves playing the role of users is configured for the work on the affordances of the objects.

The hybrid work of the innovators, underscored by the use of the double language of practical experience and measurement, produces objects which are themselves hybrid and derive from two domains: the domain in which they are manufactured and the one in which they are used. Each object carries with it both the domestic and the industrial worlds and expresses clearly in its shape the autonomy of each. The casing that the user cannot open isolates the technical parts which remain part of the industrial world, even after the object has entered the user's home, as Steve Woolgar (1990) has shown for personal computers, whereas the parts made for handling will (if functions and affordances are well conceived) be appropriated by the user in domestic practices.

Notes

1 This research, entitled 'The Social Trajectory of a Technical Object: From Its Design in the Household Appliance Industry to Its Use in the Home', is funded by the Interdisciplinary Programme for Research on Technology, Work and Ways of Life (Programme Interdisciplinaire de Recherche sur la Technologie, le Travail et les Modes de Vie – PIRTTEM) of the French National Centre for Scientific Research (CNRS), and the French Ministry of Research and Technology. This study is the French contribution to a European cross-national project on 'The Impact of New Technologies on Changing Gender Relations', initiated in 1989 by the European Centre for Coordination of Research and Documentation in the Social Sciences (Vienna Centre). The various contributions to the project have been published in a collective work: *Bringing Technology Home: Gender and Technology in a Changing Europe*, edited by Cynthia Cockburn and Ruža Fürst-Dilić (the scientific coordinator and Vienna Centre coordinator of the project, respectively).

2 It goes without saying that the company hires a local marketing research agency to conduct the survey.

3 Many consumer products are the result of innovations derived from scientific knowledge, or from technical principles imported from other fields. In the field of household appliances, an example is the microwave oven, which is constructed around the magnetron, a generator of electromagnetic waves. This device was developed as part of radar technology in the 1940s. Its heating properties were only paid attention to later, and applied to domestic technology even later. Its usefulness (fast cooking, defrosting, reheating without changing the taste) was constructed progressively (Cockburn and Ormrod, 1993).

4 It may be remembered that Marx, Taylor and the sociologists of work who have studied the relations between technological transformations, the division of labour and qualification (see, for example, the works of Freyssenet, 1977, 1990), have analysed the distribution of skills, responsibilities and actions between industrial machines and the personnel using them.

5 We may note that the machine remains a 'minor' at this level, for when the safety system is faulty, it is its manufacturer who is legally responsible.

6 The manufacturers' ideal is something like 'all the ingredients are put in at the same time and the machine does all the preparation tasks, then cooks the food, keeps check on the temperature, stirs when needed, and rings a bell when it's ready'.

7 On the role of handling in the perception of affordance, see Fornel (1993).

8 On the identification of designers with users, its dead-ends and ambiguities, see Chabaud-Rychter (1994).

9 An oblique stroke (/) in the transcription indicates the place where the speaker was cut off by the next speaker.

References

AKRICH, MADELEINE (1987) 'Comment décrire les objets techniques', *Techniques et culture*, 9.

AKRICH, MADELEINE (1993) 'Les objets techniques et leurs utilisateurs', in Les objets dans l'action, *Raisons pratiques*, 9.

BOLTANSKI, LUC and THÉVENOT, LAURENT (1987) *Les économies de la grandeur*, Cahiers du centre d'études de l'emploi, Paris, Presses universitaires de France.

CHABAUD-RYCHTER, DANIELLE (1994) 'Women Users in the Design Process of a Food Robot: Innovation in a French Domestic Appliance Company', in COCKBURN, CYNTHIA and FÜRST-DILIĆ, RUŽA, (Eds) *Bringing Technology Home: Gender and Technology in a Changing Europe*, London, Open University Press.

COCKBURN, CYNTHIA and FÜRST-DILIĆ, RUŽA, (Eds) (1994) *Bringing Technology Home: Gender and Technology in a Changing Europe*, London, Open University Press.

COCKBURN, CYNTHIA and ORMROD, SUSAN (1993) *Gender and Technology in the Making*, London, Sage.

FORNEL, MICHEL DE (1993) 'Faire parler les objets', in Les objets dans l'action, *Raisons pratiques*, 9.

FREYSSENET, MICHEL (1977) *La division capitaliste du travail*, Paris, Savelli.

FREYSSENET, MICHEL (1990) 'Les techniques productives sont-elles prescriptives?', *Cahiers du GIP Mutations Industrielles*, 45.

MARX, KARL (1960) *Le capital*, Paris, Les éditions sociales.

NORMAN, DONALD A. (1990) *The Design of Everyday Things*, New York, Doubleday Currency.

TAYLOR, FREDERICK (1971) *La direction scientifique des entreprises*, Paris, Dunod. Translation of *Scientific Management* (1911).

THÉVENOT, LAURENT (1985) 'Les investissements de forme', in *Conventions économiques*, Cahiers du centre d'études de l'emploi, Paris, Presses universitaires de France.

WOOLGAR, STEVE (1990) 'Configuring the User: The Case of Usability Trials', paper presented at the Discourse Analysis Workshop, University of Lancaster, 25–26 September.

Chapter 5

New Reproductive Technologies and the 'Modern Condition' in Southeast England

Eric Hirsch

'"Designer" mixed race baby sparks row' is the title of a front-page article in a recent issue of the *Guardian* (31 December 1993). Encapsulated in the article is the perspective (see Gell, 1988) that technology provides enabling conditions for the imagined to become aspired towards in the real world of social relations and material conditions. In the present case a black woman and her mixed-race husband are enabled to have a white egg implant so as to produce a desired outcome: a mixed-race baby. As a result of these enablements, previously implicit contexts (baby-making as a seemingly 'natural' act) are transformed into explicit contexts (intentionally designed), and this presents a challenge to accepted thoughts and practices. The widespread media coverage that attends the latest innovation in the take-up of the New Reproductive Technologies (NRTs) is testimony to the power the implications of this technology exercises on our unspoken conventions.

What the example of NRTs highlights, as does technology more generally, is how our thoughts and practices are relational: we think and/or act with other people in mind whether they are physically present or not. Intrinsic to this relationality are the relations we refer to as gender. The thoughts and actions of men and women imply the other, whether this other is physically present or not: the exclusion of women from a men's context, for example, 'includes' them by the very fact of their active 'exclusion'. In this way, gender involves a form of completeness – a male/female duality – which, depending on the cultural and historical context, is imagined as completed in a variety of forms (see Strathern, 1988). In the Euro-American context (as more generally) conjugality is a specific example of this completeness. As described more fully below, innovations in NRTs present particular challenges to accepted thoughts and practices about conjugality. Through the thoughts and narratives reported in this chapter, men and women draw on various scenarios to sustain an image of completeness in the light of transformations enabled by the NRTs. As it turned out, it was around the notion of 'modernity' that these scenarios cohered.

We have recently been reminded that the notion of modernity passed into popular usage during the mid nineteenth century. It was Baudelaire who characterized the term in the following way: 'modernity is the transient, the fleeting, the contingent; it is the one half of art, the other being the eternal and the immutable' (cited in Harvey, 1989, p. 10).[1] Although Baudelaire was addressing the emerging conventions of art during this period, his focus on a tension inherent in aesthetic sensibilities is seen to be replicated in wider social and cultural domains.

One side of the modernist tension, as transience, is exemplified in the ever-changing range of commodities produced and available for mass consumption. The values of individual choice in consumerism are part and parcel of the experiences associated with the fleeting and contingent. The sociology of Simmel, for example, and of later commentators, is concerned with examining the individual implications of this aspect of modern life in significant detail (cf. Miller, 1978). The other side of this tension, what has been referred to as the 'project' of modernity (Habermas), has intellectual origins which can be traced back to the Enlightenment: the intention behind this project was to reveal the 'universal, eternal, and immutable qualities of humanity' through the scientific domination of nature, and the development of rational forms of social organisation. However, the desire to dominate nature for rational ends also entailed the simultaneous domination of human beings (Harvey, 1989, pp. 12–13). There is, thus, a fine line to be discerned between the Enlightenment ideals of equality, liberty and democracy and the twentieth-century developments of totalitarianism (cf. Lefort, 1986).

An analogous idiom for rendering this modernist tension is characterized as the relationship between the 'individual' and 'society', where the individual – as transient and contingent – exists in relationship to society, which is enduring and transcendent. This model is a core component of Durkheim's sociology and his sociological project (cf. Lukes, 1973, pp. 19–22), but it also figures in the mundane, everyday discourse of social and political life. Much recent debate in anthropology, and social and cultural theory more generally, has asked whether this tension is still an apt characterization of Euro-American cultures; whether it can be transposed onto cultures outside this context (cf. Strathern, 1988); or whether it has been transfigured into what is now referred to as postmodernism. This is a central theme of Strathern's recent study of late-twentieth-century English kinship (Strathern, 1992). Her work forms a key point of reference for the analysis which follows.

The Study

This chapter is based on discussions with twelve married couples from Central London and a Berkshire town, where it was aspects of this 'modern condition' which were explored. The discussions, which focused on themes related to the new reproductive technologies (NRTs), evoked a particular set of tensions intrinsic to this modernism. On the one hand, men and women were prepared to accept (to greater or lesser degrees) that technology could be used to 'improve' on biology/nature. On the other hand, the couples could conceive of these improvements as acceptable so long as the changes to 'nature' were true to its principles. In other words, one could 'give nature a helping hand', as in the case of people having difficulty conceiving children, but this help should go to heterosexual couples: the 'natural' context for conceiving children.

In exploring this tension, three recurrent scenarios have emerged from people's visions. In each of these scenarios a connection can be recognized between the extremes of transience (unbridled consumerism) and the eternal (totalitarianism), and particular renderings of the relationship between individual and society. The first is of NRT connected to a form of consumerism and consumer choice (for example, conception becomes like 'baby shopping'). Here, NRT is being connected to an extreme example of practices generally current. I interpret this scenario as a particular rendering of the individual/society relationship. In this case, the individual or individualism is predominant and the interpretations of society become less evident, even hidden (cf. Strathern, 1992, p. 158). The second scenario is of NRT connected to a futuristic vision of the 'Brave New World' or the retrospective one of 'Hitlerism' or the 'master race'. In this set of scenarios, as I interpret them, society is predominant and all-powerful (cf. Lefort, 1986, p. 305). This set negates the significance of the individual and individuality (expressed in sentiments such as 'we all become standardized'). Here, the potentials inherent in NRT are extrapolated to a totalitarian vision of future society. The third scenario is evoked in the way NRT belongs to the various techniques by which a heterosexual couple seek to create the child that will be formed through the equal contributions of both the man and woman. I interpret this as making the relationship between individual and society visible, and indeed enabling it in the context of the NRT where otherwise men and women sense its subversion.

My interpretations gather together and make sense of various remarks people made. The third scenario itself brought together the other two. Indeed, the tension between reconciling the desires and choices of the individual and his/her relationship with society was an explicit and recurring theme in the discussions I held with all of the couples. Each couple, through their own idioms and with reference to their own personal experiences, attempted to sustain a notion of balance and regulation between 'individual' and 'society' made potentially precarious by developments in NRTs. I suggest that one means of achieving this, and one evidently available to these couples, was being able to draw on the scenario of conjugality in the context of the NRTs: one could improve on 'nature' while remaining true to 'nature's' principles.[2]

The Context: The Diversity of Families

The people whom I spoke with (my 'informants') come from a diverse range of family backgrounds, of religious, social and economic circumstances and of educational qualifications. All are involved in conjugal living arrangements. In this sense, conjugality can be taken as given in informants' circumstances. At the same time, however, there is a diversity in the way each couple has constituted its version of conjugality: re-marriage after divorce; foster and/or adopted children present; living close to one 'side' of the family; being distant from both 'sides' of the family, and so forth. As Strathern (1992, p. 22) has pointed out,

> While individuals strive to exercise their ingenuity and individuality in the way they create their unique lives, they also remain faithful to a conceptualisation of a natural world as diverse and manifold. Individual partners come together to make (unified) relationships; yet as parents they ought at the same time to stand in an initial condition of natural differentiation from each other. In the relationships they build and elaborate upon, it is important that the prior diversity and individuality of the partners remain.[3]

This point can be illustrated in the following interchanges.

Mary and Richard Dobbs have been married for ten years and have three children. They live in a detached, owner-occupied house in Berkshire. Richard works for the police, while Mary works in social services. Both are in their late thirties and both left school at 16.

In discussion with Mary and Richard, the conversation became animated when Richard suggested that developments in genetic engineering would enable parents to pick and choose the sort of child they wanted. Mary vigorously resisted his suggestion. Richard argued that parents would want to choose the way a child is genetically built, thus ensuring a 'perfect' child. Although not current practice at the moment, Richard suggested that developments were already going down this road. As he pointed out:

> RD: Well we're already doing it, why do you go to all these clinics and the rest of?
> MD: That's to monitor your health throughout your pregnancy.
> RD: Your health and who else?
> MD: The health of the baby.
> RD: What happens if, in the early stages, that baby is mentally ill?
> MD: You have the choice of abortion.
> RD: Some people take that choice and have an abortion.
> MD: And a lot of people don't.
> RD: So what they have done, they have picked they don't want that child because it's not perfect . . .

Mary was ready to agree that 'we' (society as embodied in scientists/ medicine) are looking for ways of helping people with infertility and of curing disease. She did not agree, however, with Richard's stronger claim that 'we' (society more generally) were 'looking to create the perfect child, the perfect person or perfect race'. To make her point more forcefully, she drew on the memory of discussions from a previous occasion (see below) when the issue of home shopping (teleshopping) was raised. In that discussion, Richard felt that people would gladly welcome these innovations in the home. But as Mary recalled:

> MD: [I]t was something that came up when we had our discussions previously that you felt people would rather sit at home and shop, would rather sit and shop at home in front of the television, than go out and shop. But I don't believe that, and I don't think that will ever happen because people will want to go out and shop because *the desire to be with other people is much stronger than using a computer to save them energy.* So I think in the same way that, something has been developed, research and so on and it may be possible to do what Richard has said, to create this perfect being, but I think pressure from society, from people, will say alright you've created that, but we don't actually want that, that's not what we're looking for. (emphasis added)

Mary was making a connection between innovations in consumerism and consumer culture with those in NRTs. Implicit in her statement is an analogy between home shopping and baby shopping. Mary is not opposed to shopping, but what becomes clear from her discussion with Richard is that shopping is not simply about the easiest mode of access (i.e. through a television/computer screen) to a desired object. It is also about the experience of acquiring the object in the context of other people. In drawing limits around developments of NRTs, Mary is drawing on another familiar domain of consumerism and the consumer culture to make her point. At the same time, Richard is making comparisons between current practice and the direction in which he perceives the technology to be developing. Like Mary, he is drawing on a particular conception of what motivates people to action and what desired results they aspire towards. In Richard's formulation, 'individualism' is the operative theme while with Mary, that of 'society' comes to the forefront.

As with the other married couples I spoke to during the research, Mary and Richard have not had direct contact with NRT. At this point, certain general remarks are in order to help further contextualize the material that forms the substance of this chapter.

The couples recruited[4] in the present research formed part of a recently completed study which had been investigating the relationship between family life and the appropriation and use of domestic technology (ESRC-PICT project; see Hirsch, 1992). My previous research experience with the families had been extensive (based on 8 or 9 meetings of several hours in each case). The research format used in the two studies was similar: a structured, but open-ended, set of questions and discussion themes. The couples had, therefore, a long-standing relationship with myself as ethnographer and with my style of eliciting information. Given the amount of background information held on each family, the present research was based on a single visit to each couple.

My discussions were conducted in the couples' homes with only the husband and wife present. The questions and themes used in the discussions were ordered in such a way as to move from the most immediate and accessible forms of experience to those presumably more distant and less familiar. The themes covered during the discussions were as follows: (a) the family as an idea; (b) children and parents; (c) technologically assisted reproduction (NRT); (d) donation/surrogacy; (e) degrees of acceptable assistance. Each discussion lasted between 2 and 2½ hours and was tape-recorded.

The couples had no problems in talking generally and hypothetically about the themes covered in the discussions. They were not being asked to speak as representatives of, for instance, their class, age group or religious affiliation, though these were all part of their diverse experiences. Rather, the subject of NRT itself offered a perspective from which the couples were able to formulate viewpoints on their own and others' experiences. My intention was to establish a context where informants could talk in the context of one relationship.

This chapter thus highlights the existence of a 'conjugal sub-text' at work in the discussions. By conjugal sub-text I refer to a specific example of a more general process. The specific example follows from the fact that, in the material presented here, the persons are related through a conjugal relationship. The general process is that people act in the context of relationships and in so doing they act with other people in mind. This is the case whether there are other persons physically present or not. Indeed, I suggest that the dialogue these couples sustained with themselves through discussion with me makes evident one dimension of what people generally are doing when speaking as individual persons: they exist as individuals within a field of relationships.[5]

As a consequence, the discussions reported here express a particular 'conjugal' perspective on NRT. At one level, I interpret the views being expressed by the couples as related to the way each person understands her/himself within their relationship. But, perhaps at a more fundamental level, I infer that the narratives reported here turn on certain axiomatic assumptions about the nature of conjugality itself.[6]

I use the term 'conjugal' rather than 'nuclear [family]' in order to stress the cultural completeness of the husband-wife pair, whether or not the pair is further completed by children (Goody, 1983). This accompanies the idea that persons ordinarily have as part of their family experience both a mother and a father. As a norm this is, of course, contested, and is a cultural, not a social, fact. It is therefore not surprising that the status of the family in English and Western European history is itself a contested issue.[7] Whether we follow Laslett (1972) and see the one form as prevailing, whether we follow M. Anderson (1980) and see a diverse range, what is clear is that the idea of conjugality strongly impinges upon what is imaginable as 'family life' (cf. Strathern, 1992, p. 24). To consider the NRT in the context of a conjugal setting is at the same time to conjure up a cultural microcosm informed by ideas intrinsic to English/Western European kinship thinking. The scenarios that were evoked in discussions with the couples emerged as a way of negotiating limits to what the men and women were prepared to present or express as morally acceptable.

Children and Parents

Christine Dole of Berkshire heard about the so-called 'virgin birth' controversy when it made its way into the media in 1991. She and her husband had discussed it at the time and both 'disagreed' with such procedures. Christine and Daniel have four children. One is from her previous marriage, two from their current marriage. They also have a young adopted son from an Afro-Caribbean family, whom they had initially fostered. For longer or shorter periods, there are always one or two foster children in the Dole home. In fact, both Daniel and Christine would like to make fostering their full-time occupation, with Daniel leaving his current job (Daniel works for an international airline; Christine calls herself a house-wife). At the moment they feel they have to add fostering to other activities. The Doles consider themselves practising Methodists.

> CD: I think every child has the right to two parents. If God had wanted us to have children being only one person we would have been able to do it . . . I know a lot of children don't have two parents but a lot of one-parent families do have contact with the other parent.

The practice of egg or sperm donation of itself did not pose a problem for Christine.

> CD: I have no problem with that. If there are reasons why either the man can't produce the sperm, or the female can't produce the eggs themselves, and they are still a couple and they still want children . . .

Daniel agreed with his wife. But as with a number of other men and women, he also drew out a darker, more nefarious side to these processes.

> DD: I have a concern, because I think this is where you start to get into genetic engineering, as far as the people who actually have the money to select the sperm and/or egg.
> CD: Oh no, I wouldn't do it like that, it would have to be, as far as I'm concerned, I think sperm and eggs should be labelled white or black or mixed race and that's as far as it should go.

But Daniel still felt there was a more powerful side to the technologies that could not be controlled.

DD: I feel pretty certain that things are going to get pretty muddled and perhaps that's why certain people are beginning to say no, the white race must be there or no we must have this or no we must have that ... perhaps that's what's actually prompting some of the work that's actually done, because there are people in power, in authority who are able to promote these things and pay for them to actually occur, who could perhaps be engineering this super-race ...

Daniel felt that the women wanting a 'virgin birth' should be counselled. He felt there were many children already born that needed adoptive parents. Christine agreed. For her, couples have children and if a single person wants a child, they should be able to adopt. This would allow, in her view, a deeper 'truth' to be revealed.

CD: [B]y saying they want to adopt they will then have lots of counselling and their reasons for wanting a child so desperately as a single person would be gone into properly.

Underlying the concerns of both Christine and Daniel were the issues of keeping certain facts or tendencies outside of the context of having children (for example, money, anonymous donating third parties, and totalitarian power). It is for these reasons they found adoption and even surrogacy, if money did not change hands, such suitable alternatives.

CD: [I]n which case, if there's no money changing hands and the surrogate had nothing to do with either parent, then basically what we're saying is that the surrogate mother gives the baby up for adoption and the couple adopt it and then in that case I don't think it makes any difference at all.

If these elements entered into the context of the child's life, certain problems would become manifest:

DD: ... whether the child is actually at some stage in the future going to have an identity crisis, going to wonder about the other party, that wasn't involved ... in their upbringing and all the rest of it.

I suggest that what the Doles (and other couples) are seeking to maintain is the idea that parents should reproduce persons that are individuals in themselves: 'that individual persons are somehow prior to ... relationship', one of Strathern's facts of English kinship (1992, p. 53; see note 3). The introduction of these other elements into the situation of a child's individuality is evidently being formed through various public and visible relationships instead of existing prior to them.

Like the Doles, Ganesh and Rajni Lunn, who live in a Westminster owner-occupied maisonette with their three daughters, had followed the item in the tabloids at the time. Ganesh and Rajni came to London from South Africa nearly twenty years ago, but their families originate from India. Their links to Hinduism are explicit in their home with daily prayers, especially on Friday evenings. Ganesh is often called to act as priest for family ceremonies. They refer to themselves as a 'modern' family and, after so long in Britain, think of themselves as having taken on many of the attitudes associated with British family life. But this form of conception went too far.

> RL: We felt it wasn't right for a woman to have a test-tube baby without having any sexual connections with a male . . .
> GL: What kind of feeling would she have, she's nothing else than a factory, like a conveyor belt conveying the completed project . . .

And in developing these ideas he adds:

> GL: Yes, it's the vision Hitler had, a superhuman race, isn't it . . . It's contrary and contradictory to the role of Nature isn't it, where you are now propagating the role of Nature.

Both Rajni and Ganesh appear to be strongly opposed to forms of NRT. Their objections, however, are less focused on the techniques themselves than on the consequences for relations between parent and child. This emerged in more explicit fashion later in our discussions when we considered the possibilities of multiple births under certain NRT procedures. As Rajni indicates, she is not against multiple births per se.

> RL: [It's O]kay right for example say a man and woman can't get together to fertilize and have babies, and the eggs are taken out from her and the sperm is taken from the man and are fertilized outside and then put back into the woman, it's still the same man and woman who's doing it, for me that's okay, it doesn't matter how many multiple births you have, it's still the same man and same woman who have produced it. The problem arises for me when there's man and woman and they have to bring a third party in to create that from the sperm bank, that worries me because then what do you tell the

child where it originally comes from, or who the father is.

The problem for Rajni, as well as her husband, was the existence of a third party outside the original mother and father pair. In pushing her point forward, she draws on the now well-established and familiar cultural icon of Louise Brown.[8]

> RL: Because when you look at our test-tube, how old is she?
> EH: Who's this, Louise Brown?
> RL: Yes, but in her case it's her mother and father, it's not brought from outside, there's no third party involved, it's just its own natural mother and father, it was only fertilized outside and put into a test tube. That's okay because she knows that is her natural father although she's been brought into this world in a different way from other children.

As in the case of the Doles, adoption was seen by Rajni and Ganesh as a preferable alternative. Although the adopted child would have the trauma of its early life outside a family to contend with, through the adoptive process this would be transformed. Ganesh felt that gradually this early emotional state would 'wear' away. He contrasted this process with that of surrogacy and, in particular, surrogacy where there was a transaction of money. Again, the image of a consumer process was evoked to characterize the negative aspects of this relationship with a child.

> GL: [I]t's like going into a supermarket and taking a baby off the shelf, putting it in the trolley, wheeling it to the cashier, paying the cashier and walking off with the child. It's not that simple.

Again, the question of the child's identity became the issue. Rajni returned to the example of Louise Brown. Although she was seen to exemplify the positive side of NRT, the way she came into the world raised problems of identity and difference. Rajni wondered whether the circumstances of her birth and the large media attention in subsequent years would cause her to become 'anti-people'; or whether people will become 'anti towards her'. These are all factors she will have to cope with, while, as Rajni pointed out, her children will not have to cope with such problems.[9]

    Whereas, in their particular ways, Christine and Daniel, like Rajni and Ganesh, were in general agreement about these issues, Megan and Nicholas Selby had very different perspectives from each other. Megan and Nicholas live in a council flat in Camden with their two sons. Megan is a part-time play instructor for the local council; Nicholas works in a small local travel agency. Megan knew they would disagree when we began to discuss the issues touched on by the research. She said the two of them had very different opinions about 'equal opps, and that sort of subject'.

> MS: I honestly don't see why they ['virgin birth women'] can't just go to a sperm bank, I don't want a relationship, I might be gay, I might be whatever you want to call it, lesbian, I want to have a child anyway.

Although she saw single women conceiving through artificial means as acceptable, Megan was not in favour of what she called 'cloning'; this is where she drew the limit. As she put it:

> MS: Sperm-bank babies, and they can choose what colour hair, skin, mentality depending on whose sperm it is ... it's a type of cloning.

By contrast, Nicholas had great difficulty in initially accommodating any aspect of these forms of reproduction.

> NS: It's not a natural relationship, it's not a relationship that's natural to have children, two females or for that matter two males, cannot produce children ...

Nicholas' expressed concern was in relation to the child.

> NS: I don't think it's fair on the child.
> MS: What's not fair?
> NS: Because that child will not have a normal relationship.
> MS: But it would be [normal] to that child but not to you.
> NS: Nor to anybody else. It's an abnormal relationship.

On this point there was no agreement between Megan and Nicholas. As is clear from Megan's earlier comments, they had certainly disagreed on this and similar issues in the past. Where they did agree was around what Megan had referred to as 'cloning', and more specifically on the use of genetic engineering to produce a particular sort of child. To elaborate her point, Megan drew on her own relationship with Nicholas; there was a virtue for society at large in the way they had paired up.

> MS: This is where people like Nicholas and I for some unknown

reason attract, it brings things into a norm. I'm so short and he's tall, and it brings the offspring to a middling size, so their offspring should continue a natural balance, and I think that if you start messing about with the genetics until . . .

NS: In its place it's fine [egg and sperm donation], if it can help a couple who want children, who can't have children naturally, to have children, great, but if it comes to the state where you're messing around with genetics to produce, you're getting back into almost the realms of the Aryan race. You're trying to create something to an ideal.

The disagreements between Megan and Nicholas stemmed from different versions of what they imagined was 'natural' or normal and what was 'unnatural'. On further reflection, and after listening to Megan's comments, Nicholas felt he was able to accommodate a particular image of NRT.

NS: If you can give a couple, who want children, the ability to have children by artificial insemination by fertilizing the egg inside, outside the body whatever then reimplanting, fine, you're giving Nature a helping hand. But if you're trying to create the master race, by fiddling around with genetics, that's wrong.

I suggest that as long as the image of a man and woman contributing equally to the child was sustained, Nicholas could imagine the acceptability of these techniques. If this type of assistance did not bring the desired result then, Nicholas insisted, the only alternative was adoption. Although the child was not the 'flesh and blood' of either parent, each could feel they were equally contributing to it as a parent. He was insistent that if the child had the genetic substance of only one parent, then the relationship between the parents would not work.

NS: Then it wouldn't last, if you've got such a, if the woman really so desperately wants children that badly, every argument you get, that you have, that will keep being thrown backwards and forwards and in the end that relationship wouldn't last.

Perspectives on Connectedness

We have just seen how couples from diverse family contexts approach the image of a single mother wanting to conceive a child without a male partner present. In each case, they negotiated possibilities and drew limits around what they were prepared to present as morally acceptable. Their thoughts were constrained by contrary images of consumerism, totalitarianism and the loss of individuality, and by the apparent desire to keep a 'natural' relationship between the individual and society through conjugality. This is true, despite the way the arguments vary; Megan Selby, for example, is prepared to allow the 'virgin birth' as acceptable, but at the same time draws limits around what she will not condone ('cloning'). When I raised similar questions not in relation to a distant and hypothetical other ('virgin mother'), but in relation to one's own reproductive substance (donation), I found men and women drawing similar conclusions – though in the course of doing so they might use different images to evoke the same three scenarios.

Natalie and Charles Simon live in a large terraced house in Islington. They have five children, two of whom are adopted. Natalie is a part-time teacher and Charles describes himself as a technologist or inventor. They also have a summer house and boat on the southwest coast.

When I discussed egg and sperm donation with them, Charles indicated he would not do this; it would be beyond any limit he was prepared to go to.

> CS: I wouldn't be prepared to put all the other resources ... donating the physical genes that's not the problem is it, as I see it?

He then elaborated on the idea.

> CS: ... I wouldn't be prepared to donate sperm because I couldn't back it up with the emotional support, all the other support that I think as a result of that donation would require. I would feel obliged to not donate a sperm but donate the whole package, the responsibility of it.

Natalie agreed in absolute terms with her husband. For both, the idea of donation evoked the image of parenthood and one could not be dissociated from the other.

Earlier in our discussion, Natalie and Charles spoke of their family life as a 'project' (their term). They conceptualized its organization in this manner: initially certain things had to be put into place (finances, a place to live). Charles also indicated that the 'project' is periodically 'reviewed'; they discuss and plan what they are going to do in the future and when it will happen. When they got married, the intention was to have children; it was some years before this actually happened, but, as Charles put it, 'it was always on the agenda'. Neither of them could imagine the disassociation of this project from their own genetic substance – the one was part of the other. In fact, during the years leading up to having their first child, they had explicitly considered the possibilities of infertility and adoption: these were options they felt needed to be considered as part of the process of carrying out their project. As it turned out, they decided to adopt in any case.

The donation of genetic substance raised the issue of the lengths to which men and women were prepared to go in order to have a child. Natalie felt uncomfortable with certain practices. She brought into the discussion the example of a friend who was unable to have children with her husband.

> NS: I have a friend who's married, her husband was infertile, she desperately wanted a child, so she had an affair with somebody else and got pregnant and had a child. As the child is growing up, she has told the child that her husband was not his natural father, but the child, I think, is incredibly confused about the relationship, he knows his mother had an affair with this other person, and he knows this other person, and if you know who donated the sperm or eggs, I think in some ways that is going to affect your relationship later on.

Charles felt that in such a situation the child was being put in the position of a 'freak': 'it has an identity of itself as something radically different and unusual from its peers'. The only context in which he could imagine the acceptability of such practices (including NRT) was one of what he called 'alternative parenthood'.

> CS: I can see it would work in a situation where you had an extended family, that you were living in an environment where several couples, with their parents and their children were all mixed up ... where a group of adults took on the collective role of parents to a group of children ... and if they went outside that environment they would have the resources, they would have the assistance of the group that they were brought up with, and they could get support ... self-identity in that way.

Both Natalie and Charles agreed that the identity of the child could be adversely affected by the various techniques of donation and assistance now possible with NRT. What was of most concern to both was the tendency to transform the basis of childhood itself. In their view, the parent has a 'mission' to help the child become a 'happy and integrated member of society'. In the context of NRT, there is a tendency to end up with a different type of child.

CS: [T]herefore you end up with a different type of child, *its mind will have been formed by relationships which are different from a child that was created by other means.* (emphasis added)

When I discussed gamete donation with Eileen and Phil O'Leary, a different set of connections were evoked. The O'Learys live in a semi-detached house in Berkshire with their four children. Their eldest son is currently sitting his A levels and plans to attend university next year. Eileen has been a housewife for most of her married life but has recently started working in social services; Phil started his own business during the late 1980s after working for over a decade in a large London department store. They were both raised as Catholics although Phil now considers himself an agnostic.

EH: Would you be prepared to be a donor with your sperm?
PO: I haven't got any now, it's irrelevant.
EH: Oh, you've had a vasectomy?
PO: Yes.
EH: But assuming . . .
PO: I think I would have.
EO: Now, I wouldn't let Phil do that willingly, now you said you wouldn't mind, I would actually give that some thought, that sounds really selfish doesn't it? I was quite possessive then!

And a short while later Eileen expanded on her initial reaction.

EO: It was almost like he was being unfaithful, the initial feeling was oh, he was being a bit free and easy . . .

In this context, Phil indicated that by donating sperm he would be doing his 'bit for society', but for Eileen the thought evoked an initial reaction of unfaithfulness. It was as if Phil were prepared to commit adultery: to behave in a very individual and selfish way. The initial contrast between Eileen and Phil's attitude in this context bears comparison with Megan and Nicholas Selby in the last section. It will be recalled that Megan was prepared to accept a number of innovations associated with NRTs that Nicholas found unacceptable. Eileen, however, appears to adopt a more conservative perspective than her husband. (I mention this here to caution against a reading of the narratives presented here as corresponding to the views associated with either 'men' or 'women'.)

EO: [I don't agree] that a single parent should automatically be able to go to a sperm bank and have their eggs fertilized ... it's a dodgy business for later on in life for that particular child.

Again, Eileen's reflections on techniques of donation lead her to consider the possible effects it has on the child's mind: 'it just sounds awful coming from a sperm, coming from a freezer'. Phil, by contrast, has a more accepting, if slightly cynical, attitude towards these developments. On the one hand, he finds it difficult to separate these techniques from other controversial research in science and its technological implementation.

> PO: And you really can't differentiate between biological experimentation like that and filling the world with nuclear arms, because it's the very same thing, science is following research as far as it will go.

On the other hand, this view is wedded to one which senses an inevitability to these trends, and their negative if somewhat desired outcomes.

> PO: When you get into it, the very fact that it's done, for instance, if somebody goes to a sperm bank, somebody goes to a baby shop to get a baby ... what I'm saying is look at the lovely guarantees you've got, it won't be abnormal because they've screened the embryo to make sure there's nothing wrong with it, before it's implanted ... it's not Nature's work any more. It's somebody getting a microscope and saying oh, don't like that one, that one's not perfect, get rid of that one, or people saying, I'm not having that embryo it's a girl. Then you can literally end up going shopping for a baby.

Whereas Eileen felt a sense of adultery and betrayal in Phil's casual offer to donate sperm, Phil sensed a certain inevitability associated with developments in NRT which led to a close connection between babies and consumerism. Neither Eileen nor Phil thought NRT should be abandoned. Rather, they suggested that NRT presented the possibility of novel forms of relationships (particularly linked to anonymous donation) which challenged our existing morals. The image of a child as the product of two known parents was at the centre of their conceptions.

In discussion with a London-based couple, Lynn and Frank Irving, an analogous reference was made to adultery. Lynn and Frank live in a council flat in Camden with their daughter and son. Frank sells insurance while Lynn describes herself as a housewife, but also does voluntary work at their son's school. Both are Jewish. I asked Lynn her thoughts about human egg and sperm donation.

> LI: At one stage I used to think yes, it was nothing, I hadn't really thought about it and even suggested to a friend of mine . . .
> EH: What did you suggest?
> LI: That she should have artificial insemination.

At this point the husband, Frank, immediately added 'Test-tube adultery'.

Eileen's response focused on unfaithfulness with an anonymous other; Lynn's advice to a friend to seek an anonymous donor suggested to Frank adultery, albeit in a test tube. By none of these three couples could sperm be imagined as an entity divorced from various social/sexual relationships; even Phil's donation to 'society' led to an image, given voice by his wife, of potential illicit sex.

Lynn then went on to add:

> LI: But then, thinking about it years later, I don't think it's a good idea. I think it comes to a point in one's life where you have to accept your limitations, and if you really can't have a child from your partner, and it's absolutely impossible, if you can't adopt a child . . . and if there isn't a child to adopt, well I think one has to accept their limitations.

Lynn argued that when one was able to face up to these limitations, the next possible option was to consider adopting a child. We also discussed the fact that the number of children available for adoption was in relative terms not very large. Even so, they both insisted that an anonymous donation was unacceptable. If NRT had to be brought into the process, then it should only involve the substance of the husband and wife.

> LI: I don't object to fertilization within the test tube, with a husband and wife's fertilization . . .
> FI: I[t] keeps it within its own context both genetically, biologically and psychologically, they say it is us, it needed some artificial assistance, but it's us that actually produced it, it's our baby, it's not 50 per cent somebody else.

Earlier in our discussion, Lynn and Frank described to me the way they felt connected to their children. As in the case of many of the couples, they did not mention a genetic connection (it was ideas of love, responsibility, support, respect and so on that were usually mentioned).

> EH: But before, when we were talking about the way you felt you
> were connected to your children ... you didn't really mention that at
> all.
> FI: But you take it for granted. It's only when you're suddenly
> confronted with the possibility it could not be your child.

Lynn then suggested the following analogy:

> LI: Look, imagine [a roof] and you're holding it up with [two]
> pillar[s], those pillars are not joined together, they are apart, they are
> standing apart, but they are still part of each other because they have
> one aim to hold that roof up, as one pillar collapses, then the other
> can't support that beam, so even though they are separate, they are
> still one, so are children. Even though you're separate, you are still
> one, do you understand what I'm getting at? But you cannot think of
> that child all the time as an extension of yourself, an extension of
> your character, of everything within yourself, they are a separate
> individual but they are still part of you.

As we have seen in other conjugal contexts, what one reproduces as a parent
is a separate yet 'connected' individual. Both Lynn and Frank are suggesting
that the advent of NRT brings the potential for those ideas of love,
responsibility, and so forth, that are explicitly associated with (parents) being
connected to a child, as becoming 'disconnected' from their previously
implicit foundation in a genetic base.

Unlike Lynn, Mark Lyon did not give advice to a friend to seek an
anonymous donation. But as with Lynn Irving, his perception of these
matters changed over time. Mark and his wife Shirley live in an owner-
occupied semi-detached house in Berkshire. They have three daughters and
one son. The eldest daughter recently completed her GCSEs. Shirley works
as a director's PA in a computer firm; Mark has a middle-management
position in a multinational technology company. They fostered children in
the past, before the birth of their first child.

Mark explained his change of attitude as being linked to an article he had
read.

> ML: I used to think this was fairly socially acceptable, the act of
> sperm donation, medical students of the sixties used to do this to earn
> some extra money to pay their way through college, they used to

donate sperm and this was used in AID [artificial insemination by donor] ... but then I actually read, a couple of years ago, some references to people who had grown up and had discovered that this was how they had come into the world. Now this was about the time that adopted children in this country were given freer access to their original birth certificates ... at the same time, a story surfaced from people who were products of insemination by donor and it was really quite revealing, it took me aback, in that these people were actually angry with their sperm father, as they called it, because they said what sort of careless thing to do, to go in, to donate sperm, walk away with some money, and not give another thought to what was to follow on from that, to never know the consequences of that.

Shirley Lyon shared her husband's feelings on this issue.

SL: I think it's sad in the case of the people who've grown up and discovered that the person you think is your natural father isn't ... and the fact that the husband, father, that must be quite something to accept the fact that your wife's going to have a baby but genetically it's not yours ...

Mark and Shirley both stressed the potential unhappiness created by the techniques of sperm donation. On the one hand, the child may discover (or in fact be told) that s/he came into the world as a result of another person's genetic material. On the other hand, the husband, for example, may have to live with the fact that the child he loves and values is 'not really his'. In light of the difficulties associated with such artificial techniques, I suggested to Mark and Shirley that perhaps they should be discontinued. Although they both acknowledged that numerous problems, both inter- and intra-personal, resulted from the use of the techniques, neither of them suggested that the techniques should no longer be available.

SL: No, because I don't think everybody that happens to, I mean when you have a child, even if it isn't, when you raise a child from a baby, and you've loved it and cared for it, you taught it all the things that you value and you hope that it will grow up to be a confident human being, then I feel that it does, that child is part of you whether or not you made it in the first place.

Shirley was insistent that if the parents had considered the situation with a great amount of thought and discussion, and had prepared themselves for all the later consequences, then they should be fine. But she added that it took a special sort of person (especially on the part of the 'father' or 'mother') to be able to bring a child into the world in this way.

We continued this line of discussion for some time, after which I asked Shirley and Mark whether they thought such donations should be from a known person or should be anonymous. Mark suggested that with an anonymous donor the whole process might be easier to accept. He said that one heard stories about those who chose traits they desired in the child, even though the donor was anonymous. Mark's comments sparked a connection in Shirley's mind. She was immediately reminded of a conversation she had with a neighbour a few years ago. Her recollection of this conversation also connected with her earlier comments on techniques of sperm and egg donation. Although a potential source of sadness and confusion for all parties concerned, such techniques, she felt, should not be discontinued: if the child is given enough love and care s/he will 'be a part of you whether or not you made the child in the first place'.

> SL: What Mark said before took me back, just a flash in my mind, to a conversation I had with a ... next-door neighbour of mine ... and her sister had been adopted. Now I didn't know that because those two girls looked so much alike I would never have known that they weren't natural sisters ... we had a conversation about it and they said we guess we just grew alike, it was so strange.

I asked Shirley why this *particular* recollection was brought to mind.

> SL: This business of saying well I'd like to have the donor who donated the sperm, if he could have blue eyes and brown hair or whatever, a ginger moustache ... maybe when people are living close together, they do look alike, maybe it's the way they cut their hair, or their facial expressions or the way they stand, I don't know.

Mark then succinctly elaborated on Shirley's insight.

> ML: Your expectations, so you expect it, *you see what you want to see* ... (emphasis added)

Differences of Opinion

How one perceives a child born under circumstances of donation and/or surrogacy became a point of disagreement in my discussions with Mary and

Richard Dobbs. It will be recalled from earlier in this chapter that they had different perspectives on the long-term possibilities made available by developments in genetic engineering: Richard suggested that parents might be attracted by the possibility of producing a genetically perfect child, while Mary argued that although this might be technically possible, it was not what people generally wanted.

It emerged during the course of our conversation that Mary had considered, at some point in the past, being a surrogate mother for her sister. Her sister had had a miscarriage and the medical diagnosis given afterwards seemed to suggest that she suffered from a rare disorder which might prevent her from giving birth to children (it subsequently transpired that she was able to have children and she now has two). Mary said she cared very much for her sister and knew the sort of feelings that exist when one wants to have a baby. At the time, Mary discussed the possibility of acting as a surrogate first with her sister and then separately with Richard. The conversations were recalled by Richard and he said that his views had not changed since that time. In essence, he was not in favour of Mary acting as a surrogate for her sister.

> RD: Mary's my wife, Mary has my children, not somebody else's.

Richard said that he would feel alienated from this child, knowing that it was a part of Mary and had nothing to do with him. When Mary asked him to think about the *reasons* she had for considering taking on this role, Richard replied:

> RD: I hear what you're saying, very commendable, but at the end of the day you and I are number one and it is us we should think about.

What underlined these differences were opposing attitudes to the intentions behind donation itself. Richard felt it should be given and received anonymously, while Mary said she would want to know whom her eggs were being used to help; she would want the recipient to know her.

> MD: I would like to know who I am donating it to and why.
> RD: You don't think you'd have feelings for that kid when it's born?
> MD: No, I don't think I would, I might have a closer relationship possibly, but I can't speculate on that, but I wouldn't be doing it for that reason, the overriding feeling would be . . .
> RD: You've just hit a point there, a closer relationship with that child.

MD: I don't know, but one can't always view things from one's own perspective can one, one has to look at things from other people's point of view.

Much of the subsequent discussion revolved around how one would 'look' at a child that was a product of the donation of either sperm or egg.

RD: ... I'd see him every birthday, christening, you know what I mean, and I think if it was my child, I think every time I saw that child one thing that would go through my mind ...

Mary then directed our attention to the fact that we had failed to consider the perspective of the child in these matters:

MD: ... the one person we haven't actually talked about is the child and their feelings at the end of the day, and how would that child feel, growing up and it might be that mum says well I want to tell you this because I want to be truthful to you about you and where you come from but Richard is really your dad.

Although Mary did not initially consider this to be an important considera-tion from her adult perspective, when she began to view matters from the perspective of the child many more complications emerged than first seemed to appear. Richard suggested that such information might come out into the open, given certain circumstances, and be used in a hurtful manner.

RD: All it needs is an upset in the family, you could turn round and say that child is mine, all sorts of nasty things could come out, like the father could not produce the child, it's not my child, we don't know who the father is because it's all anonymous.

Richard and Mary perceived numerous tensions and potential conflicts arising from new forms of reproduction and the technologies associated with them. A number of the issues they raised in their discussion, particularly the distinction between a father and a 'real' (in their view, genetic) father, are not necessarily confined to developments associated with NRT. On both points, there is an overlap between the discussion I had with this couple and the one I had with another couple, Winnie and Ted Murphy; however, the Murphys come to the discussion from a particular family background.

Winnie and Ted Murphy live in Berkshire. They have an owner-occupied semi-detached house and share it with one of the two children from Ted's previous marriage. They also own a caravan in southwest England. Both Winnie and Ted have been married previously. They have been in their present marriage for six years. Ted is in his mid fifties and has recently taken early retirement from his job as a trade union official; Winnie is a nurse and recently completed a university degree. The eldest child, Caroline, started a course at university last year, while Sam is studying for his A levels and still lives at home.

The tensions that were expressed by Mary and Richard Dobbs – especially around the 'unequal' contribution to a child's birth (whether genetically or through gestation) – also became evident when Winnie and Ted discussed the same set of issues. In this case, however, they emerged from a baseline different from that of the other families. During the early part of our discussion, Winnie and Ted were asked to offer some thoughts about their family. As with the other couples, a distinction was soon introduced between immediate or close family and relatives (cf. Firth *et al*, 1969, pp. 89–98). Winnie spoke of immediate family as being about close contact, the people we know better than others, as compared to relatives who are more distant. But Ted soon introduced a further distinction which seemed to complicate matters.

> TM: It is more than closeness ... immediate family would include my mother and father because we are part of them. From them we have been created and my brothers share that creation because they come from the same womb, so I would see that as immediate family. I see our children as being immediate family because they are from our creation. But your aunts and uncles haven't got that kind of relationship.

Ted's attempt to encompass both their thoughts with this comment contradicted a fundamental aspect of his conjugal experience with Winnie: that 'their' children were not a product of their 'creation'. Winnie soon put another gloss on his remark.

> WM: I don't know that I necessarily see it like that, I think it's more to do with closeness you have with certain members of the family.

She then expanded on this point.

> WM: Well, how much you sort of share with them, like although I won't see my sister's baby a lot, not closeness in the sense that you

see them a lot, but I speak to them a lot, we share all sorts of childhood experiences and things like that. I don't know whether it's necessarily simply just coming from the same womb, because I see Caroline and Sam as my kids, but they're not, do you know what I mean? But they are still classed as family.

The implicit tension between a 'biological/natural' connection with the children and a 'social' connection was a recurring theme throughout our conversation. At several points, Winnie stressed that although Caroline and Sam were not her biological children, Caroline, in particular, considers her to be the mother: 'Mothering has been me, she sees that as me.' Ted agreed with Winnie on these points throughout the discussion. However, it was his periodic recourse to a conception of parenthood based on 'biological' facts which frequently led Winnie to stress the non-biological dimension of parenting. For example, I asked them to consider those factors which could prevent one from being a parent. Ted immediately started to answer but was cut short by Winnie.

> TM: Apart from biological things . . .
> WM: I don't think that's true because we've just said all that. I'm parenting although I'm not the biological mother, that's nothing to do with it.

Again, after we had covered the topics of donation and technologically-assisted forms of reproduction, this same tension emerged later with respect to dimensions of maternal surrogacy. Both Winnie and Ted agreed that people should seek out adoption – trying to give a home to children who have no parents – as opposed to choosing artificial means of bringing a child into the world. But Ted suggested that there was a thin line dividing adoption and surrogacy: in a surrogate birth, the child has to be signed over by the biological mother and in this way there is little technical difference between it and adoption. He then went on to make an additional point:

> TM: I don't know, but I would find it very difficult to come to terms with, as the child is growing up, to see the features of the mother, appearing in the child, and they're not your features.[10]

Ted's comment was again unsettling for Winnie, particularly as her relationship with Caroline and Sam seemed to replicate the difficulty he had identified for himself. To distinguish her own experience from these other forms of parenting, Winnie brought into the discussion what she called 'cultural inheritance': the 'cultural thing' people pass on to one another. She was not able to elaborate on this idea, but it was clear she was making a distinction between what one acquires through culture and what in this case she called a 'nurturing [biological] mother'. But again, this holds as true for adoption and being a stepmother.

In order to overcome the dilemma and distinguish surrogacy from the experience of Winnie *vis-à-vis* the children, Ted stated that surrogacy arrangements are tainted by a commercial attitude.

TM: They see children as a market.
WM: Just another commodity to be bought and sold on an open market.

This agreement signalled a joint perspective. Both step-parenthood and adoption could be seen to be sustaining the link, however partially, between the 'natural' and 'social': what they share is the way they keep relationships separate from aspects of money and the market.

Markets, Materialism and Morality

Winnie and Ted, as with the other couples I spoke to, attached negative consequences to developments in NRT. Reference to Brave New World and Hitlerism emerged time and again during our talks. This totalitarian scenario was evoked precisely when the possibilities of choice and selection were made apparent by the techniques associated with NRT: the idea that one could now select and construct 'the perfect race'. In fact, Winnie even suggested that if we lived in a different, perhaps non-capitalistic society, these same fears would not be evident. However, given the world we live in, one cannot but feel that it 'has sinister implications'.

Some of these same concerns were expressed by Gloria and Paul De Guy, also of Berkshire. But the conjugal context from which they were expressing their views was very different from that just considered. Gloria and Paul live in an owner-occupied detached house with three young children. Gloria calls herself a housewife and Paul works in a management capacity for a large telecommunications company. They both consider themselves devout Catholics and their Catholic beliefs impinged strongly during our discussion.[11] In fact, I attempted to discuss several of the themes associated with donation, surrogacy and NRT, themes I explored with the other couples, but the conversations were curtailed very quickly: Gloria and Paul were totally 'against' them as a matter of religious principle. They discussed the possibilities only long enough to register their disagreement. Gloria summed up her thoughts in the following way:

> GD: I, myself, am torn in two, I find it very hard, on the one hand a part of me believes that yes, you have to use whatever knowledge and intellect you have to solve all manner of human problems and one of them would be infertility. However, having said that, I think infertility would be very low down my scale of priorities of helping the human race, in that particular situation it's a question of God's will. If you're meant to have them, you will and it is unreasonable in my mind to go to the lengths that apparently one has to conceive a child.

Gloria, in particular, saw developments in NRT as part of a wider trend in society. She did not see NRT as an innovation that came about and then had effects on the attitudes of people (as suggested by comments of other people I spoke to). Rather, it reflected a selfishness that was intrinsic to society and allowed people to expand the areas where they could be selfish.

> GD: ... it's yet another way of getting round life, of doing what they want to do, putting themselves, their own needs absolutely first: I want a baby, I'm upset, I'm going to do whatever it takes to do it, like I want a car, I'll go and get a bank loan and I'll get a car. It's like another possession, another thing they want and they will move heaven and earth to get it.

It is the image of unbridled consumerism that Gloria and, to a lesser extent, Paul picked up on: 'a danger of seeing [a baby] as yet another material possession'. She perceived a trend where children just become the next thing in the long list of material possessions one is supposed to have. This is the process Gloria sees at work in relation to NRT.

> GD: ... I don't for a moment wish to be unkind to the couples who genuinely are bitterly disappointed and would love to have it for the right reasons, but for many it isn't that, it's like you get a car, a dishwasher and then a dog and then you think what next ... so I think there is that sort of danger to it, that one perceives them as the thing to have, the thing to do.

For Gloria and Paul, if children come 'naturally' within the married state, then this was another matter altogether. All attempts to artificially assist the process were wrong. Gloria put it in strong terms: 'I feel that the whole field of procreation ought to be left alone'.

These same issues were not so cut and dried for Maria and Geoff Williams. Both are trained pharmacists and work in two of the local hospitals. They have a daughter and son and live in a semi-detached, owner-occupied house in Berkshire. When we began to touch on some of the issues described for the De Guys, Geoff indicated that such matters had been familiar to them for a long time, given their medical background and working environment. Maria supported his comments by referring to Louise Brown and the relatively long period that has elapsed since her birth. Geoff was even prepared to suggest that these matters were an 'accepted fact'. Maria was not prepared to go quite so far. She perceived a worrying side to these developments which could not just be glossed over. In particular, she drew on the image of genetic engineering and, more specifically, the possibility that men and women will be able to decide in the future what sort of child they want. This is a suggestion we have come across in various ways already. Geoff concurred with Maria, while at the same time arguing that all of these developments would have to occur under strict controls. For her, it was the danger of 'it being completely taken over by science'; Geoff stated it from a different perspective.

For him, the advent of trust hospitals in the NHS meant that the market mechanism could be used to provide men and women with these 'services' if they so desired. It would be a matter of supplying people with what they want. His half-joking manner was offset by his experience of 'market forces' having been introduced into his own sector of the hospital.

> GW: A trust hospital might go for something like 'special offer this week – red-headed boys'.

For Maria, it all 'smacked of the Aryan race'. Geoff felt less threatened.

> GW: It would be possible from a scientific point of view. Lots of things are possible now, it's just they wouldn't morally be accepted
> . . .

While Maria was most concerned with the potential 'standardization' of children in the context of NRT, Geoff could imagine the potential of innovative hospitals and maternity wards operating in a new market-led environment.

> GW: Which comedian was it, Leslie Crowther wasn't it? He had a

girl, and another girl, how many girls did he have, four or five girls, what he would have done for a boy, everything except have a sixth girl. Now if he was put in a position where he could have said, if we do this, you'll definitely have a boy, who's to say he wouldn't have gone for it? Who's to say that if we had Ellen and then we'd had another daughter, and I'd say oh I want a son, if that had been available, say okay we'll do this and we'll definitely have a boy, that we wouldn't have gone for it?

MWi: But I think we would have been prepared to accept that we were going to have another child, and if the child was a girl it would still be our child.

But as Geoff readily acknowledged, all of the developments would be constrained by the current morality and what people thought was morally acceptable. Maria was less convinced by the effectiveness of controls.

MWi: It's difficult to say what the point is though, isn't it? Because what would be sound now, in ten years time, the improvements in science and the improvements in technology, who's to say the barriers won't move?

The problem of morality and its change over time was also a theme that Denis White highlighted towards the end of our discussion. Denis and Margaret live in an owner-occupied semi-detached house in Berkshire with their four young children. Denis works for the Post Office; Margaret describes herself as a housewife and also does some paid child-minding.

Margaret made it clear towards the beginning of our discussion how important children were to her. It was a topic she had discussed with Denis before they got married; she did not see any point in getting married to someone who did not want children. Although they never considered adopting children, it was an option that would have arisen very quickly.

MWh: I mean obviously if we couldn't have had any, then I would have gone anywhere to find out how I could get them.

During the course of our conversation, Denis and Margaret drew on scenarios that were evoked by several of the other couples. They made connections between techniques of sperm and egg donation with images of catalogue shopping, genetic engineering the 'the master race'. At the same time, they both agreed that a 'conventional' couple (husband and wife) should be given 'all the help that medical science can give them': an image of 50 per cent or equal shares coming from each partner in a relationship was their underlying model (they also extended this idea to an adopted child where each can give equal shares, as well as a test-tube baby, where equal shares of substance could be given). Again, as with many of the couples, neither Margaret nor Denis had explicitly considered all of the themes and their variations before I raised them during our conversations. It is in this light that Denis made the following observation towards the end of our discussion:

> DW: A lot of it really is to say, through these questions, are people's morals or understanding keeping up with the changes in medicine and you know, do people feel all these changes are for the good and are we ready for them? Medicine is racing well ahead; do we morally feel we are in agreement with what they're doing? We probably need time to catch up with the medical people where things will change over the years. *I suppose, given enough time, we will all start to think differently.* (emphasis added)

The problem for Denis, as for several of the other men and women who raised this same possibility, was that no matter how hard these developments are thought about, discussed and even resisted, given enough time, they would change what we are prepared to imagine as thinkable and acceptable. There is a certain inevitability attached to the future that is supposed for such ideas and one that makes change almost inescapable.

Conclusion: What Kind of Limits?

Throughout the discussions I had with the couples reported in the pages above, concern was expressed that the way we conduct our most familiar relationships would change dramatically with the advent and greater use of the NRT. Two recurrent scenarios were evoked to express concern, even fear, about how NRT should be appropriated (except in the one family where religious principle prevailed). Each contained images of limits, though the particular images on which people drew were as diverse as their experiences. Then again, concern was expressed that NRT could lead to children being just another aspect of the individualist, consumer culture, so that conception would be reduced to just another feature of shopping and consumption. On the other hand, couples were concerned by the possibilities inherent, as they saw it, in NRT producing a master race, where the powerful are in too strong a position to impose what their vision of society should look like in the future. In either case, the modernist relationship between 'individual' and 'society' is potentially subverted. As one might expect in conversations with people in the context of conjugal relationships, their stated imaginings of how NRT should be appropriated also had a particular conjugal bias. The third scenario offered hope through regulation. NRT should be appropriated so as to sustain the image of a child as a product of a known and present mother and father.

The idioms, however, that the couples use to negotiate their concerns are drawn from domains we would not ordinarily associate with the realms of conjugal reproduction: the market (consumerism) and the state ('big brother'). In fact, much of Euro-American history of kinship has been concerned with tracing the development of a *separation* between this private domain and the public domains of the market and state (cf. Strathern, 1992, pp. 103–4, 187–92). This suggests that the conception of limits intrinsic to Euro-American kinship is not in fact as separate from these other domains as first appears.

Kinship implies a form of regulation. What is implicitly being regulated according to informants' images are the 'biological foundations' of the relationships referred to here as 'family' and 'relatives'. This was the image that Winnie and Ted Murphy were struggling with in articulating their respective roles as step-parent (no biological connection) and parent (biological tie). When the foundations are imagined as no longer regulated, concern is expressed: for example, the possibility that techniques of anonymous donation could conceivably enable a brother's sperm to be received by his sister. This particular potentiality became visible to Winnie and Ted at the end of our discussion.

> WM: They couldn't possibly make that kind of error surely, like my brother could go along and donate sperm and I could innocently pick that sperm up? There must be some kind of regulation.

And Ted immediately followed with:

> TM: The only way you could do that is knowing the name of the donor isn't it? I had never thought of that you know. This thing about incest really throws all the thing out, all the things we've been saying about, oh yes, we'd come to terms with that, when you throw it in, you don't know who the donors are. We've been saying we shouldn't know who the donor is because it makes life easier for everybody else.

In the everyday thoughts and perceptions of the couples reported here (as more generally), family and kinship is conceived as a domain separate from wider political and economic structures. However, when assumptions underlying conceptions of family and kinship are made explicit, their intrinsic connection with the domains of market and state becomes visible. In other words, when the basis of our most familiar relationships comes to appear potentially unregulated, then political and economic domains, by virtue of this intrinsic connection, become so as well.

Debates about the regulation of the market, as much as those about regulating the state, are public and wide-ranging. We do not think twice about offering an opinion as to whether more regulation or less is desirable. What is less evident, even hidden, is the manner in which these debates imply a particular conception of relatedness that we commonly understand as family and kinship. In this way, the concern of Denis White expressed in the previous section, and of other informants, is a genuine concern. As debated by parliamentarians, or as discerned by clinicians, medical developments are racing ahead of the ordinary man and woman. As Denis sees this, it takes time to catch up with these changes and in the process our thoughts are transformed. Yet perhaps it is not just our thoughts that are changing, in the way Denis suggests, but the previously *implicit* contexts to which they have to be *explicitly* focused, and the images by which they are summoned.

We have seen, through the material presented in this chapter, that men and women struggle to sustain a perspective on the present in the face of innovations that seem to threaten their accepted ideas and practices. In the future, NRT might be more readily available and 'acceptable', but it will not be 'our' thinking and practices that have necessarily changed as a result, so much as the areas and domains where they are *visibly* applied. These are issues that will continue to be debated, both politically and ethically – framed by the agencies of the market and state – and to which concepts of family and kinship will remain intrinsically connected.

Notes

I would like to thank the women and men who allowed me into their homes to discuss the topics reported in this chapter. All their names have been changed.

A slightly different version of this chapter appeared in J. Edwards, S. Franklin, E. Hirsch, F. Price and M. Strathern, *Technologies of Procreation: Kinship in the Age of Assisted Conception* (Manchester, Manchester University Press, 1993).

1   I was reminded of this passage in Harvey (1989) by a productive comment from Ronnie Frankenberg.
2   It should be noted here that it would be a mistake to conclude from the material

presented below that informants were opposed completely (with exceptions noted) to the development of NRTs, or to their take-up by the general public. What are being highlighted are connections made explicit by NRTs, to domains conventionally conceived as separate from kinship and family. The concerns expressed are as much a product of the connections being made visible as of the connections themselves.

3   Here, Strathern is referring to what she calls the second 'fact' of modern kinship; the first 'fact' is the individuality of persons (1992, p. 14), while the third 'fact' is that individuals reproduce individuals (1992, p. 53).

4   The families for the ESRC-PICT research project were initially recruited through local schools. Contact was made through the head teacher who was asked to recommend families for participation in the research. An initial meeting was then arranged at which time the families could decide whether they wanted to participate further in the research.

5   Allen Abramson has suggested that one of the recurring themes *implicitly* at work in this sub-text is the 'self-externalization of parental biology in one's own children'. I would argue that this conceptualization becomes *explicit* in the light of NRT. As a number of informants indicated, it is taken for granted until one is 'confronted with the possibility it could not be your child' (see p. 130; cf. Schneider (1992) for an insightful description and elaboration of these processes). I am grateful to Allen Abramson for his very helpful comments on this chapter.

6   Jeanette Edwards, personal communication. I am grateful to her for comments on this chapter.

7   Had this study been intended as a contribution to the sociology of the family, then it would have been appropriate to elicit material from the perspective of other families, or to have contextualized the present selection in relation to them.

8   Several men and women evoked the example of Louise Brown in the discussions. It is significant to note that she has become a cultural icon for what is possible for *people*: her introduction into a number of discussions is first and foremost because she can be cited as a real human being.

9   Both Rajni and Ganesh could imagine, under strict moral constraints, the increased take-up of NRT in British society. However, Ganesh insisted that, in Indian culture, the possibility of anonymous genetic material would not be thinkable: 'Now they want to know, if it's an anonymous sperm, will you know which caste it comes from? So it's completely out of the question, they will never accept it. Never accept it, even if they are given 100 per cent verity it's a high caste, they still won't accept it.'

10 Ted's conception of surrogacy in this instance was based on the use of the surrogate's eggs as well as her womb.

11 I have indicated the religious affiliations for several of the couples reported here. Only in the case of the De Guys, however, did religious beliefs become an explicit and inhibiting issue with respect to the topics of this research.

References

ANDERSON, M. (1980) *Approaches to the History of the Western Family 1500–1914*, London, MacMillan.

FIRTH, R., HUBERT, J. and FORGE, A. (1969) *Families and Their Relatives: Kinship in a Middle-Class Sector of London*, London, Routledge and Kegan Paul.

GELL, A. (1988) 'Technology and Magic', *Anthropology Today*, vol. 4, no. 2, pp. 6–9.

GOODY, J. (1983) *The Development of the Family and Marriage in Europe*, Cambridge, Cambridge University Press.

HARVEY, D. (1989) *The Condition of Postmodernity*, Oxford, Blackwell.

HIRSCH, E. (1992) 'The Long Term and the Short Term of Domestic Consumption: An Ethnographic Case Study', in SILVERSTONE, R. and HIRSCH, E. (Eds) *Consuming Technologies: Media and Information in Domestic Spaces*, London, Routledge.

LASLETT, P. (Ed.) (1972) *Household and Family in Past Time*, Cambridge, Cambridge University Press.

LEFORT, C. (1986) *The Political Forms of Modern Society*, translated and introduced by J.B. Thomson, Cambridge, Polity.

LUKES, S. (1973) *Emile Durkheim*, London, Allen Lane.

MILLER, D. (1987) *Material Culture and Mass Consumption*, Oxford, Blackwell.

SCHNEIDER, D. (1992) Comment on 'Virgin Births and Sterile Debates: Anthropology and New Reproductive Technologies' by C. Shore, *Current Anthropology*, 33, pp. 307–10.

STRATHERN, M. (1988) *The Gender of the Gift: Problems with Women and Problems with Society in Melanesia*, Berkeley, University of California Press.

STRATHERN, M. (1992) *After Nature: English Kinship in the Late Twentieth Century*, Cambridge, Cambridge University Press.

Chapter 6

Networking Constructions of Gender and Constructing Gender Networks: Considering Definitions of Woman in the British Cervical Screening Programme

Vicky Singleton

Sociology has historically been 'driven by an ambivalent wish to learn of and intervene about injustice' (Law 1992). 'We need to be able to cherish certain kinds of intellectual, political, and psychic discomforts, to see as inappropriate and even dangerous certain kinds of clear solutions to the problems we have been posing' (Harding, 1986).

Introduction

In 1989 I was offered a studentship to study public understanding of science.[1] After spending a year searching for an empirical focus for this work, personal experiences as a lay participant in the British Cervical Screening Programme (CSP) led to an intense interest in the programme and my research site was set. Reviewing approaches to the sociology of scientific knowledge, I introduced myself to Actor Network Theory (ANT). Directed by Michel Callon and Bruno Latour, I followed scientists and technologists around as they constructed electric vehicles, scallops and microbes (Callon, 1986a, 1986b; Latour, 1987, 1988c). I began to see how ANT might be useful as a way of structuring my analysis of the public/science relationship within the CSP. This chapter traces how I have used ANT and how I have developed the approach through its application to the CSP. It also demonstrates ways in which I feel ANT might be a useful tool for feminists approaching science.

The more I engaged with the discourses of ANT the more I became enamoured of the approach, in particular its radical non-dualistic nature and its concomitant emphasis of the contingent nature of scientific knowledge-claims. Nevertheless, in applying ANT to the CSP I found myself in an ambivalent association with the approach, especially when I considered that the CSP is for women. Feminist researchers have shown that woman has a particularized association with science and technology (e.g. Ehrenreich and English, 1979; Harding, 1986; Merchant, 1980). How could I incorporate the historicity of women's oppression by medical technologies and medical experts into my historically contingent analysis of the CSP? In answer I applied ANT to offer a woman-centred analysis, focusing on how 'woman as an actor' is defined within, and evolves through, the CSP actor network.[2]

Drawing on this application of ANT, this paper explores possible commonalties and tensions between feminist approaches and ANT. I suggest that feminist approaches and ANT, as diverse as they both are in their own right, appear to have similar theoretical developmental trajectories, to be discussing similar issues, expressing analogous ambivalences and facing the same dilemmas, at this historical moment. Feminism is struggling to find ways of describing and explaining the experiences of woman that are neither wholly essentialist 'biological', nor purely social constructivist (Lowe and Hubbard, 1983). That is, feminism is trying to develop ways of thinking outside the traditional subject/object, nature/culture dichotomies. ANT, as applied within this paper, offers a way of capturing how woman's biological and social experiences are interwoven. As an approach that attempts to transcend conventionally given dualisms, ANT responds to some of the concerns of feminism. However, thinking outside traditional dichotomies throws up another series of concerns and dilemmas, common to both ANT and feminism, that surround a problematic of speaking for others and representing multiformity and plurality.

The British Cervical Screening Programme

The CSP was first constructed as a national service in 1966 by the British government. It is a preventive health initiative. 'Healthy' women routinely undergo a cervical smear test (CST) during which a sample of cells from their cervix (neck of the womb) is obtained, smeared onto a glass slide, and fixed and preserved for subsequent laboratory analysis. The laboratory analysis detects cytological changes and categorizes them along a continuum from normal, through inflammation, to pre-cancerous changes or invasive carcinoma. The objective of the CSP is to detect pre-cancerous changes to allow for their treatment, so preventing the development of cervical cancer and mortality. There is a medical consensus that cervical cancer is linked to sexual activity, if not sexual promiscuity.[3] Hence all women who are sexually active are defined as a priority group in terms of participation in the CSP.[4]

Applying Actor Network Theory to the Cervical Screening Programme

ANT looks at science and society as co-evolving from the definition and positioning of non-human and human entities into a network of associations – an actor network (Callon *et al.*, 1986; Callon, 1986a, 1986b, 1987; Latour, 1987; Law, 1987). Through detailed case studies ANT looks at how scientific/technological artefacts or knowledge-claims become, or do not become, indispensable to the worlds in which they circulate, and to which they contribute.

Using ANT terminology, the British government could be seen to have simplified and juxtaposed a series of entities into a network of associations that make up the CSP. That is, the existence of the CSP is bound up with the construction of a certain world in which various entities play an assigned role – assume a simplified 'black-boxed' identity. For example: lay women between the ages of 20 and 64 are defined as at risk from cervical cancer and as concerned about their own health to the point of attending for a CST; the laboratory is defined as carrying out quick and accurate interpretations of cervical cell samples; medical practitioners are defined as obtaining cervical cell specimens quickly and painlessly; and cervical cells are defined as easily and painlessly obtainable and as changing in predictable and detectable ways in relation to cervical cancer.[5] As long as each of these diverse entities adheres to its defined role the CSP actor network is a successful construction and becomes indispensable to women's health. Thus, according to ANT, I can suggest that the CSP 'can be compared to a black box that contains a network of black boxes that depend on one another for their proper functioning as individuals and for the proper functioning of the whole' (Callon, 1987, p. 95) – a black box being defined as 'a simplified entity that is nevertheless a network in its own right' (Callon *et al.*, 1986, glossary).

ANT provides a way of approaching science without assuming *a priori* distinctions between, for example, science and society, human and non-human entities, valid and invalid knowledge. The approach refuses to consider any dichotomies *a priori*, rather it offers a way of mapping their construction. The entities involved with the construction of artefacts or programmes are viewed as 'heterogeneous' and the construction of a network involves the intermingling of concepts from a variety of repertoires including the social, economic, technological, scientific and political (Callon, 1986b). Indeed ANT rests on three tenets: generalized agnosticism – analytic impartiality as to whatever actors are involved in controversy; generalized symmetry – the use of an abstract and neutral vocabulary to understand the conflicting viewpoints of actors; and free association – the repudiation of *a priori* distinctions between the social and the natural or the technological.

Despite the very snug fit of ANT to the CSP, I have certain reservations. The original case studies of actor-networkers seem to represent *either* triumphant constructions *or* disastrous defeats. Either the entities are successfully enrolled into a particular network and the constructed artefact becomes indispensable, or the entities challenge, problematize and betray their defined identity and the construction fails. However, the CSP can be seen as both a successful construction and a failure. It has been in existence for almost thirty years and is referred to by some commentators as a triumph.

> The word cancer is an emotive one. For many years cancer was synonymous with death; the detection of the disease was usually at a late stage and the treatments were few and, for the most part, able only to relieve the suffering a little.
>
> During the last two decades, however, there have been enormous advances in the detection as well as the treatment of cancer. With the most modern screening techniques it is now possible to detect and to treat potential cancer of the cervix in its pre-cancerous state. Cervical cancer is therefore perfectly curable in its early stages. . . . (Chomet and Chomet, 1989, Introduction)

However, the CSP is also referred to as a failure, mainly because an average of 2,000 women per year continue to die from cervical cancer (Roberts, 1982; Johnston, 1989). Furthermore, although the programme is publicly represented as straightforward, controversy has hit the programme in many areas, including disputes over the presumed natural progression of cervical cell abnormalities to cervical cancer, false CST results, disagreements over the causes of cervical cancer, and suggestions that the CST is not an accurate indicator of the degree of cervical abnormality (see Singer and Szarewski, 1988, for an overview). The CSP seems to be an example *par excellence* of a black box as defined by Callon *et al.* (1986), that is, an entity that is both simplified and complex, stable and unstable. But can ANT allow me to capture how the CSP has become indispensable despite its predicaments?

Actors' Ambivalence

Elsewhere I have suggested that an initial response to the above question can be found through exposing the ambivalent discourse of the various actors involved in the CSP (Singleton, 1992; Singleton and Michael, 1993; Singleton, in press). All the actors demonstrate a commitment to their role within the CSP and stress its value, while also highlighting various problems with the programme generally, and specifically with their own simplified identity within it as defined by the government. I have argued that each actor in the CSP is engaged in complex, on-going processes of problematizing, negotiating and redefining their own and other actors' identities. Indeed, we can conceptualize each actor in the CSP not only as a network in its own right, but also as an internal network-builder. Actors demonstrate their membership in many worlds at once as they draw upon a multiplicity of resources to negotiate their identity within the CSP (Star, 1992). To offer an example, a laboratory pathologist can also be a General Practitioner, a lay participant and a feminist activist; and the movement of entities between the different worlds that they are a part of seems to allow the CSP flexibility, which in turn contributes to the maintenance of the programme. Consequently, I have suggested that the ability of actors to hold contradictory perspectives can be seen as necessary to the durability of the CSP.

Entering the CSP from a variety of actorial perspectives at once exposes the ambivalence and multiplicitous identity of actors. Along with Fujimura (see Star, 1992) I suggest that these multiple perspectives are missing from ANT in its traditional form. In sum, ANT did not adequately incorporate the multiformity and negotiation of identity into its narratives and analyses. Rather, the narratives of actor-networkers, which in the main followed only the scientists and the network-builders, and constructed coherent, very persuasive, accounts, seemed to occlude ambivalence, multiplicity and instability. However, more recently the issue of how networks within an actor network overlap and interact has begun to occupy many writers commenting upon ANT. Such writers are becoming more concerned with the complex 'network-ness' of actors' identities, and with how networks become stabilized over time, than with the simplified 'black-boxed-ness' of identities and the contingent stabilization of networks.[6] For example, Star (1992) asks questions about how standards and multiple selves can be incorporated into networks along with the processes by which identity is negotiated. In part this question is about how actors as simultaneously black-boxed, unified identities and complex, decentred networks can be incorporated, and how network stability and transformation can co-exist. One response to this, as outlined above, is to emphasize the importance of adopting a multi-perspectival approach that goes inside constructed actor networks and looks at the responses and interaction of the entities therein (Singleton, 1992). Similarly, Schwartz Cowan (1987) and Akrich (in press) have focused upon the consumer/user as opposed to the network-builder.

Incorporating Difference: The Basis for a Dialogue between Feminism and ANT

It seems that the question of how to incorporate 'difference' into narratives may now be central to many analysts working with ANT (for example, Callon, 1991; Latour, 1991; Law, 1991). ANT began by levelling differences through highlighting the heterogeneity of entities – by transgressing many of the disciplinary dichotomies cherished in sociology, such as nature/culture, subject/object, non-human/human, science/society. However, ANT is now concerned to try and incorporate differences, for example in the forms of the multiple perspectives on a network, the multiformity of actors and on-going negotiation processes. For me, this theoretical developmental trajectory relates closely to that of some forms of feminism. Feminism championed sexual difference as its starting point to emphasize women's oppression and pursued a levelling of differences between women in order to find a collective voice (e.g. Firestone, 1970). That is, feminism constructed woman as a black-boxed, unified actor in its fight against women's oppression. However, in its many forms, feminism has developed to challenge the inevitability of sexual differences and also to expose and celebrate differences between women and within woman (e.g. Di Stefano, 1990; Eisenstein and Jardine, 1980). Questions of how to conceptualize difference have occupied feminist thinkers for some time and a closer look at how feminists have dealt with the 'theme of difference', particularly when approaching science, may prove helpful to actor-networkers.

Moreover, within my actor-network approach to the CSP it seems essential to consider the significance of the factor that the CSP is for women, especially when women in the CSP are the recipients of comments from male practitioners such as the following, which was an attempt to encourage this woman to have a CST: 'It's not a rape, it's a seduction. You can always say no.' (KS, 4.93)[7]. Feminist analyses of science are unanimous in their assertion that science is not only 'social', more specifically it is gendered and sexist (Fee, 1983; Harding, 1986; Merchant, 1980). Directly relevant to the CSP is the wealth of feminist empirical and theoretical literature looking at medical technology and the female body. The editors of a recent collection *Body/Politics*, state:

the essays in this collection attest to the persistence and power of the discourses of science to define the feminine body as the object of knowledge par excellence – as subjected rather than subject, and hence as the site of crucial feminist struggle in the realms of both politics and theory. (Jacobus *et al.*, 1990, p. 6)

However, the decision to consider, specifically, the role of woman in the CSP conjures up many dilemmas within me. As previously stated, ANT denies the analyst the comfort of drawing upon the existence of dualisms, such as male versus female, and oppressor versus oppressed, prior to analyses of specific constructions of the science/society relationship. For ANT, power is a consequence rather than a cause of action. Power relations are the consequence of defining and associating entities (Latour, 1986). I could be in danger of directly contradicting the principles of ANT by bringing a male/ female dichotomy and assumptions about a pre-existing power relationship into a non-dichotomous approach. It may be useful to look more closely at the relationship between ANT and feminist approaches and to consider how they might inform one another.

Ambivalent Interactions between ANT and Feminism

In some respects ANT provides a way forward for feminists approaching science yet simultaneously it epitomizes the paradoxes they are dealing with at this moment in time. One starting point for looking at this ambivalent interaction is the subject/object dichotomy. The question of how to conceptualize 'difference', both in sociological and feminist studies of science, has been answered by some analysts by incorporating 'the other', 'the object', of science into their narratives. For ANT it is the non-human that has been reconceptualized and reincorporated. For feminists, the object of science has been consistently coded as 'woman', hence woman has received the same treatment. Jacobus *et al.* (1990), in their text subtitled *Women and the Discourses of Science*, refer to the oppressive and exclusionary effects of the subject/object split and to the consequent 'compensatory emphasis in feminist theory on the desiring and speaking feminine subject' (p. 7).

This 'giving voice to the object' (or subjectifying the object) may provide a starting point for collaborations between feminist studies of science and ANT. However, perhaps ANT highlights a dilemma for feminists that a 'compensatory emphasis on the feminine subject' may be incompatible with the eradication of dualisms and the deconstruction of sexual differences. As Callon and Latour note, 'The recognition of the historicity of differences, their irreversibility, their disintegration, and their proliferation passes by way of a bitter struggle against the assertion of one great ahistorical difference (1992, p. 356).

Considering the work of Jardine (1985), ANT might even be conceptualized as a feminist approach to science. Jardine explores the commonalties and tensions between 'feminism' and 'modernity'.[8] She suggests that modernity and feminism, in their many and diverse forms, are both instances of the process of 'gynesis', that is, a process of rethinking involving reincorporation and reconceptualization of the master narratives' own 'nonknowledge' or 'space'. For Jardine, this space has consistently been coded as woman. Thus gynesis is defined as 'the putting into discourse of "woman"' (Jardine, 1985, p. 25). Gynesis is not necessarily about woman, it is about giving voice to the spaces, the other, the feminine. With its concern to give voice to the spaces of empiricism – the object of science, the non-human – ANT could be seen as an example of gynesis, as giving voice to the symbolic woman, and hence as compatible with feminist concerns. On the other hand, ANT could be seen as non-feminist, if not sexist, because it refuses to acknowledge a symbolic link between 'the object' and 'woman'. In its very reconceptualization and reincorporation of the other, ANT levels differences and eradicates the presence of woman. Jardine (1985) highlights this paradox as one with which feminism is faced when it meets the discourses of modernity: texts that attempt to overcome dualisms and to 'give voice to the object'.

Back in 1980 Jardine defined *the* theoretical question entwined with feminist responses to difference: 'Is there a way to think outside the patriarchally determined Same/Other, Subject/Object dichotomies diagnosed as the fact of culture by Simone de Beauvoir thirty years ago, and, in the process, still include woman as a presence?' (Eisenstein and Jardine, 1980, p. xxvi). It seems that this 'theoretical' question is as pertinent to present-day feminism as it was when Jardine posed it: at least it seems directly relevant to feminists approaching science at this historical moment, and to the relationship between feminism and postmodernism. The same question posed slightly differently has been the focus of ANT. ANT is a way of thinking outside the scientifically determined science/society, same/other, subject/object dichotomies that have been diagnosed as the 'fact' of culture by sociologists of scientific knowledge. However, in the development of this new way of thinking the 'social' has no presence – or rather no particularized, special presence. This issue has been the focus of some critiques of ANT from within sociology of scientific knowledge (SSK). For example, Shapin (1988), in a review of Latour's (1987) text on ANT, writes:

The constraints which Latour places on himself and his programme arise from the same source as his valuable contributions to the discipline. Both stem from his opposition to conventionally given *dualisms* that have bedevilled the social studies of science and allied enterprises. (Shapin, 1988, pp. 546–7, emphasis in original)

For ANT, by necessity, the social can no longer have a presence because it is constructed through the very scientific hegemony one is trying to explore. The social, the scientific, truth, etc. are the consequence of scientists' actions rather than the cause. With the loss of dualisms comes the loss of social explanations of scientists' actions and the challenge to scientific hegemony associated with such explanations. I suggest that this echoes the dilemma faced by some feminist theorists, both in 1980 and now. Furthermore, the above reflects my own ambivalence towards ANT. ANT could be seen as compatible with feminist concerns – as an example of the process of gynesis. However, Jardine (1985) states that the object produced by this process is a gynema – a horizon rather than a person or thing – and that

[The] *gynema* is a reading effect, a woman-in-effect that is never stable and has no identity. Its appearance in a written text is perhaps noticed only by the feminist reader – either when it becomes insistently 'feminine' or when women (as defined metaphysically, historically) seem magically to reappear within the discourse. This tear in the fabric produces in the (feminist) reader a state of uncertainty and sometimes of distrust – especially when the faltering narrative in which it is embedded has been articulated by a man from within a nonetheless still-existent discipline. (p. 25)

Perhaps I notice in the texts of ANT a woman-in-effect. Certainly it seems that woman magically appears in the discourses of ANT as 'the object' given a voice. Moreover, as Jardine suggests, this 'discovery' produces a state of uncertainty and distrust in myself, especially as the main texts of ANT are those of men who are embedded within, and engaged in a discourse with, SSK – a discipline which some have claimed has neglected consideration of gender, race and class (Harding, 1986; Law, 1991). Like Fujimura (see Star, 1992) I am enamoured of the philosophically radical nature of ANT but I am also interested in taking a stand. So too, some feminist writing about postmodernism is concerned that just at the historical moment when women are finding a powerful voice, the concepts of 'a' truth and taking a justifiable stance have become suspect (Flax, 1990; Di Stefano, 1990). ANT may offer a way for feminists to think about the woman/science relationship outside patriarchally determined dichotomies but this way of thinking may be, at best, degendered and politically impotent and, at worst, politically potent through (its claim to) being degendered.

To summarize, ANT may allow us to go beyond a search for *a* cause of women's oppression, that can lead to the oppression of voices different from our own. ANT allows us to see woman as an 'effect' and to map how biological and social woman co-evolve from the construction of technologies.[9] In this way ANT provides one possible response to Lowe and Hubbard's call for feminists to provide ways of demonstrating that 'people's biological and social experiences are intimately interwoven' (1983, p. xii). We can look at 'woman as an actor' in programmes such as the CSP. Furthermore, through developing the approach to incorporate multiplicity and ambivalence, ANT may be able to address some of the issues raised by some feminists discussing postmodernism. Indeed, I suggest that the next section of this chapter, in which I focus on feminists', women's health activists' and lay women's definitions of woman in the CSP, may fit well with the proposals of Flax:

> Feminist theories, like other forms of postmodernism, should encourage us to tolerate and interpret ambivalence, ambiguity, and multiplicity as well as to expose the roots of our needs for imposing order and structure no matter how arbitrary and oppressive these needs may be. (Flax, 1990, p. 56)

Making Gender Visible within the CSP Actor Network: Feminists' and Women's Health Writers' Definitions

The aim of much feminist and women's health writing about the CSP is to increase women's knowledge, to encourage women to share experiences and to enable women to take control of their own health and treatment (e.g. Barnett and Fox, 1986). The majority of this writing does not engage in analyses of the efficacy of the CSP, rather it focuses on redefining woman and cervical cancer *within* the CSP. Various aspects of the programme, such as medical definitions of the cause of cervical cancer, are problematized in order to promote women's participation. That is, feminists and women's health writers are committed to problematizing the CSP in order to redefine the identity of woman, but they are also committed to maintaining the programme. The resultant ambivalence is described by one feminist commentator as follows:

> Women with pre-cancerous or cancerous changes of the cervix have now become victims par excellence. The screening women campaigned for offers them early detection at the price of being labelled.... (Robinson, 1981)

> Neither the ethics, the efficacy, nor the adverse effects of screening have been adequately discussed by women's organisations. Of course, we need better organised screening and more money for health care. But isn't it time for women to ask why the medical profession advocated a policy of screening but denied women information ...? Why did the information that women's promiscuity 'caused' cervical cancer get through to the public whereas the risks of male promiscuity, the textile industry for women workers, men's dusty jobs or the pill did not? (Robinson, 1987, p. 51)

Feminists and women's health activists stand, albeit uncomfortably, both committed to and betraying the CSP. As a consequence of their commitment to the health needs of women they find themselves failing to problematize aspects of the programme for fear of threatening its existence. However, as the above quotation demonstrates, by problematizing the identity of medical professionals – as sexist and biased – feminists can overcome this dilemma. The CSP can be maintained as valuable and effective, we just need to rid medical science of its bias.

Coping with Non-Participation

A further example of the ambivalence of feminists and women's health writers is how they define women who do not participate in the CSP. Their definitions emerge as the same as those of medical professionals: non-participants are defined as ignorant in some way.

Much research on the CSP has focused on why 2,000 women each year continue to die from cervical cancer. Due to the CSP, cervical cancer is described as 'totally preventable' and deaths from this disease as avoidable and unnecessary (Singer and Szarewski, 1988). This usual explanation of the continued mortality is that women fail to attend for a CST. This has led to an abundance of work investigating why women do not attend. Many researchers have reached conclusions similar to this feminist writer: 'These problems stem in part from women's own fear and lack of knowledge' (Doyal, no date, p. 3). Consider another example from a women's health text:

22,000 women every year die from cancer of the cervix, ovary and breast. Yet in many cases these conditions could be easily detected, treated and often cured – if only women had the knowledge to know that something was wrong, that something could be done, and the confidence to demand that action be taken. It could be argued that for many of these women, fear and lack of information disable and kill, more than the diseases themselves. (Hayman, 1989, p. 2)

This quote appears to blame the woman's own knowledge and fear for her own disability and even death.

In much of this literature non-participation in the CSP is presented as a consequence of lack of information and recommendations are made for increased education (for example Savage *et al.*, 1989). As I stated earlier, the aim of many feminist and women's health texts is to increase women's knowledge. But there seems to be a very fine line between, on the one hand, informing and empowering women, and, on the other, imputing ignorance and undermining women's decisions not to participate, especially when the underlying assumption is that the CSP is valuable and a good thing for women.

Within medical professionals' definitions of women who do not attend there are numerous references to lack of knowledge. A variety of medical professionals refer to women who do not attend as 'recidivists'. The dictionary definition of a recidivist is 'one who lapses into crime'. Non-attendance is, for the most part, seen as an inappropriate, even immoral response. It emerges as synonymous with ignorance and fear, and attendance as synonymous with intelligence. Some medical professionals also spoke of 'the worried well', defined by one GP as 'middle-class ladies who swamp the system often by having unnecessary, very frequent smears' (Dr F, 479).

Women appear to be treading a fine line between attending, not attending and attending too frequently. However, the overriding definition of women is that they are ignorant in some way, be it of needing a smear at all or of how often they need to have a CST. Another medical practitioner is worth quoting here: 'Women's understanding is frequently very limited. Women's knowledge and understanding of their physical body is very limited. Most would not know what a cervix is ... To most women it [the vagina] is just a hole' (Dr DL, 259). Considering such remarks it is possible to understand why women's health writers and feminists are at pains to stress the need to increase women's knowledge. They are engaged in a discourse with medical professionals as much as with women. As one writer states,

Knowledge is power. Knowing what is happening to you makes you far less vulnerable, and means that you can cope with what is going on. Understanding the facts and knowing what you are talking about when speaking to a doctor means that you can address her/him with authority. (Quilliam, 1989, p. 79)

Nevertheless, the effect of such emphases can be that feminists and women's health writers find themselves, at one level, validating the very definition of woman – as ignorant – that they are, at another level, problematizing. It is interesting that it seems to be, on the whole, only a few male medical professionals who consider women's non-attendance as a valid response and the dissolution of the CSP as a reasonable option (e.g. McCormick, 1989).

Tolerating Multiplicity and *Imposing Order*

Feminists, women's health writers and researchers are committed to the continuation of the CSP. However, they are also committed to problematizing aspects of it. The struggle for the recognition of women's health needs has been, and continues to be, a bitter one with little time for reflecting on the implications of the provisions that have been fought for with such strength and perseverance. Further, as more technologies emerge, the CSP seems to have become increasingly stable and to be assured an almost triumphant identity. In a feminist critique of reproductive technologies, Spallone (1989) states that 'infertility could be managed *now* by better primary health care for women, screening for pelvic inflammatory disease and cervical cancer' (p. 27, emphasis in original). It is both interesting, and perhaps disconcerting, that in a consideration of the issues raised for women by the new reproductive technologies we may neglect, or even invalidate, previous medical technologies and the relationship between women and medical science that is evolving through their use. Whatever the implications of the new reproductive technologies for women, it is possible to suggest that they may have served to increase the stability and durability of the CSP. One might suggest, drawing on ANT, that the CSP is enrolled into these new actor networks as a black-boxed actor.

To offer a final example of the dilemmas faced by women's health writers and feminist researchers, some texts problematize woman's identity in the CSP through highlighting the invasive nature of the test. However, this aspect of the CSP and woman's identity is usually problematized only in relation to it being a deterrent to women's attendance (Saffron, 1987; Doyal, no date). Further, many of these writers highlight women's priorities as a factor influencing their participation in the CSP.

> Many middle-aged women think of themselves as less important than their husbands or children and do not go for a cervical smear to protect themselves in their own right. This attitude will only be changed as the general struggle against women's oppression grows stronger. (Saffron, 1987, p. 46)

Many of the lay participants and non-participants that I have spoken to have demonstrated how the complexity of their lives affects their participation in the CSP. However, Saffron clearly implies that women's non-attendance reflects a failure to prioritize their own health. This in turn is defined as an inappropriate attitude in need of change. A women's health text presents an almost opposite perspective on this issue, but demonstrates the same underlying commitment to the CSP. From this perspective, woman is defined as having a 'duty' to participate in the CSP.

> Well women care recognises that women need to look after themselves, if for no other reason than to allow themselves to be better carers of their families. A worried, ailing mother is hardly likely to be able to give better attention to her partner and children than a confident and fit one. More important to many people is the fact that women have as much responsibility to themselves as to others, and have the right to put their own well-being on an equal or more prominent footing. . . . Well women care is 'empowering': not only does it give us responsibility for our lives, it gives us far more control. (Hayman, 1989, pp. 4–5)

It seems that in much of the feminist and women's health literature on the CSP empowering woman means engaging them in the CSP and its dominant discourse, medical science. There is a circularity to this approach which can lead to silencing the voices of some women and valorizing the voice of medical professionals. The experiences and views of women who choose not to participate nor to prioritize the CSP seem to be undermined by feminists and women's health activists. More importantly, the commitment of these actors to the CSP can lead to occlusion of the multiformity of 'woman' and the diversity of 'women'. Feminists and women's health writers can be seen as constructing their own CSP actor networks from within the CSP. Woman is redefined – as active and empowered – but she is also re-black-boxed – simplified and unified.

Lay Participants' and Non-Participants' Definitions

'It's just not high on my list of priorities'

Many lay women spoke about two worlds, that of the medical profession and their own, and they frequently defined the former as male. These women implied that this world made inappropriate judgments about them, specifically related to their being women. For example, many women spoke about medical practitioners' unrealistic expectation of the availability of their time and the consequent inadequacy of the provision made for them within the CSP, such as inappropriate appointment times. One participant perceived inferences about having 'wrong priorities' when she had difficulty attending. She concluded that 'ultimately they do not acknowledge what a woman's life is like' (VS, 3.90)[10].

Many women spoke of the difficulty of getting to appointments that fitted in with their own world and that of the medical practitioners as well as with their menstrual cycle. Women are requested not to attend during a menstrual period. Further, they introduce menstrual variability as a complicating factor affecting attendance. Moreover, the interests of 'woman' are often different to those attributed to her within the CSP. Many women made comments such as the following about the CSP: 'it's just not high on my list of priorities' (AJ, 11.90)

'You must be stupid not to go'

Women demonstrated the difficulty of attending due to other commitments whilst defining women non-participants as ignorant or inappropriately indifferent: 'Well you must be stupid not to go. Mind you it is mainly those women with less education isn't it?' (ID, 10.90). The discourse of lay participants and non-participants in the CSP suggests that they often internalize certain definitions of non-participants – that they 'cannot be bothered', or are ignorant in some way. A woman who had decided not to participate in the CSP, despite defining the CSP as not a priority to her, also stated, 'I suppose I'm stupid not to go really' (AJ, 11.90).

'It's like being in a jam factory, you are processed'

Women expressed their discomfort over the loss of control that they felt when participating in the CSP. They often referred to 'being processed', or being patronized and excluded from decision-making. Women could readily infer the CSP's 'routinization' of women through which they would be treated like a helpless object on a factory conveyor belt. This was linked to feelings that 'woman in the CSP' is divorced from her body. The CSP simultaneously defines the *inability of woman*, and the *ability of medical science*, to understand her own body. 'They say you don't know if anything is wrong with you but I am sure that I would know' (MS, 2.90).

'She thought I was going to go hysterical or something'

Women frequently stated that medical professionals 'hid things from them', on the assumption that they would panic, get upset or not understand. During my fieldwork a variety of medical professionals expressed concerns about women being prone to 'panic', becoming neurotic, and being unable to cope with information. A public health physician described women as unable to cope with uncertainty:

> At an individual level people can rationalize. But they will only cope with knowledge of uncertainties until they get an abnormal result, then it becomes totally irrational. I mean I have seen intelligent, well-motivated women almost psychotic when they have an abnormal test. (Dr BU, 122)

One medical consultant at a medical conference stated with regard to the CSP that 'we have created a nation of neurotic women' (Dr J., NAC, 1990). It is interesting to note here the words of a woman non-participant: 'I do feel quite strongly that people in this day and age get themselves paranoid and all screwed up about things because there are so many tests' (MS, 2.90). As a non-participant this woman would probably be defined as irrational, fearful or lacking knowledge.

Medical practitioners frequently described women in the CSP as wanting certainty and reassurance. However, they also defined woman as having unrealistic expectations of the CSP and medical science. For example, while stating that 'the public perception of what screening is all about is over-ambitious', a public health physician also stated: 'What women want is somebody to take away the uncertainty that she has. The patient wants reassurance' (Dr DU, 20). Similarly, a consultant cytopathologist, rather ambivalently, stated:

> Expectations of medicine are too high, well they should be shouldn't

they, well they shouldn't expect perfection but they do. People believe that nothing should ever go wrong ... they have totally unrealistic expectations of what doctors do ... there is this curious thing about medicine that uncertainties, mistakes don't exist. It's very difficult to deal with. People feel that it just shouldn't be – that science, including medicine, is perfect. (Dr Y, 5)

However, within the CSP, information is simplified and hidden from women: 'In attempts to reassure someone we tend to oversimplify things' (Dr EU, 600). Perhaps more importantly, such definitions of woman are ultimately bound to maintaining the credibility of the CSP: 'If women get a detailed letter explaining about the uncertainties in the test they will all be coming saying, "Doctor, do I really need this?"' (Dr CU, 101).

'I thought it was supposed to be all straightforward!'

It is not surprising that some women feel that they receive contradictory messages. These messages were related to, for example, uncertainties in diagnosis and treatment. But women's inferences about contradictory messages were also a consequence of their experiences of inconsistencies between women's expectations, the 'public' portrayal of the test as straightforward and painless, and women's experiences of indeterminacy, ambiguity and pain. Often these 'mixed messages' resulted in women feeling confused or betrayed, and in some cases they resulted in a decision not to participate in the CSP. Other women emerged from the confusion with a re-evaluation of their own knowledge. For example, following numerous repeat CSTs and various interpretations of their results one woman stated: 'I was beginning to think I knew more than the doctor ... I thought it was supposed to be all straightforward!' (EL, 7.90)

'It's for our own good'

Having stated all of the above women appeared to feel guilty when not participating or failing to attend for an appointment. Many women spoke of widespread commitment as they were encouraged to go by friends and relatives. One participant stated: 'I can understand with something like the smear test. I mean they should make women have it. I mean it's for our own good and it's certain isn't it?' (AM, 11.90).

Some women move from within the CSP to outside the CSP and back again as they uncomfortably assume an identity of neither participant nor non-participant. For example:

> So I opened the letter and read it and thought, no I'm not going to do that, I just couldn't face it again and I mentioned it in work. I work mostly with women, and they all said, 'Oh, you've got to go, you'll have to go, and you can't not go'. Anyway I so much didn't want to go but I thought that perhaps I should go that I actually, instead of tearing the letter up, which is what I would normally do, I stuck it in the pending try and it's still pending. It's been there about a month now. But in fact I'm not going to go back. (MS, 2.90)

Lay Woman's Ambivalence and Multiformity

Woman assumes an ambivalent identity within the CSP actor network. Many lay participants and non-participants feel that the CSP is a good thing and that they ought to participate. Simultaneously, the identity of 'woman as an actor' in the black-boxed straightforward government CSP is betrayed as a simplification. They demonstrate the multiformity of woman, both in terms of the intrinsic multiplicity of women and in terms of differences between women. Participants and non-participants stressed the complexity of their lives and the diversity of roles that they adopt. Furthermore, they problematized the CSP through introducing the variability of menstrual cycles, within the individual woman as well as between women, as affecting participation in the CSP. 'Woman' is exposed as sociologically and biologically black-boxed within the government CSP and 'women' as inappropriately homogenized.

> With things like smear tests they must aim it at some sort of middle-class woman who doesn't work, who's got her kids doing something else all day so that she hasn't got them under her feet, and she's got nothing better to do than go along and have a smear test. (MS, 2.90)

Considering the above it is possible to see some women's non-participation in, and/or problematization of, the CSP, not only as a reasonable response, but further as a part of negotiating their identity and asserting their individuality.

The Price of Order: Constructing Woman's Ignorance

Within the CSP actor network woman is defined as unable to cope with indeterminacy, as disliking uncertainty and as needing reassurance from 'expert' professionals (see also Posner and Vessey, 1988). Such definitions evolve and become increasingly stable through the functioning of the CSP actor network. Woman is shielded from uncertainty and information is hidden from her, and the CSP is 'publicly' portrayed as straightforward. However, woman is then defined as ignorant and naive, as having unrealistic expectations of medical science and the CSP. Further, woman is defined as prone to hysteria and panic if she 'reacts' to uncertainty or information when she meets it. Moreover, we can see here how social and biological definitions of woman co-evolve through, and are negotiated within, the CSP actor network.

As I demonstrated earlier, such definitions of woman can be found, not only in the discourse of medical actors, but also in that of feminists and women's health activists. The latter's emphasis on empowering women within the CSP can be seen to culminate in a paradox. Woman is defined as needing to engage in the dominant discourse of the CSP in order to valorize her own knowledge and discourse. Their view of the empowerment of woman involves woman changing her priorities and adopting those of the CSP. It is worth noting the remarks of one 'non-participant' here: 'I am quite happy to make my own decisions' (MS, 2.90). Empowerment can mean deciding not to participate and refusing to engage in the discourse of the CSP. Through the processes of empowering women, feminists and women's health activists may be validating the very identities and associations that they are, elsewhere, problematizing. Further, they may find themselves undermining and occluding the voices and experiences of some women, and excluding others, as they construct their own CSP actor network with its simplified black-boxed definition of woman.

Star (1992), in her critical application of ANT, makes the point that any actor network excludes some entities and annihilates some forms of knowledge. Moreover, she stresses that the important point is to consider *what* is excluded and annihilated. While, from the above analysis, the feminists' and women's health activists' CSP actor network emerges as inevitably inimical to women, woman does emerge as active instead of passive and empowered instead of oppressed. In many respects feminists and women's health activists offer a voice to that which has been excluded from, and annihilated by, the government CSP actor network: for example, women's experiences of the programme and women's multiple priorities. However, they do so as a part of constructing their own CSP actor network in which woman is re-black-boxed and unified. Consequently, the feminists' and women's health activists' CSP actor network, like the government CSP actor network that it is critical of, excludes some voices, occludes diversity and annihilates some forms of knowledge. Considering lay women's discourse about the CSP has highlighted some of the things that are excluded by the feminists' and women's health activists' network. For example, some women have demonstrated that they are neither participants nor non-participants in the CSP actor network (or they are at once participants and non-participants). These women refuse to assume a unified black-boxed identity. In the words of Star (1992), they occupy a 'high-tension zone', being neither excluded from, nor enrolled within, the CSP.

The above reflects a much wider problem in feminist theory and feminist analyses of science. I refer to the problem of conceptualizing and incorporating difference. Within feminist studies of science, there are those suggesting a new feminist 'standpoint' based upon the 'special characteristics of woman and distinct from traditional male scientific empiricism. Others are talking and writing of ridding science of its male bias through increased female participation (Harding, 1986, reviews this literature). Both approaches have their critiques. In the case of the latter, which Harding refers to as feminist empiricism, Longino's (1989) remarks are appropriate: 'Feminists – in and out of science – often condemn masculine bias from the vantage point of commitment to a value-free science' (p. 212). Some of the feminists writing on the CSP whom I quoted earlier can be seen to be in the same paradoxical position. They problematize the CSP with reference to the sexist nature of medical science. However, they also propose the possibility of a value-free non-sexist medical science/CSP.

Considering proposals for a feminist standpoint, this concept has also received critical comment as being 'falsely universalising' (Harding, 1986, p. 26). Harding questions: 'Can there be a feminist standpoint if women's (or feminists') social experience is divided by class, race, and culture?' (1986, p. 26). As I suggested above, feminists in the CSP may be engaged in constructing a feminist standpoint, as they simplify and unify woman into their own CSP actor network.

Feminist postmodernism challenges the assumptions on which feminist empiricism and the feminist standpoint are based. This fragmented approach begins with fractured, decentred identities and is profoundly sceptical 'regarding universal (or universalising) claims about the existence, nature and powers of reason, progress, science, language and the "subject/self"' (Harding, 1986, p. 28). However, this 'approach' implies that we cannot profess one true feminist viewpoint. In relation to the CSP, it demonstrates the dilemma of feminists and women's health writers: attempting to give voice to the 'decentred-ness' of woman may threaten the CSP.

In essence, feminists and women's health activists commenting on and enrolled in the CSP are committed both to questioning and validating the CSP. They are committed to redefining the identity of woman in the CSP. They present the CSP as a good thing for women, as indispensable to women's health, and as a rare concession to the particular health needs of women. However, the CSP is also constructed as a demonstration of the domination and subjugation of woman by medical science. The multiformity and complexity of woman's identity is exposed by feminists and women's health activists, and governmental and medical definitions of woman are betrayed as inadequate simplifications. However, woman is also simplified by feminists and women's health activists in order to maintain the CSP – paradoxically in order to prioritize the needs of woman and to empower her. The CSP emerges as a forum for two apparently contradictory discourses. On the one hand, it affords a demonstration of the ways in which women are dominated and oppressed by medical science (and society). On the other hand, it allows for, and demonstrates, the reconceptualization of woman, the incorporation of her own voice into medical science, and the re-valorization of her knowledge and experiences. This could be conceptualized as the co-existence in the CSP of 'woman-the-object' and 'woman-the-subject'.

Network-Building and the Fate of Difference

In applying ANT as a woman-centred approach to the CSP I have been able to capture some of the ambivalence, ambiguity and multiplicity of lay woman and of feminists and women's health activists. Furthermore, I have been able to explore how and why these actors, while demonstrating their own and others' multiplicity and 'network-ness', and despite a concern to 'give voice to woman', also have a need to impose order and to simplify woman which results in the occlusion of difference and diversity. In essence, the 'problem' that ANT has allowed me to elucidate in relation to representing woman in the CSP is one of incorporating difference, both within woman and between women. As I have suggested, this problem is also reflected in feminist approaches to science more generally. Furthermore, considering the present concerns of analysts working with ANT that I mentioned earlier, this problem is also one that ANT is itself prey to. Feminists and women's health activists in the CSP, along with feminist theorists commenting upon the woman and science relationship, and sociologists commenting upon the science/society relationship, can all be seen to be engaged in network-building. Moreover, it seems that the 'fate of difference' when building networks is not a happy one: network-building involves simplifying diversity and levelling differences.

The above 'problematic' is one that plagues other areas of sociology and feminism – the problem of 'speaking for and representing others'. Law conceptualizes these issues in mainstream sociology as ones of distribution and suggests that sociology historically has been 'driven by an ambivalent wish to learn of and intervene about injustice (1992, p. 1). Putting ANT and feminism into dialogue with one another has, for me, exposed the importance of, and ambivalence produced by, the issue of where to put our own political commitments into the analytic frame. It seems that political concerns to intervene about inequitable distributions of power do not always sit comfortably alongside concerns to learn of those same distributions.

With non-dualistic approaches such as ANT we are left with certain forms of narrative: with stories which describe rather than explain, which emphasize their own historical contingency, which attempt to say something about what things may be like now and that they could have been otherwise. But these narratives say nothing about what things should be like or have been like. It often seems that, consequently, we are left with no political voice, no place from which to stand and claim that our own knowledge-claims are more valuable than any others. In sum, by applying ANT to the CSP and through associating it with feminism I have become aware of the analytical tension inherent in using such an approach – the tension between political and intellectual commitments (or rather, the tension between the dual political concerns of the politics of gender and the politics of the academe). In creating the conversations that I have the multiplicity of my own identity and the incompatibility of my own commitments have become increasingly salient to me.

Accepting Ambivalence and Exposing the Roots of A Need for Order

My concluding suggestion is rather like that of Harding (1986) when she calls for the acceptance of the validity of destablization, paradox and dissonance; although, contrary to Harding, I do not describe the value attached to coherent theorizing as a patriarchal construct, because feminists, sociologists and scientists alike seem to value coherent theorizing as a means of enrolling others and validating their own voices. However, as analysts we can choose to adopt a principle of analytical ambivalence. We can attempt to recognize our own 'multiple membership in many worlds at once' (Star, 1992), and to use approaches such as ANT to certain ends, but then go on to develop them through ourselves actively engaging in network-building (they may be 'academic networks', 'gender networks', or networks in which the two concerns co-exist).

As analysts we are constrained by particular analytical principles and motivated by particular political aims which both demand coherence and the narrative clarity that is associated with conventional academic inquiry and writing. Coherence is prioritized as desirable and valuable and ambivalence becomes something negative and politically impotent. Considering the discourse of actors in the CSP has suggested to me an opposite conceptualization of ambivalence – that it is inevitable, and can be a useful force. However, this begs the question of how to incorporate this into our narratives. Notions of celebrating multivocality and plurality of epistemologies bring with them non-universalization and non-totalizing theory. Needless to say, as various writers point out, these concepts themselves form an epistemology, a master narrative (Poster, 1984). Perhaps, as Latour (1988a) suggests, forms of master narrative cannot be avoided. Consequently, according to Latour (1988a), we should recognize writing as a powerful persuasive tool and draw up all the tactics available to us to convince our readers. This may be a more productive response to the dilemmas that we have created for ourselves than the circularity of reflexivity or deadening silence but, for me, it is not an adequate response. Recognizing the inevitability and usefulness of master narratives, and accepting our need to impose order, need to be coupled with exposure of the roots of these needs and acceptance of the potential usefulness of ambivalence and instability. Finding ways to achieve this in our research and narratives is a challenge which is yet to be met adequately and ANT may be a useful tool in this process.

Notes

An earlier version of this paper was presented at Brunel University, at the Conference on European Theoretical Perspectives on New Technology: Feminism, Constructivism and Utility in September 1993; and at University of Manchester Institute of Science and Technology in January 1994. I am grateful for the comments received from the participants of these workshops.

1 I am grateful to the Science and Engineering Research Council who provided funding (1988–91) for the research that this paper draws upon.
2 In many respects I conceptualize 'woman as an object' in the CSP actor network. It could be argued that there is no equivalence between artefacts/natural phenomena as objects and woman as object. For example, women do have a 'voice' – a recognizable subjective quality. Nevertheless, I attempt in this chapter to illustrate

how woman can be conceptualized as both subject and object in the CSP. That is, it is the contingency of definitions of 'an object' that is of interest. Various studies have suggested the historicity of the 'natural phenomenon as object'. For example, Merchant (1980) traces how Nature was seen 'as subject' to be entered into discourse with, then was subsequently conceptualized 'as object' to be manipulated and controlled. Michael and Grove White (1991) suggest that there has been a contemporary shift in conceptualizations of Nature to 'Nature as subject'.

3 McPherson (1985) and Savage and McPherson (1983) review the medical literature and demonstrate that while there is uncertainty over this issue there is medical consensus that cervical cancer is linked to sexual activity and multiple sexual partners. McPherson comments, 'Women who get cervical cancer (or their partners) should not *necessarily*, however, be labelled as promiscuous' (1985, p. 6, emphasis added). One wonders whether it is ever necessary to label women who develop cervical cancer as promiscuous.

4 Laboratory staff analysing cervical cell samples are instructed to report on finding any sign of the presence of Human Papilloma Virus or Herpes Virus and women are subsequently placed in a high risk category and requested to attend for CSTs more frequently (laboratory fieldwork, 1990–92). Both of these diseases are defined as sexually transmitted.

5 The CSP actor network is constructed from government documents (HM(66)76; HC(84)17; HC(88)1).

6 In April 1992 I attended a fascinating workshop at Keele University organized by John Law and Leigh Star, the focus of which was discussions about how networks within networks overlap and interact.

7 The initials and numbers attributed to this and subsequent quotes identify the interviewee and interview transcript. I interviewed a number of medical practitioners between 1989 and 1992.

8 Jardine, at some length and with considerable difficulty, attempts to clarify her use of the word 'modernity' (1985, pp. 22–4). She states that the word 'postmodern', as it is commonly used in the United States of America, most accurately applies to the specific set of writers, and the concepts, that she draws upon.

9 Further, the analysis of the CSP that I develop in this chapter demonstrates that ANT may be able to speak to another issue raised by Lowe and Hubbard (1983). They suggest that we need to consider, not only how woman is defined in certain ways by science, but also how woman then adopts the behaviour assigned to her and so, in some ways, sustains her own oppression. ANT allows me to illustrate this 'self-fulfilling oppression' by looking at how woman in the CSP adopts the role assigned to her and consequently validates that role, even though it may be one in which her own knowledge and experience is subjugated to that of medical professionals.

10 The initials and numbers attributed to this and subsequent quotes refer to the lay woman interviewed and the date of interview.

References

AKRICH, M. (in press) 'Semiotic Scenarios: Configuring the Cable TV Interface in France', to appear in FROST, R. and PFAFFERDEGAR, B. (Eds) *Material Discourse, the Meaning of Human Artefacts*.

BARNETT, R. and FOX, R. (1986) *A Feminist Approach to Pap Tests*, Vancouver, Vancouver Women's Health Collective.

CALLON, M. (1986a) 'Some Elements of a Sociology of Translation: Domestication of the Scallops and the Fishermen of St Brieuc Bay', in LAW, J. (Ed.) *Power, Action and Belief*, London, Routledge, pp. 196–233.

CALLON, M. (1986b) 'The Sociology of the Electric Vehicle', in CALLON, M., LAW, J. and RIP, A. (Eds) *Mapping the Dynamics of Science and Technology*, London, Macmillan, pp. 19–34.

CALLON, M. (1987) 'Society in the Making: The Study of Technology as a Tool for Sociological Analysis', in BIJKER, W.E., HUGHES, T.P. and PINCH, T.J. *The Social Construction of Technological Systems*, Cambridge, Mass., and London, MIT Press, pp. 83–103.

CALLON, M. (1991) 'Techno-Economic Networks and Irreversibility' in LAW, J. (Ed.) *A Sociology of Monsters*, London, Routledge, pp. 132–161.

CALLON, M. AND LATOUR, B. (1992) 'Don't Throw the Baby Out with the Bath School! A Reply to Collins and Yearley', in PICKERING, A. (Eds) *Science as Practice and Culture*, Chicago and London, University of Chicago Press, pp. 343–68.

CALLON, M., LAW, J. and RIP, A. (Eds) (1986) *Mapping the Dynamics of Science and Technology*, London, Macmillan.

CHOMET, J. and CHOMET, J. (1989) *Cervical Cancer. All You and Your Partner Need to Know about its Prevention, Detection and Treatment*, Wellingborough, Grapevine.

DI STEFANO, C. (1990) 'Dilemmas of Difference: Feminism, Modernity, and Postmodernism', in NICHOLSON, L.J. (Ed.) *Feminism/Postmodernism*, New York and London, Routledge, pp. 63–82.

DOYAL, L. (1985) *Women's Health and Cervical Cancer*, London, Women's Health Information Centre.

EHRENREICH, B. and ENGLISH, D. (1979) *For Her Own Good: 150 Years of the Experts' Advice to Women*, London, Pluto Press.

EISENSTEIN, H. and JARDINE, A. (Eds) (1980) *The Future of Difference*, Boston, G.K. Hall.

FEE, E. (1983) 'Women's Nature and Scientific Objectivity', in LOWE, M. and HUBBARD, K. (Eds) *Woman's Nature*, New York, Pergamon Press, pp. 9–28.

FIRESTONE, S. (1970) *The Dialectic of Sex*, New York, William Morrow.

FLAX, J. (1990) 'Postmodernism and Gender Relations in Feminist Theory', in NICHOLSON, L.J. (Ed.) *Feminism/Postmodernism*, New York and London, Routledge, pp. 39–62.

FUJIMURA, J. (in press) *Crafting Science, Transforming Biology: The Case of Oncogene Research*.

GARRY, A. and PEARSALL, M. (Eds) (1989) *Women, Knowledge, and Reality: Explorations in Feminist Philosophy*, Boston, Mass., and London, Unwin Hyman.

GREAT BRITAIN, MINISTRY OF HEALTH (1966) *Population Screening for Cancer of the Cervix*, Health Memorandum, HM(66)76, London, Ministry of Health.

GREAT BRITAIN, DEPARTMENT OF HEALTH AND SOCIAL SECURITY (1984) *Screening for Cervical Cancer*, Health Circular, HC(84)17, London, Department of Health and Social Security.

GREAT BRITAIN, DEPARTMENT OF HEALTH AND SOCIAL SECURITY (1988) *Cervical Cancer Screening*, Health Circular, HC(88)1, London, Department of Health and Social Security.

HARDING, S. (1986) *The Science Question in Feminism*, Milton Keynes, Open University Press.

HAYMAN, S. (1989) *The Well Woman Handbook: A Guide for Women Throughout their Lives*, London, Penguin.

JACOBUS, M., KELLER, E.F. and SHUTTLEWORTH, S. (Eds) (1990) *Body/Politics: Women and the Discourses of Science*, New York and London, Routledge.

JARDINE, A. (1985) *Gynesis: Configurations of Woman and Modernity*, Ithaca and London, Cornell University Press.

JOHNSTON, K. (1989) *Screening for Cervical Cancer: A Review of the Literature*, Health Economics Research Unit Discussion Paper 04/89, Aberdeen, University of Aberdeen.

LATOUR, B. (1986) 'The Powers of Association', in LAW, J. (Ed.) *Power, Action and Belief*, London, Routledge, pp. 264–80.

LATOUR, B. (1987) *Science in Action: How to Follow Scientists and Engineers through Society*, Milton Keynes, Open University Press.

LATOUR, B. (1988a) 'The Politics of Explanation – an Alternative', in WOOLGAR, S. (Ed.) *Knowledge and Reflexivity: New Frontiers in the Sociology of Knowledge*, London, Sage, pp. 155–76.

LATOUR, B. (1988b) 'Mixing Humans and Nonhumans Together: The Sociology of a Door-Closer', *Social Problems*, vol. 35, no. 3, pp. 298–310.

LATOUR, B. (1988c) *The Pasteurization of France*, Cambridge, Mass., Harvard University Press.

LATOUR, B. (1991) 'Technology is Society Made Durable', in LAW, J (Ed.) *A Sociology of Monsters*, London, Routledge, pp. 103–31.

LAW, J. (Ed.) (1986) *Power, Action and Belief: A New Sociology of Knowledge?*, Sociological Review Monograph no. 32, London, Routledge.

LAW, J. (1987) 'Technology and Heterogeneous Engineering: The Case of Portuguese Expansion', in BIJKER, W.E., HUGHES, T.P. and PINCH, T.J. (Eds) *The Social Construction of Technological Systems*, Cambridge, Mass., and London, MIT Press, pp. 111–34.

LAW, J. (Ed.) (1991) *A Sociology of Monsters: Essays on Power, Technology and Domination*, Sociological Review Monograph no. 38, London, Routledge.

LONGINO, H.E. (1989) 'Can There Be a Feminist Science?', in GARRY, A. and PEARSALL, M. (Eds) *Women, Knowledge, and Reality*, Boston, Mass., and London, Unwin Hyman, pp. 203–16.

LONGINO, H.E. and HAMMONDS, E. (1990) 'Conflicts and Tensions in the Feminist Study of Gender and Science', in HIRSCH, M. and KELLER, E.F. (Eds) *Conflicts in Feminism*, London, Routledge, pp. 164–83.

LOWE, M. and HUBBARD, R. (Eds) (1983) *Woman's Nature: Rationalisation of Inequality*, New York, Pergamon Press.

McCORMICK, J.S. (1989) 'Cervical Smears: A Questionable Practice?', *The Lancet*, July, pp. 207–9.

McPHERSON, A. (1985) *Cervical Screening: A Practical Guide*, Oxford, Oxford University Press.

McPHERSON, A. and ANDERSON, A. (Eds) (1983) *Women's Problems in General Practice*, Oxford, Oxford University Press.

MERCHANT, C. (1980) *The Death of Nature: Women, Ecology and the Scientific Revolution*, New York, Harper and Row.

MICHAEL, M. and GROVE WHITE, R. (1993) 'Talking about Talking with Nature: Nurturing "Ecological Consciousness"', *Environmental Ethics*, 15, pp. 33–47.

NICHOLSON, L.J. (Ed.) (1990) *Feminism/Postmodernism*, New York and London, Routledge.

O'SULLIVAN, S. (Ed.) (1987) *Women's Health: A Spare Rib Reader*, New York and London, Pandora.

PICKERING, A. (Ed.) (1992) *Science as Practice and Culture*, Chicago and London, University of Chicago Press.

POSNER, T. (1987) *An Abnormal Smear: What Does That Mean?*, London, Women's Health and Reproductive Rights Information Centre.

POSNER, T. and VESSEY, M. (1988) *Prevention of Cervical Cancer: The Patient's View*, London, King Edward's Hospital Fund for London.

POSTER, M. (1984) *Foucault, Marxism and History: Mode of Production Versus Mode of Information*, Cambridge, Polity.

QUILLIAM, S. (1989) *Positive Smear*, London, Penguin.

ROBERTS, A. (1982) 'Cervical Cytology in England and Wales, 1965–80', *Health Trends*, 14, pp. 41–3.

ROBINSON, J. (1981) 'Cervical Cancer: A Feminist Critique', *The Times Health Supplement*, 27 November.

ROBINSON, J. (1987) 'Cervical Cancer – Doctors Hide the Truth', in O'SULLIVAN, S. (Ed.) *Women's Health*, New York and London, Pandora, pp. 49–51.

ROYAL COLLEGE OF OBSTETRICIANS AND GYNAECOLOGISTS, ROYAL COLLEGE OF PATHOLOGISTS, ROYAL COLLEGE OF GENERAL PRACTITIONERS and FACULTY OF COMMUNITY MEDICINE (1987) *Report of the Intercollegiate Working Party on Cervical Cytology Screening*, London, The Royal College of Obstetricians and Gynaecologists.

SAFFRON, L. (1987) 'Cervical Cancer – the Politics of Prevention', in O'SULLIVAN, S. (Ed.) *Women's Health: A Spare Rib Reader*, New York and London, Pandora, pp. 42–9.

SAVAGE, W. and MCPHERSON, A. (1983) 'Cervical Cytology', in MCPHERSON, A. and ANDERSON, A. (Eds) *Women's Problems in General Practice*, Oxford, Oxford University Press, pp. 179–202.

SAVAGE, W., SCHWARTZ, M. and GEORGE, J. (1989) *A Survey of Women's Knowledge, Attitudes and Experiences of Cervical Screening in the Tower Hamlets Health District*, Whitechapel, London, The London Hospital.

SCHWARTZ COWAN, R. (1987) 'The Consumption Junction: A Proposal for Research Strategies in the Sociology of Technology', in BIJKER, W.E., HUGHES, T.P. and PINCH, T.J. (Eds) *The Social Construction of Technological Systems*, Cambridge, Mass., and London, MIT Press.

SHAPIN, S. (1988) 'Following Scientists Around', *Social Studies of Science*, 18, pp. 533–50.

SINGER, A. and SZAREWSKI, A. (1988) *Cervical Smear Test: What Every Woman Should Know*, London, Macdonald Optima.

SINGLETON, V. (1992) *Science, Women and Ambivalence: An Actor-Network Analysis of the Cervical Screening Programme*, University of Lancaster, unpublished PhD thesis.

SINGLETON, V. and MICHAEL, M. (1993) 'Actor Networks and Ambivalence: General Practitioners in the Cervical Screening Programme', *Social Studies of Science*, 23, pp. 227–64.

SINGLETON, V. (in press) 'Resourcing Negotiation: The Role of the Laboratory in the British Cervical Screening Programme', to appear in BERG, M. and MOL, A. (Eds) *Differences in Medicine*.

SPALLONE, P. (1989) *Beyond Conception: The New Politics of Reproduction*, Hampshire and London, Macmillan Education.

STAR, S.L. (1992) 'Power, Technologies and the Phenomenology of Conventions: On Being Allergic to Onions', in LAW, J. (Ed.) *A Sociology of Monsters*, London, Routledge.

WOOLGAR, S. (Ed.) (1988) *Knowledge and Reflexivity: New Frontiers in the Sociology of Knowledge*, London, Sage.

Chapter 7

Competition and Collaboration in Male Shaping of Computing: A Study of a Norwegian Hacker Culture

Tove Håpnes and Knut H. Sørensen

Introduction

The perception of knowledge as gendered is at the centre of feminist theory. This has been a critical position, allowing feminists to undermine existing bodies of knowledge as male-biased and to argue the need for more women in knowledge-producing institutions. The main bulk of the literature has been concerned either with epistemological issues or with the way particular discourses perceive women. However, there is also a growing body of literature concerned with gender and the practice of science. Science is analysed and criticized as the outcome of a masculine way of relating to nature (Keller, 1983; Bleier, 1986; Harding, 1986; Tuana, 1989), but also as a hostile environment to women (Rossiter, 1982; Zuckerman *et al.*, 1991).

Feminist studies of technology have to some extent followed the same pattern (Wajcman, 1991). The observation that most designers of technology are men suggests that technology is shaped accordingly as a carrier of masculine values. However, there are few empirical investigations of these claims and the findings are ambiguous (see, for example, Berg, 1992a; Sørensen, 1992; Cockburn, 1992). The sociology as well as the history and philosophy of technology have largely ignored gender issues, while feminist studies have focused on the uses of technology (e.g. Olerup *et al.*, 1985; Lie *et al.*, 1988).

Recent contributions from the social studies of technology do not easily lend themselves to gender-sensitive reinterpretations either. The contingencies of emerging technologies are many, and, in some sense, the social shaping of technology is overdetermined. A reanalysis of, for example, Thomas Hughes' (1983) study of Thomas Edison shaping the emerging system of electricity would face great problems in differing between the effects of Edison as a man versus Edison as an American versus Edison as a capitalist versus Edison as a person with particular cognitive characteristics.

However, in our opinion, the most substantive problem arises from the implicit understanding in most of the literature on gender and technology – that gender is the dominant force of the relationship. Masculinity or maleness becomes a pre-given factor that shapes technology, independent of the process of design and development. The task is thus reduced to establishing the correlation between the given features of maleness and (some of) the characteristics of the resulting technology.

The approach contrasts with constructivism as it is currently practised in technology studies (Bijker and Law, 1992). This may of course be less of a problem for feminism than for constructivism, but it would be interesting to establish some common ground of research. Also within feminism there is a growing uneasiness with gender categories as pre-given (Haraway, 1991). A challenge common to feminist and constructivist studies of technology would be to analyse design and development of technology as simultaneous constructions of gender and technology (see Berg, 1992b).

This article is a response to this challenge. Through an analysis of a male, Norwegian hacker culture we want to explore the interrelationship between gender and technology, or, to be more precise, between maleness and computing. Is it possible to see the gender identity of hackers as independent of their style of computing, and vice versa?

Feminist Studies of Technology: Constructivist Links and Political Challenges

Constructivist studies of technology have mainly, but not exclusively, grown out of science studies (Bijker 1993, Woolgar 1991, Sørensen 1993a). At least in Scandinavia, feminist studies of technology have a rather different ancestry, coming out of industrial sociology and labour process theory (see Lie *et al.*, 1988). Research into so-called office automation in the late 1970s and the early 1980s was a breakthrough for gender and technology as a research issue. The main argument forwarded was that the introduction of new technology was usually to the disadvantage of women. Their qualifications were neglected, their promotion possibilities decreased, and their work was degraded (West, 1982; Game and Pringle, 1983; Lie *et al.*, 1988).

The emerging discourse on gender and technology focused on three sets of conditions: the sexual division of labour, workplace and union politics, and the patriarchal nature of technological design (Sørensen, 1988; see also Wajcman, 1991). When women were victimized by technology, this could be explained by a sexual division of labour which marginalized women in relation to technology. It might also be the outcome of women's marginal position in unions and in workplace politics. Women could also be victimized by technology because it was designed by and for men, shaped by male values, and mediating patriarchal subordination of women (Hacker, 1990).

This discourse was assumed to contribute to the struggles of working women, and it was considered important to prove that technology was gendered, not gender-neutral. The accounts concerned properties of industrial systems and structures of women's subordination, but they were also anti-determinist in the sense that they emphasized local conditions when accounting for socio-technical changes (Cockburn, 1985; Lie *et al.*, 1988).

Male shaping of technology has been deconstructed by applying concepts like *control* and *hierarchy*. Male technology is assumed to reproduce male designers' hierarchical thinking and their aim to control users or Nature (Merchant, 1980). There has also been a concern with the destructive aspects of technology, highlighted by designers' tendency to use violent metaphors in describing their work (Easlea, 1981). Keller's (1985) model of gendered science could serve as a different point of departure. With reference to object relation theory, male scientists are seen as emphasizing *objectivity* and *autonomy* through their *distance* from their research 'objects'. Also, Keller argues, the meta-discourse of modern science is heavily gendered in its use of metaphors.

The contrast is 'a feeling for the organism' (Keller, 1983, 1985), an 'ethics of care' (Gilligan, 1982) or more generally, an emphasis on caring as a basis for design and development of technology (see Sørensen, 1992). Keller (1985) carefully argues the case of gender-free science (and technology, by implication), but in most instances a 'feminization' of science/design is seen as an important goal.

Some of the problems with such arguments have been outlined by Wajcman (1991). Working with binary oppositions like woman and man easily produces a kind of essentialism or romanticism related to biological sex. Moreover, most of the literature on the issue is either normative or speculative. However, there is some evidence that women try to develop or design technology differently from men, but this is the result of a tendency to choose different problem fields rather than solving problems/producing designs that are different (Sørensen, 1992).

There are several analytical and methodological challenges here. First, there is the issue of describing the kind(s) of masculinity displayed in a given context of development or design of technology. This raises problems of reflexivity, but also of reductionism and reification (Morgan, 1992). Second, there are the preconditions of arguing the translation of masculinity into the artefact or system that is designed. This raises the problem of identifying certain physical properties of the design as either feminine or masculine, without returning to the more popular system of polarities of large/small, clean/dirty, heavy/light, etc. (Sørensen and Berg, 1987; Sørensen, 1992)).

On the other hand, we may approach the problem as being a study of culture. That would imply that our main interest would be to analyse a given group or community to see how it was gendered, e.g. in terms of recruitment, career systems and ideology, and less so in terms of how this shapes or does not shape the designs or the work of the group (see Traweek, 1988, 1992).

This would allow a broader conceptualization of the interrelationship between gender and science/technology. Male work-cultures are often characterized by competition and conflict, games and an emphasis of mastery (Morgan, 1992; see also Wajcman, 1991). Physical features of technology like size, noisiness or greasiness may enter the definition of masculinity at the shop floor (Willis, 1977); other features could enter in academic settings.

There are different strategies for approaching these problems. The most obvious one would be to look for situations where gender is implicated in controversies about science or technology. Another possibility is to compare the conditions of male and female researchers, the problems they work with, their methods, their networks, their relation to users, their values, and so on. A third route would be to analyse the socialization of students to identify gendering processes in the university community.

We have chosen to study gender and technology through a group of students who see themselves as computer hackers. They are a strictly male and very marginal community, extreme in their engagement with computers. One of the reasons we became interested in this group was the conclusions from a study of female computer science students. They used the hackers as a metaphor for all the things they did not like about computer science: the style of work, the infatuation with computers leading to neglect of normal non-study relations, and the concentration on problems with no obvious relation to the outside world (Rasmussen and Håpnes, 1991; Håpnes and Rasmussen, 1991). Thus, the hackers emerged as a possibly important example of an extremely masculine technological culture. Moreover, the situation of student hackers could be an interesting example of what Turner (1974) calls *liminality*, a transition from an outsider to an insider of computer science. This means that relations are more fluid, easier to change, but also easier to observe than in ordinary situations. Obviously, hackers are not representative of technological research communities, but they may teach us something about them.

On the Margins of Computer Science

In science and technology studies the concept 'hacker' describes a particular infatuation with computers usually found among young men in a university environment. An early critical discussion is Weizenbaum (1976). He was very much concerned with the computer bum who is interested in nothing but computers: 'The compulsive programmer is convinced that life is nothing but a program running in an enormous computer, and that therefore every aspect of life can ultimately be explained in programming terms' (Weizenbaum, 1976, p. 126).

Sherry Turkle (1984) approaches them as a sub-culture, describing their way of life, their identity and relationship to computers. She is in particular concerned with the computer's ability to act as a medium of projection and reflection, to be an object to think with: 'A relationship with a computer can influence people's conception of themselves, their jobs, their relationships with other people, and with their ways of thinking about social processes' (Turkle, 1984, p. 168).

Hackers thus become a *deviant* group, a counter-culture defining itself in opposition to 'the dominant modes of computer science'. The culture is partly explained with reference to students' experience at the Massachusetts Institute of Technology (MIT): their insecurity and self-hate is produced by the efforts to be transformed from a 'nobody' into a 'somebody', the expected result of an MIT education.

However, Turkle also sees it as an issue of gender. The hackers are male MIT students, not female ones. The community is expressing a macho-culture, not by means of physical appearances, but through a highly competitive striving for mastery and control. The hackers subject themselves to increasingly violent tests which make the culture peculiarly unfriendly to women. There is also a flight from relationships with people to relationships with machines, more characteristic of men than of women (Turkle, 1984, p. 216).

An intriguing aspect of the hacker culture is how we should characterize their activities. Formally, hackers are (usually) students of computing. This suggests that it is a student culture, a setting where one is trained to achieve computer virtuosity. On the other hand, hackers' uses of computers are by no means just straightforward applications. In fact, some of them design software used by others.

This feature highlights a very important point: the distinction between design and application is by no means as clear-cut as usually is assumed in science and technology studies. When people integrate an artefact or a piece of knowledge into their culture, this is not passive consumption, it is an active act of *domestication*. The artefact or the knowledge has to be appropriated, of course, but it also needs to be incorporated and given a place in the practical and symbolic order of the person(s) performing the domestication (see Silverstone *et al.*, 1992; Sørensen, 1993b).

The aim of our study of Norwegian hackers is thus threefold: first, to analyse this particular culture to learn about the interaction between gender and computers; second, to improve our understanding of how users of an artefact construct the artefact, so to speak, as an ensemble of technical and cultural elements through processes of negotiations with human and non-human actors; and third, to assess the notions of a universal hacker culture, brought about by computers and other media.

Our study of hackers is based on an ethnographic approach in order to get comprehensive and broad information. We used participant observation, though only for a few nights. During this period we discussed our observations with the hackers, both in groups and with individual members. Most of the discussions took part in front of the terminals, because the hackers preferred to illustrate their activities and strategies on a computer to be sure that we understood their explanations. We have also conducted longer interviews with individual members of the group. We think this has given us a good opportunity to grasp their mode of thinking and living in the way they see themselves.

Young Men Negotiating Gender and Computers: Being Visible as an Individual

The sorry image of the computer hacker as a young male workaholic, non-social, and totally immersed in programming is mainly an American one. There are good reasons to expect that the location, for example, in a Norwegian culture would make hacking different or even non-existent. When we approached a group who called themselves 'the Software Workshop', we found a computer-based counter-culture recruited from students from physics, computer science and electronics at the Norwegian Institute of Technology. They did in fact define themselves as 'hackers', emphasizing that this was an international phenomenon which they recognized from books and articles. Moreover, they saw themselves as the 'real hackers' in contrast to the electronic hardware manipulators and the

PC-freaks among computer scientists. The 'real hackers' meet at one of the computer labs. Here, they gather in the evenings to work during the night.

The hackers are, biologically speaking, a male group. Their designs are consequently, in a very elementary way, signifying maleness. However, we cannot infer much from this. These males construct computer applications as well as an image of themselves, relative to other students.

The first night when we visited the 'Software Workshop', we saw young men sitting in front of computer terminals. The only sounds came from busy fingers typing away on keyboards, interrupted by sudden bursts of electronic sounds from computer games. We were almost afraid to disturb them, but it turned out that the hackers were more than willing to talk with us about themselves and their work. They very much wanted to introduce us to the intricacies of their sub-culture, and to guide us through the world inside their machines. And we tried to follow them.

The hackers emphasized that they saw themselves as one of the best computer clubs in Norway. They worked with large and ambitious programming systems, and their knowledge provided a basis for making sub-programs and smaller systems on order from companies and clients. Their self-image was as an alternative computer culture. They wanted to be different from 'the rule-based mainstream computer culture'. To emphasize the differences, they saw it as very important to be 'visible', as a group as well as individuals. Also within their own sub-culture, it was essential to communicate their individuality. Difference could be symbolized by their dress or haircut, or communicated through particular interests or personality traits. For example, we met the only 'religious' hacker, the 'fastest programmer' and even the only 'normal' hacker.

The term 'normal' usually signifies those on the outside, the people who are not immersed in computers like they are. This is a way in which the hackers may turn on its head their common experience of being classified as special or 'abnormal' because they spend so much time and effort with computers:

> A lot of others think that this community distinguishes itself in a negative way. They see us as exhibitionists. But we are not. It is more that we want to gain distinction because we are clever. I want people to know who I am, not to disappear in the mass.

They confirm this specialness through communicating that being fascinated by computers means to be different. This is why you may stand out within the sub-culture by being described as 'normal'. As a group they communicate their common culture through a particular style of living. They prefer to work in the evenings and at night, and they use a sub-cultural language shaped by their digital activities. It is also important for them to make it clear that they dislike the university system. The best thing about the university is the opportunity to work with powerful computers. They get access to good work stations, large amounts of computer power, good systems and software. They describe themselves not as good students, but as clever computer users.

We would like to know how hackers construct their masculinity in terms of their work with computers, their internal relations, and their relations to other groups. The way that technical and cultural elements, including gender, are negotiated into the construction of networks, may be observed through the interaction among the hackers and the machines. We want to show that the masculinity of hackers is not a simple reflection of a general masculine culture or the computer. It is a product of the efforts to construct networks of men and machines.

Domestication by Tampering: Freedom and Creativity

How is it that individuality is such an important characteristic of the identity of the hackers, and thus of their construction of masculinity? To understand this, we have to look more closely at how they relate to and negotiate with computers. We have chosen to focus on their style of working with the machine, and how they interpret the machine and their own identity in terms of the interaction with the machine. Most of the hackers have been interested in computers since they were 10–12 years of age. Quite early they began to feel special. Mads' story is typical:

> In my class, we were a couple of kids that got hooked on computers. It made a difference at that time, to be a computer freak or not. Many people do not understand how it is because they are not interested themselves. What we did, appeared to be dull to quite a lot, and thus they assumed that we were dull also.

Before they started with computers, many had played a lot with mechanical or electronic sets. They had disassembled radios and watches to see what was on the inside and how they could be reassembled and developed. In this way, they had developed a taste for tampering with machines. The computer offered new possibilities to integrate new elements, either by developing the computer or through the making of software. Programming became a main activity. In the hackers' accounts, comics and science fiction also stimulated their interest in computers. Here, they met with figures and heroes able to invent machines that could do the most fantastic things. This was the raw material of dreams and a source of new ideas to be tried out on their computers.

Their strategy of learning is to tamper, to try and fail, and to read about ideas and possibilities in computer magazines and manuals. Programming and a taste for science fiction are important elements in their accounts of themselves. *The Hitchhiker's Guide to the Galaxy* is required reading for those wanting to join the culture. They see it as an extremely funny book. In general, science fiction is relaxing and entertaining, an escape from reality, but also an opportunity to fantasize and think creatively.

Games are a third source of inspiration, to play computer games for many hours in a row, often several playing together. Usually, the computer games display general characteristics of boys' games. It is the activity, the action, which is important, roles are distributed and exchanged, and there is an element of competition. Some win, some lose, and the action offers challenges, speed and excitement. All this is found in computer games too.

They continue to play computer games also as members of the 'Software Workshop'. Simple games are recreations or models from which to make their own games with more advanced niceties and possibilities. However, to be a real hacker, games cannot be your main activity. Only Multi-User Dungeon – MUD – is constructed as 'real fun', and consequently as a proper hacker activity. Playing MUD may go on for months because of the challenges the game seems to offer in terms of gaining skills and resources. The game is played by the user of computer networks. Thus, several people may play simultaneously with or against each other. Participants may come from different countries. One exciting possibility offered is the ability to spy on the other players, if you have learnt the trick. You may also communicate with the other players, leave messages or obstructions, and thus 'bug' the rest. What counts as an extra sophistication is that you do not know the identity of the other players. You construct your own identity in the game. The ultimate aim is to become a wizard by scoring huge numbers of points. This is evidence that you are a master of the game.

Competition and Control, Excitement and Fun

When games are the object of negotiations around the machine, we find a competitive style. There is competition either between the hacker and the game software, or between the hacker and other players. The important thing is to gain control through understanding the system and being able to manipulate it to win. Competition may also be a part of the internal activities of the sub-culture. Who makes the most brilliant Othello-game? In their accounts, this is seen as play, not work. It is considered to be fun, and to stimulate creativity.

At the same time, they compete about endurance – for how many hours in a row they are able to do programming. In this area, we find personal as well as community records. Kim told us about Anders:

> I nearly thought he had disappeared, but no – he came back, pale and sallow, and told that he had made a new record. He had been programming for 42 hours in a row, then he went into his room and slept for 17 hours.

The word 'asceticism' is mentioned as a central element in such perseverance. You do not give up until the problem is solved. Thus, they may work very long hours at the computers. They forget about time and eating. In their accounts, this is not only a matter of excitement. It results from a determination to succeed. The trick is to be enduring and patient. However, forgetting about time does create practical problems. To help out, Roar designed a program that produced a warning message on the screen in the late afternoon: 'The shops are closing in ten minutes'.

Programming is a main task, but to master programming is not a goal in itself. It is a precondition of designing software products. One of the hackers put it like this: 'If you want to build a whole house, it is not enough only to learn how you hit the nails.' To design a product may mean anything from developing a whole software package for drawing to making a small function to be put in a program or a system. The hackers are into very different kinds of problems. Some may be interested in graphics, some in fractals, and some in how you combine pictures with movement and sound.

The fascination with machines and programming is explained as a result of the possibilities offered to them by the computer. The interesting part is not to find out how things have been made, but how it is possible to design them: 'You have a problem or an idea, let's see if we are able to run it or solve it through the machine.' They are motivated by the excitement and fun. The joy of working is in the process itself. Kim describes his fascination in these terms: 'With computers you don't think the same things over again. There is always variation, always new possibilities emerging. That is the exciting thing about computers, the lack of repetition. Computers are variation.'

Many hackers describe their style of working with computers as experimentation, searching for solutions, coaxing and trying and then seeing what it looks like. They much prefer trial-and-error to well-structured methods out of manuals or existing software. They explain their preference by pointing out that they dislike being controlled. It is better to try it out directly with the machine, or to ask others in the community.

They perceive themselves as creative computer users, in contrast to standardized computer professionals. The style of work and their understanding of themselves is expressed through the way in which they define computers and computer systems. PCs are 'disgusting', IBM computers are 'wicked', Macintoshes are 'snobbish', and they hate programming languages like Pascal and Cobol. Such programming languages represent uniformed and rule-regulated systems. They are replete with 'barriers' that block their wish for individuality and artistry, or, as they put it themselves, 'We depend on freedom from "walls" when we do programming.' They want the structure to be in their mind, not in the software. Success should depend on abilities, their capacity to think logically and abstractly.

Their favourites are the programming language C and machine code. They say that this gives them greater freedom to construct their own approaches, to find 'brilliant' solutions. PCs are considered as tailor-made to a uniform use. They have a lot of 'strange' characteristics. In the hackers' accounts, they have no consistent design, only a lot of parts clashed together. Thus, they do not like them. They are the machine of others, they are outside their culture. Macintoshes are snobby because they look brilliant in terms of design and graphics, but they are considered to be slow and full of structures and barriers. Macintoshes are associated with architects, marketing people, and women.

Even if the joy is in the work process itself, they say that it feels glorious to be the one who masters the machine, the one who is able to control it and the processes that are being run. One of the hackers put it this way: 'In relation to the machine, I am the boss, and it feels grand to win over the machine.' To win means to be able to control, to be able to solve the problem that initiated the work. They see the relation to the computer as neither personal nor close, like the MIT hackers in Sherry Turkle's account of them.

> Most of us look at the computer as a thing, to be manipulated. People, on the other hand, exist for cooperation. What is fascinating to us is the *potential* in the machine. You may nearly put anything into it.

The hackers are using concepts like manipulating, control and winning over the machines. They are characteristic of the approach to computers that Turkle (1984) calls 'hard mastery', described as typical of boys. At the same time, our hackers say that it is important to have an artistic approach, to be creative, to try things out, to see what fits, elements similar to Turkle's 'soft mastery', more typical among girls using computers.

Competition and Collaboration

While their approach to computers has competitive features – to win over the machine and internal competition – their knowledge about computers and their products are available to all members of the hacker culture. To help each other and to use each other's products make them become more able and to reach further in their inventiveness:

> As a group, we are more powerful than as individuals. For example, the drawing program that Roar designed, there is a lot of me in it too. Things he has taken from what I know and have made. . . . From this point of view, cooperation is more characteristic of our group than competition. The computer field is in fact too large for competition. But of course, there are elements of competition in the group, for example we did have this Othello-program contest. But we have come to see that to progress, we have to learn from each other.

They dislike internal secrets related to computers, and they are ardent adversaries of the practice of the mainstream culture of copy protection and copyright. This is reflected in the collaborative features of their approach to computers. You do not just contest the machine to be able to master it. You have to learn to understand the logic of hardware and software too. There is a process of domestication going on between man and machine, a process which demands collaboration of the two parties. In this way, the hackers manage a dual relationship to the machine, to activities and approaches, and to each other. They have a style of work and a way of interacting which is simultaneously competition and collaboration.

Still, even if there are many common features in their style of work, the hackers also emphasize distinguishing individual stylistic elements. This is related to their keenness to achieve visibility as persons. They manage and communicate their individuality through the tasks on which they are working, and through their style of interaction with the machine:

> We work rather differently, too. Some just sit down, work on a program and tumble with the bits and pieces until they arrive at a solution. My approach is characterized more by the way I look at the whole problem, analyse it to simplify it as much as possible, and then

I start running things on the machine.

The hacker culture provides more than an opportunity to interact with machines. When they are tired of programming or need a break, they often see a movie together or drop by a pizza bar to eat and talk about movies, science fiction books and computers. According to the hackers, new members are offered a community and a group of friends. While each person's individuality should be provided for, they see it as very important to take care of the community. The sub-culture should be congenial, and the members should be open towards each other. They protect each other in particular through a caring based on tolerance and solidarity. Kim exemplifies this when he tells us about one of the members with what he sees as psychological problems:

> The fact that he has problems in relating to people, and that he is not all well – that makes him very easily aggressive. The result is that he may become rather difficult. But here, in this community, there are at least some people who share his interest in computers. Therefore, we have chosen to be lenient towards his behaviour. There's no point in dismissing, it is better to help. Because, he is good with computers and he is able to show it here. We do it like we try to emphasize his qualities, then we try to calm his more negative expressions.

The combination of competition and collaboration, of individualism and caring, may be typical of male middle-class groups, inside or outside of science and technology. What we see here is probably a useful corrective to the picture of male scientists as being dominantly competitive and individualist. Without some collaboration and caring, a group or a community would find it difficult to exist. Even in settings of competitiveness and individualism, there may be an undercurrent of collaboration and caring which is important to the work performed.

Men, Women and Machines

The hackers have not thought much about why they are a purely male group. To them, it is a mystery that no women are interested in computers the way they are. Nevertheless, they have learnt that computer hacking is something women and girls want to keep at arm's length:

> The first thing you learn as a computer boy is: Never talk to girls

about computers! They get this kind of desperate expression. I believe they think it's too complicated, they cannot stand to listen to it. All of us belonging to this hacker community have learnt that. When girls don't understand what we say, they lose interest. I don't understand it.

Consequently, the hackers have defined women as being on the outside. However, that does not imply a point of view that women are generally different from men:

In the Software Workshop community, we are a minority also among men. So some women don't seem to be that different from some other men.

As a group, women are associated with, among other things, Macintosh machines. That is of course outside the interest sphere of hackers, but they tell us that through working with Macintoshes, they believe more girls could learn to become more interested in computers. Macintoshes are perceived as simpler to use (far simpler than the SUN workstations and terminals which the hackers employ themselves). That is because they are well-structured and rule-based. Moreover, Macintoshes are seen as related to activities like the *application* of graphical programs, to the designing of text and use of graphics, things which are defined in their culture as feminine. Their own work with graphics is not defined as application. They *design* graphics.

The hackers do not understand the absence of women, but it does not bother them much either. They do not believe that they 'frighten' away women. Some have visited the workshop, not as computer users, but as girlfriends. The hackers may relate to girls outside the hacker community, but as one of them said, they do not consider it important to 'chase or look for women either'. Here, there are some differences among hackers. Some have girlfriends, some emphasize that they have no relation to women or things outside the hacker culture. It is the life at the Software Workshop and the enthusiastic interest in computers that are their common denominator.

They know little too about how women interpret and evaluate computers and computer science, for example what female computer science students at the same university see as interesting and what they would like to do. They do not know that these women call them 'key-pressers', a concept used to signify people whose only great interest in life is to do programming for the sake of programming. To the female students, the hacker figure signifies all the fears and horrors of computer science. They construct their femininity in relation to computers through defining hacking as bad and constructing their own approach to computer science antithetical to what they see as a monstrous love of computers for their own sake.

Male Computing and Computing Males

The most striking feature of the hacker culture we have analysed is its many ambiguities. It is competitive, but also collaborative. It is directed toward control and manipulation of the machine, but is also artistic and interactive. It is considered playful, but also useful. The hackers play games, but also design products. They strive to achieve individual visibility and recognition as well as community.

What emerges is a more complex male culture of computing than could be imagined from the literature. We find hierarchy, competition, distance and control, but also more 'feminine' characteristics. This is the result of the way computers and masculinity are allowed to interact in the rather freewheeling hacker culture. Computers as well as masculinity are constructed as sufficiently flexible to allow these contradictions. The computer, and computer science in the hackers' interpretation of it, seem to encourage modification of traditional masculine values like being competitive and in control. On the other hand, the construction of approaches to the computers draws upon these traditional values. Contradictions in the constructed masculinities are also found in the uses of computers. The approaches are neither hierarchical, competitive, and manipulative nor interactive, collaborative and network-like. They are both.

It is interesting to compare the male hackers' accounts with those of the female computer science students at the same university. They perceive the hackers as too obsessed with computers, too immersed in abstract technicalities, and not sufficiently engaged in the solution of practical problems (Håpnes and Rasmussen, 1991; Rasmussen and Håpnes, 1991). The hackers see the women (and most other male computer science students) as mainstream, caught by structures and rules.

This is a gendered controversy above all about how to work with computers. There may be disagreements in terms of the quality of software, the relative importance of, for example, user-friendliness and elegance, but they are not so pronounced. The Norwegian hackers are not that absorbed in the abstract, 'erotic' (Hacker, 1989) qualities of computers. They are also interested in computer applications, although their definition of usefulness seems to differ from that of the female students. What emerges is not a dualism of male and female, because we may observe at least two different male cultures of computing – probably several. Still, the cultures are gendered in a thorough and important way.

The complexity of the hacker culture is also evidence of the flexibility of computers as a cultural medium. The hackers have developed what we will call *a strategy of domestication* in their relationship with computers. They incorporate them by tampering, by trial and error, combined with the use of written resources like computer journals and manuals. They try to develop and maintain creativity by playing games and reading science fiction. Also, in their use of computers, the hackers emphasize qualities like understanding and control to achieve a kind of freedom in their problem-solving. Still, the outcome in terms of style of work is different. Even a similar strategy of domestication does not produce only one way of using computers.

The same phenomenon may be observed on the symbolic level. The hackers use their style of computing to distinguish themselves not only from the non-hackers but also from the rest of the community. However, a style of computing may not be sufficient, so many also use dress, haircut, and personal style to make sure that their individuality comes across. What comes out of the process of domesticating computers is a web of artefacts and styles, of machines and identities. The persons change, as does computing. The tampering novice seems to acquire new skills, but also to learn the value of community and collaboration in experimenting with and improving upon computer software. The skills and his style of work becomes part of the gender identity of the hacker, while this identity seems to influence the way he operates within the field of gendered polarities such as hierarchy versus equality, competition versus collaboration, and control versus creativity. The result is contingent on the construction of masculinities, but not determined by them.

The domestication strategy of the Norwegian hackers is obviously influenced by the international discourse about hackers. This discourse is a resource from which they get cultural models. Some of the common characteristics, like working at night, may be accounted for by a common situation as marginal users of a limited resource – computers. On the other hand, the interest in science fiction is probably an indication that this literature manages to address issues generally appealing to boys and young males interested in 'modern' technology. Compared to Turkle's description of American MIT hackers, however, the Norwegian hackers appear as less extreme and more 'feminine'. This may be due to differences of interpretation, but it could also be argued that it reflects some dissimilarities between American and Norwegian cultures.

References

BERG, A.-J. (1992a) 'The Smart House as a Gendered Socio-Technical Construction', STS working paper 14/92, Trondheim, Centre for Technology and Society.

BERG, A.-J. (1992b) 'Technological Flexibility – Bringing Gender into Technology, Or Was It the Other Way Round?', STS working paper 15/92, Trondheim, Centre for Technology and Society.

BIJKER, W.E. (1993) 'Do Not Despair: There is Life after Constructivism', *Science, Technology, and Human Values*, vol. 18, no. 1, pp. 113–40.

BIJKER, W.E. and LAW, J. (Eds) (1992) *Shaping Technology/Building Society*, Cambridge, Mass., MIT Press.

BLEIER, R. (Ed.) (1986) *Feminist Approaches to Science*, New York, Pergamon Press.

COCKBURN, C. (1985) *Machinery of Dominance*, London, Pluto Press.

COCKBURN, C. (1992) 'The Circuit of Technology: Gender, Identity and Power', in SILVERSTONE, R. and HIRSCH, E. (Eds) *Consuming Technologies: Media and Information in Domestic Spaces*, London, Routledge.

EASLEA, B. (1981) *Fathering the Unthinkable*, London, Pluto Press.

GAME, A. and PRINGLE, R. (1983) *Gender at Work*, London, Pluto Press.

GILLIGAN, C. (1982) *In a Different Voice*, Cambridge, Mass., Harvard University Press.

HACKER, S. (1989) *Pleasure, Power and Technology*, Boston, Unwin Hyman.

HACKER, S. (1990) *'Doing It the Hard Way': Investigations of Gender and Technology*, (Ed. SMITH, D.E. AND TURNER, S.M.), Boston and London, Unwin Hyman.

HÅPNES, T. and RASMUSSEN, B. (1991) 'Excluding Women from the Technologies of the Future?', *Futures*, December.

HARAWAY, D.J. (1991) *Simians, Cyborgs, and Women: The Reinvention of Nature*, London, Free Association Books.

HARDING, S. (1986) *The Science Question in Feminism*, Ithaca, Cornell University Press.

HUGHES, T.P. (1983) *Network of Powers*, Baltimore, Johns Hopkins University Press.

KELLER, E.F. (1983) *A Feeling for the Organism: The Life and Work of Barbara McClintock*, New York, W.H. Freeman and Company.

KELLER, E.F. (1985) *Reflections on Gender and Science*, New Haven and London, Yale University Press.

LIE, M. *et al.* (1988) *I menns bilde. Kvinner-teknologi-arbeid*, Trondheim, Tapir.

MERCHANT, C. (1980) *The Death of Nature: Women, Ecology and the Scientific Revolution*, San Fransisco, Harper & Row.

MORGAN, D.H.J. (1992) *Discovering Men*, London, Routledge.

OLERUP, A. *et al.* (Eds) (1985) *Women, Work and Computerization: Opportunities and Disadvantages*, Amsterdam, Elsevier.

RASMUSSEN, B. and HÅPNES, T. (1991) 'The Production of Male Power in Computer Science', in ERIKSSON, I.V. *et al.* (Eds) *Women, Work and Computerization*, Amsterdam, Elsevier Science Publishers B. V.

ROSSITER, M.W. (1982) *Women Scientists in America: Struggles and Strategies to 1940*, Baltimore, Johns Hopkins University Press.

SILVERSTONE, R., HIRSCH, E. and MORLEY, D. (1992) 'Information and Communication Technologies and the Moral Economy of the Household', in SILVERSTONE, R. and HIRSCH, E. (Eds) *Consuming Technologies: Media and Information in Domestic Spaces*, London, Routledge.

SØRENSEN, K.H. (1988) 'Maskinenes siste offer. Om produksjonsteknikk, kvinner og arbeidsmiljø', in LIE, M. *et al. I menns bilde. Kvinner-teknologi-arbeid*, Trondheim, Tapir.

SØRENSEN, K.H. (1992) 'Towards a Feminized Technology? Gendered Values in the Construction of Technology', *Social Studies of Science*, vol. 22, no. 1, pp. 5–32.

SØRENSEN, K.H. (1993a) 'Constructivism and the Analysis of Technology: A Pragmatic Approach to a Sociology of Technology', STS working paper 2/93, Trondheim, Centre for Technology and Society.

SØRENSEN, K.H. (1993b) 'Domesticating Technology: Artifacts in the Hands of Users', STS working paper 5/93, Trondheim, Centre for Technology and Society.

SØRENSEN, K.H. and BERG, A.J. (1987) 'Genderization of Technology among Norwegian Engineering Students', *Acta Sociologica*, vol. 30, no. 2, pp. 151–71.

TRAWEEK, S. (1988) *Beamtimes and Lifetimes: The World of High-Energy Physicists*, Cambridge, Mass., Harvard University Press.

TRAWEEK, S. (1992) 'Border Crossings: Narrative Strategies in Science Studies and among Physicists in Tsukuba Science City, Japan', in PICKERING, A. (Ed.) *Science as Practice and Culture*, Chicago, University of Chicago Press, pp. 429–65.

TUANA, N. (Ed.) (1989) *Feminism and Science*, Bloomington, Indiana University Press.

TURKLE, S. (1984) *The Second Self: Computers and the Human Spirit*, New York, Simon and Schuster.

TURNER, V. (1974) *Dramas, Fields, and Metaphors: Symbolic Action in Human Society*, Ithaca, NY, Cornell University Press.

WAJCMAN, J. (1991) *Feminism Confronts Technology*, Cambridge, Polity.

WEIZENBAUM, J. (1976) *Computer Power and Human Reason: From Judgement to Calculation*, San Francisco, W.H. Freeman.

WEST, J. (Ed.) (1982) *Women, Work and the Labour Market*, London, Routledge and Kegan Paul.

WILLIS, P. (1977) *Learning to Labour*, London, Gower.

WOOLGAR, S. (1991) 'The Turn to Technology in Social Studies of Science', *Science, Technology, and Human Values*, vol. 16, no. 1, pp. 20–50.

ZUCKERMAN, H., COLE, J.R. and BRUER, J.T. (Eds) (1991) *The Outer Circle: Women in the Scientific Community*, New York, Norton.

Chapter 8

Negotiating a Software Career: Informal Work Practices and 'The Lads' in a Software Installation

Margaret Tierney

Introduction

This chapter addresses how software careers are differentially shaped by the local social network which pertains in a medium-sized Irish software development installation. By looking at the structures and devices by which staff in this company become identified as 'good material', I explore how certain skilled staff, most especially 'the lads', are better placed than others to successfully negotiate a rewarding career strategy in software.

The concept of the career is a useful means of capturing the issues surrounding both an organization's software work practices and their employees' attempts to optimize their chances of progression within their occupational field. The single most valuable negotiable resource an organization offers its skilled employees is the career, that is, the routes and devices by means of which particular people are allocated to do particular jobs, and the subsequent linking of those jobs into a chronological sequence. Heimer offers a useful account of how the career is a jointly negotiated resource:

> When we talk about control over a career we are really talking about control over a series of elements that determine whether a person's abilities are developed, whether such development is noted and recorded, and whether the person has access to information about jobs, and potential employers have access to information about him or her. (Heimer, 1984)

Some of the career elements she notes include:

- being in an organization which structures jobs into a sequence. The clearer such structuring is, the better, for a clear ladder allows workers to plan their career.

- occupying jobs which may (or may not) enable them to learn the skills that will lead to promotion. A good career job would be one which, though it may itself be highly routinized, places the worker in close social proximity to jobs which are more difficult, varied or responsible. In such a job, the worker finds many opportunities, both formal and informal, to learn on-the-job.

- having access to information about relevant jobs. For instance, a job such as software consultancy requires the worker to meet with clients who could well become potential future employers. Thus, this kind of job is more likely than, say, back office programming to yield information about employment opportunities elsewhere.

- being able to negotiate how information about the worker's abilities, training and experience is collected by the organization and is made available to others both upwardly and laterally.

In this chapter, I consider the relationship between work practices and emergent software careers by means of one detailed case study, conducted in a software installation in Dublin in 1987. As we will see, in the important negotiation sites over the formation of a software career, viz. the recruitment, promotion and managerial practices of the organization, informal rather than obviously graded pathways, are more in evidence. In this context, the social networks which pertain in a software installation become an extremely important site for workers to demonstrate their worth; gain a reputation; acquire new forms of expertise; and so advance their careers.

The Case Study

The company, established in the early 1970s, is the Irish office of a multinational hardware company. It is relatively large, and its operations refer to the development, marketing and support of the firm's minis and micros within the country. Amongst its 120 technically-skilled staff, over fifty are in the Software Division. Software activities include the development and maintenance of systems together with business analysis activities. This firm actively seeks 'quality' software labour, since its staff must be technically knowledgeable about the firm's products, as well as conversant with handling client organizations across many different industrial sectors.

Thus, its staff enter with high expectations of being able to negotiate, over time, the kinds of activities they do. They expect to be able to enhance and alter their expertise so as to make themselves more valuable to their employer and to increase their potential power to trade themselves on the external labour market. Given the firm's size and its range of software activities, coupled with high employee expectations, this case study offers us scope to look at a hierarchy of software job-holders at different stages in their careers as they jockey for position within the firm's internal organizational structure.

The Software Division is split into four sections: Pre-Sales Support, Customer Support, a small R&D unit, and Software Supply and Development Unit (SSDU). SSDU have a staff of twenty, of whom four are women. It is this section which deals with large customer projects, either at the proposal, development or maintenance phases, though some staff work independently as maintenance programmers on small business micros. The largest team in 1987 was a group of eight who were installing thirty distributed minis for a large government department. This section – the main focus for this study – had the largest mix of people of differing experience and formal qualifications.

The culture of this firm's software division is premised upon maximizing informality, so long as that does not jeopardize the company's image to clients. The rhythm and rhetoric of the office feels like the very apotheosis of a clean, advanced, skilled and meritocratic workplace. To the observer, for instance, the main social division of this office is not centred around a distinction between management and staff. Managers do not have separate offices, and managers and staff have equal access to the division's private seminar rooms. Providing the worker is not due to meet clients that day, s/he may wear jeans and may choose to work any hours which suit. A kind of gung-ho ambition is openly celebrated in this installation. In the speech and mannerisms of the staff, assertiveness is more apparent than modesty. The work matters. It takes up most of the conversational space in the office, the canteen and the pub. The senior management of the company like to see their staff as go-getters: 'Our guys have to be hungry for work. We won't take less.'

Reflecting this company's approval of assertive ambition, most managers adopt Responsible Autonomy rather than closely interventionist strategies in monitoring software work (see Friedman, 1989): Ultan, the Senior Project Manager of the SSDU, described his staff as 'real thorough-breds. Just given them a nudge and they're off. They eat and drink the business.' He rarely intervenes directly in setting out minutely-itemized work targets. Though worksheets are filled in by staff and managers alike, their purpose is to aid the costing out of a piece of work, rather than to measure productivity. Instead, all the members of a team on a given project meet weekly to establish (jointly) the task objectives for the following week, and their spatial proximity to each other ensures that 'we're talking to each other all the time'. Ultan said 'I trust them. I must trust them. It's the only way to get work done here.'

In addition, this company attempts to encourage a 'professional' labour process by means of minimizing the number of formal authority chains between junior and experienced staff. Like many of its kind, this firm prefers to deploy informal recruitment and promotion strategies based on gradual observation of an employee's abilities to work with team-mates and with clients (see Causer and Jones, 1990; Ginzberg and Baroudi, 1988; Kanter, 1984; Winstanley, 1986). In place of a highly-visible series of graded steps which would serve to denote the salary, rank and status of staff relative to each other, there are instead only three identifiable grades in this office:

(a) junior staff, who have the prefix of Trainee before their job title, a tag which is dropped after they have served a year or two with the company.
(b) experienced staff, whose job titles may either reflect the kind of work they normally do (e.g. Programmer, Technical Support) or which reflect the image the company wishes to present to clients when these staff are out on the job (e.g. titles such as Software Co-ordinator or Customer Service Executive appear on the business cards of staff who would otherwise just describe themselves as programmers).
(c) supervisory staff whose titles contain the term manager (e.g. Project Manager, Pre-Sales Support Manager).

These three grades provide the basic parameters within which individual negotiations over salary, job content and responsibilities are conducted. Thus, a Trainee Programmer will not earn more than the upper parameter set for the grade, though s/he may be earning considerably more than a fellow Trainee. Likewise, experienced staff members may be made fully responsible for the successful completion of a piece of work, and bargain for the salary and status which ensue from that, without being managers per se.

In common with most software installations, the firm demands formal educational credentials when recruiting junior staff though the exact kind of credential (degree, diploma, conversion course) varies hugely. Women are (almost) as likely to be recruited at junior entry ports as men. However, since most of the incumbent middle-level staff and all the managers are men, sexual discrimination within the company expresses itself in terms of assumptions made in assigning particular people to do particular jobs (see Collinson and Knights, 1985; Rubery, 1978). The relatively low number of female software staff in SSDU was, indeed, often remarked on. One member of staff said:

> I was very surprised when I came here to find so few women.
> Granted that computers is male-dominated. But in most places there
> is a tendency to have a certain quota of women. I suspect that
> management find that it improves the working area and improves the
> atmosphere. The programmers like having women around. (Fergus,
> Customer Service Executive)

His surprise is couched in terms of how the presence of women normally
improves the ambiance for the workers – the (male) programmers.

Assumptions of this kind become critically important in regulating both
the quality and the amount of work-related information trading done in the
normal course of doing software work. If – as here – that work is conducted
with a minimum of formal authority chains and an overtly arm's-length
managerial control strategy, the resultant informality of a labour process of
software peers can become a minefield for those who do not fit comfortably
into the dominant local social network. Let us turn now to the detailed
organization of software work in this company, so as to monitor how
particular workers manage to enhance (or fail to enhance) their opportunities
for upward or lateral movement over the career.

Doing Software Development Work

Software development as conducted in this company encompasses three
different types of activity. The first stage of work is the business specification. Fergus, a 27-year-old Customer Service Executive, is primarily
employed to work on this area. When an in-principle sale has been made, his
liaison work with Sales involves writing detailed 'internal' and 'customer'
costings for the project – costings which are quite frequently arbitrarily
arrived at, since they depend on a feel for how much a client may be
persuaded to pay, and which programmers will be available for assignment
to the project. His work with clients means assessing how the project could
be best accommodated into their practice. This, too, is a highly skilled
activity which demands a feel for the business, based primarily on not over-
selling the client. Correctly gauging how to pitch the benefits of a new system
to a client is fundamental to the profitability of the Software Division. If too
much is promised, the client will badger the company, long after implementation, for extra enhancements which quickly escalate the actual cost of the
project. The Customer Service Executive post carries great kudos within the
company and post-holders such as Fergus command enormous respect from
managers and staff alike.

Responding to a client's decision to buy is not the only type of 1st Phase software work. Tom, for instance, is an ex-engineer who joined the company after a six-month graduate conversion course. His title is Trainee Programmer, and he was employed for the specific purpose of developing the company's PABX system in a direction which their telecommunications client has not directly asked for. Tom works alone, answerable only to a Project Manager. His task is to flesh out a potential access control facility, producing various detailed options which the senior management of Sales may later act upon. This kind of 1st Phase work – though technically interesting – places Tom in a relatively marginal position within the software division:

> I suppose I'll never really make it big here because this place is completely market-oriented. You rarely get a chance to do something really radical. I suppose I come closest to the ideal ... but we're not in the business of coming up with new ideas really.

The second phase of software development work refers to the production of the systems specification for a project. For a large government project, the spec was put together over six months by fifteen different people. Where business specifications typically involve staff in direct negotiations with the senior Finance and Accounts managers of client firms, 2nd Phase work means talking to middle management or junior users in the client firm, who can answer specific queries about the work practices the technical project affects.

This kind of work is done by Alan who is Technical Support for the minis being installed on the government project. In his terms, 'a good systems analyst is just somebody who is well-organized and knows what questions to ask', a skill which is only gradually learnt on-the-job. Indeed, in this company, Systems Analyst is not a discrete job title, but simply reflects the kind of work which the more senior programmers engage in.

Part of the task of being well-organized is to document the specification so as to make it accessible to everybody concerned, but if documentation means making the design skeleton very explicit, it is also a contentious aspect of the job. In practice, in this company, most documentation of either systems or, later, programming specifications, is left to just one or two people – usually the newest recruits (Ann and Sean). Ann and Sean were both recruited at the same time as Tom from the same graduate conversion course.

They had been preceded a month before by Ultan, the Senior Project Manager. Ultan (36 and married with children) was engaged in turning the spec into a working set of linked computer installations. This meant delegating someone to train the government staff; getting the operating system tested and installed; and getting the individual pieces of application software designed, developed, tested and then accepted by the client. He allocated Ann to do the overall systems documentation and all the necessary training of users. Ann is 34 and also married with children. She is an engineering graduate but found it difficult to get full-time engineering work and she turned to part-time lecturing in a local technical college in the evenings. Her title in the company is Trainee Programmer, as is Sean's. Sean is 19. Like Ann, he claims he has not yet done any 'real programming work'. His job is to document the programs designed by the more experienced programmers in the team – Michael, Declan and Fintan.

It is these last three who were mainly doing the 3rd Phase development work – the program specification. Though in many software installations this detailed level of design work can serve to isolate programmers from the users since, in principle, this kind of work can be turned into a wholly back room function (see Friedman, 1989), this is not the case in this office.

So as to enable all programming staff to acquire experience in systems analysis and business specification activities, 3rd Phase programmers enjoy frequent interactions both with the client (on site visits during implementation) and with colleagues who have been allocated to 1st and 2nd Phase tasks. Thus, Michael, Declan and Fintan are 'key workers', in Ultan's terms, not simply as far as the company is concerned but also as far as the client is concerned. For the purpose of site visits, Michael's business card carries the title of Software Co-ordinator though he is 'just a sort of a programmer' in the office. The structure of, say, Michael's job has enabled him to blur the distinction between the machine-oriented activities of writing programs and the customer-oriented activities of dealing with implementation hitches on site visits.

In sum, though software development work as conducted in this company is roughly divided into three phases of activities – with distinct skills being brought to bear for each phase – we can see how the loosely-specified tasks of business and systems programming and analysis provide opportunities for staff to overlap their work with each other. Sales spills into business specs which in turn spills into systems spec and so on: the boundaries of distinct jobs are unstable. In this company – as in many others with a similar collegiate style of management – there is no coherent way to define what, say, a programmer does, since the definition changes depending on the role of the person who is doing the defining. In the absence of a standardized meaning for what a job is worth (in terms of its salary, status and task content), it becomes interesting to monitor how hierarchies of skill nevertheless come about. For this, we need to look more closely at the division of labour, with respect to the firm's main business.

The Division of Labour and the Structuring of Software Jobs

Three of the company's four software units are 'market-oriented', to use the buzz word I was surrounded by. The exception is R&D. These eight people are undoubtedly the most isolated software group, since they report directly through one senior manager to the parent head office. The work they do is technically interesting and highly skilled, yet nobody – including Tom who was the nearest thing to a purist in SSDU – envied them their isolation. Mary (Technical Support for the operating systems on the company's micros), for instance, said:

> It's really closed environment up there [in R&D]. It's not good for a lifetime. Granted, the guys up there are really excellent, and there is that bit of admiration. Most of us are a wee bit awed by them. But R&D people find it difficult to negotiate. All they have is their brains. No flair. No experience to talk of. No exposure. Sales and Marketing, now that's different. They don't get too much admiration but they get lots of money and lots of responsibility. That's where the action is.

The 'action' for this company lies in finding and developing software product and service niches. The best jobs in a company such as this are those which provide the most opportunities for acquiring and exercising skill as market-oriented technical problem-solvers. Since this kind of business know-how can only be learnt on the job, Mary's comment that R&D staff get 'no exposure' and have 'no flair' is especially pertinent. Her perspective echoes a repeated finding of US research on the consequence to technical workers whose expert labour is radically divorced from the main business activities of the firm. The content of their work may be intrinsically satisfying, and their expertise may exactly match the highly specialized contours of the jobs they hold. Such jobs and such job-holders may even be indispensable to the firm – both R&D and the provision of user training are good examples of this (see Davies, 1985; Griffiths, 1981) – but so long as they are marginal (i.e. overhead) rather than core (i.e. profit-producing) activities, the job-holders may find it difficult to climb a skill hierarchy, either vertically towards management, or horizontally towards more 'core-type' work within the firm's internal labour market (see Bailyn, 1977; Kanter, 1984).

Within the SSDU the division of labour is fluid: projects are held distinct from each other, though many of the programming staff may be quickly moved across projects, depending on the pressure of work. The organizational map of who is working on what changes from week to week. Meanwhile, though, we find clear exceptions to the fluidity of staff movement in SSDU. Tom, to take one example, was specifically employed to work on the exact task assigned to him, on the basis of his specific competence in a particular area.

In addition, we find variation not just in the division of labour but in the way in which software development jobs are structured. On one hand, we have seen the three-phase approach to large-scale development work: the jobs built around large-scale projects involve different combinations of staff working on distinct phases – some doing analysis, some programming, some documenting, and so on. On the other hand, small projects are wholly owned by the programmer assigned to them. All four of the section's free-floating micro programmers – Frank, Conor, Dave and Peter – undertake applications for their individual small business customers, from beginning to end. That is, they each design, write, code and test the application under their care.

It is the crucial issue of experience which illuminates what might seem an erratic policy on how labour is divided and jobs are structured. Those who were directly recruited for their relevant experience (e.g. Ann for her lecturing experience, Tom for his Access Control thesis at College) are not generally shifted across projects. In contrast, programmers who entered the company with various credentials but little or no work experience are frequently shifted between projects and/or the tasks they are assigned, to offer a mix of design and programming work.

There would appear to be three major patterns of job structuring within this company. The R&D jobs are dependent on recruiting highly specialized graduates into very specific 'occupational' job niches, in the sense that the R&D jobs are structured to exploit the graduate's specialist technical expertise. This kind of job-holder has few opportunities for learning the company's business (i.e. incorporating an 'organizational' component into their skill base). If such job-holders wish to progress their career, they will need to leave the company for a similar (though, presumably, better) specialist 'occupational' job elsewhere.

The second pattern of job structuring is evident with recruits normally coming in at middle or senior rank ports of entry, who are hired for their specific skills and competences in various aspects of the business outside their immediate technical knowledge, for example, Ultan for his managerial experience gained in other software houses; George, an ex-technical sales rep from a rival company, joining Pre-Sales Support. These particular workers (and no others) come with a particular kind of know-how which makes them valuable to the company. They are not a general resource – unlike, say, contract staff or junior programmers – but possess a career track record, which the company can exploit. Their jobs, in a sense, are custom-built to fit them.

The third pattern of job structuring most typically characterizes the organization of software work in the firm. Here, most of the staff have been recruited through a single junior port of entry. Though most of them initially carry the same job title – Trainee Programmer — the kind and quality of work experience they gain is dependent on which tasks they are assigned to. These jobs, which are designed to facilitate a gradual process of learning-by-doing, are the most interesting for the purposes of this paper.

In this company, access to doing more skilled forms of work (ones which demand a greater combinatory range of technical and business competences) only becomes available through a silent career route which begins with programming: it is the worker's gradual acquisition of appropriate experience which guarantees their eventual allocation to doing analysis-type work. In this quiet context of learning-by-doing in a company which eschews formal graded promotion steps, the seemingly arbitrary allocation process of any available junior workers to any necessary job becomes immensely important in shaping the worker's subsequent career chances.

Informality and 'The Lads' in the Formation of Software Careers

Though management control over the labour process is premised on responsible autonomy strategies, there is always more than one way for control to be exercised over the way work is done (see Storey, 1985). In an overtly informal, collegiate workplace such as this company espouses, one potent means of control, unproblematically assumed by management and staff alike, refers to the social relationships which are brought into the workplace from outside (see Collinson and Knights, 1985). The social ties between the lads – transplanted quite 'naturally' into job-related networks – provides them with a resource for shaping their present and future work which is not available to those outside the circle. Usually without any conscious discrimination, it is nevertheless the lads who do best at strengthening the organizational component of their skill base over time.

The lads are easy to identify – in SSDU, they include Fergus, Jack, Michael, Declan and Fintan – but hard to define. They are young and single (or, at least, childless), though not all young men belong to the lads: Frank is excluded (he was considered 'a bit of a wally') and Sean is struggling on the perimeter (he is socially awkward and a teetotaller and he does not play football). They enjoy mutually good relationships with the managers (most of whom are ex-lads anyway) and with the women they collectively like. Their conversational style is bantering and frequently witty. They move in a group. They eat lunch together, either outside or in the canteen, but never issue general invitations to anyone to join them. At lunch, they are passively welcoming if some of the women go to sit with them, but they themselves would never voluntarily join a women's table. They drink together one or two evenings in the week, they play poker, and most play soccer regularly (though not necessarily with each other).

The lads constitute the dominant grapevine through which crucial pieces of seemingly extraneous bits of work-related information are traded. One example is the negotiation of the Performance Bonus. Since the company is organized as a 'professional' office, nobody is paid official overtime, though quite considerable amounts of overtime are done. Instead, staff and managers are paid a performance bonus every six months, which is partially dependent on the half-yearly audited profit position of the company as a whole. However, for each individual, it is also dependent on how their own project has originally been costed out. As Fergus pointed out:

> Not that many people know exactly how those costings are done. I mean, I'd tell the lads here and that. But it doesn't go up on the notice board or anything. Anyway, my bonus is always good. I mean, I know how the sales costings are done – sure, I *do* them half the time! – and they are just guesses. If they tried to cut my bonus for some wacky reason like that a project had gone over its estimated cost, I'd kick up murder.

But not everyone knows (or can successfully argue) that the costings are wacky – only Fergus, and whomever he chooses to tell.

The Employee Appraisal provides another example of how the network of the lads offers extra information to its members in negotiating their working conditions and likely activities for the upcoming year. Fergus explained:

> It's a really good system in the end. OK, you're in there on your own for maybe three hours. But it keeps you on your toes. It's a test of how well you can negotiate. Like, I usually work about sixty hours a week. For ten weeks last summer, I worked over a hundred hours a week for that whole period. But I wouldn't look for a one-off payment or anything like that. It would weaken my career in the long

run. I'd lose my flexibility. Instead, I go up there and I say 'I want a 20 per cent pay rise'. They say 'Why?'. I say 'I've worked an average of x hours over this time, and I've done this and that and the other. How do you intend to recompense me?' If I'd settled for a bonus, they'd say 'But we've paid you already'. This way, they must acknowledge me. They can see for themselves how I can bargain, negotiate and so on. They can see what I am worth to them out in the field. It really sorts out the men from the boys.

While Conor (whose first appraisal was due) was being groomed on good tactics by Jack and Michael, people like Frank or Ann or Sean were not. And haggling – whether with customers or your own management – is a skill that is learnt. It is surely an advantage to find yourself in a network where you can quietly pick up tips about how to be one of 'the men' – tips which extend well beyond the immediate pay bargaining foibles of your own management. For instance, in SSDU, exposure to learning how to solve novel or difficult problems comes in the form of ploughing through company standards manuals on your own, or being (informally) offered assistance from your peers. The lads, who are buddies anyway, find it easier to offer and receive the latter (more useful) kind of help.

Through practices such as these, the lads act as an important, albeit informal, means of stratifying access to skills, rewards and job opportunities from within the internal labour market of the company. Since they are in the best position to capitalize on the firm's semi-formal structuring of work, we can see why the absence of an extensive, standardized promotion ladder is an environment which they value, since for them it does not constitute a barrier.

Career Moves and The Lads – Tearing along the Dotted Line

The informality which characterizes software development work in this case study is not peculiar just to this company. Kanter (1984) schematizes career steps within and between high-tech firms as a series of 'dotted lines' rather than formal structures: she argues that the lack of acknowledged supervisory layers simply disguises alternative expressions of authority chains. For example, Fergus did not have any apparent managerial function when he proposed to set up a new EPOS project, yet it was emphatically his work. He initiated it; he requested an assistant from Ultan and got Jack – a 23-year-old Trainee Programmer and one of the lads – onto the job; he exercises authority for overseeing how it is done; and he teaches Jack, along the way, how to do it himself.

The dotted lines which characterize the structuring of software work will not only affect the shaping of career routes within a firm, but will also have implications for how a worker fares on the external labour market (see Gabriel and Holzapfl, 1981). Two of the career resources Heimer (1984) notes are access to information about other jobs, and the dissemination outwards and upwards of knowledge about a worker's competences. The informality of exchanging news about jobs in a dotted-line environment means that a network such as the lads can act as an important local power site in the spreading of information about other jobs (see Grieco, 1985). For example, one of the programmers had gone on holiday to Australia and decided to call in to the company's branch office there. (The Irish offices of this multinational do not advertise vacancies in branch offices abroad.) He was promptly offered a job – and four other jobs as well. We can readily see how it was somewhat in his personal gift both to recommend certain other colleagues for interview, and to notify whomever he wanted that jobs were going. Five people left in one month to go to Australia, as it happened, all of them lads.

The informal dotted-line network chains will also extend outside the company. Those who are marginal to the network will be less well placed to pick up word on the considerable number of 'hand-picked' jobs, mainly in small firms, which are not formally advertised (see Granovetter, 1984). Ultan, for instance, had set himself up to be head-hunted into this company by telling his contacts in other firms that he was looking for a change. This company's senior management heard of this – indeed, the grapevine is a most efficient recruitment channel since it is based on the trading of personal contacts (see Preston, 1986; Winstanley, 1986) – and Ultan was interviewed and hired. Since small high-tech firms are a major source of high-skill employment abroad, especially in the US and England (see Anderson, 1982; Hall *et al*., 1985; Oakey, 1984), those who are marginal to the dominant information network may be somewhat disadvantaged in gradually trading up their jobs, based on a usual strategy in software of moving *between* firms to shape a career.

As lateral moves between firms constitute a most important route for career advancement in software, an ironic situation can arise in the differential formation of software careers: namely, those who are marginal to the lads may find themselves 'stuck' in primary jobs, while their laddish colleagues flit lucratively through an upwardly spiralling series of seemingly secondary peripheral jobs (see Brusco and Sabel, 1981; Rubery and Wilkinson, 1981). However, there are two major provisos to be made against this kind of general proposition on external labour market movement.

First, women are not, of course, excluded from giving or receiving job-related information through the social networks of the office. The lads do not constitute a conspiratorial network. The major constraint on women's mobility in the external labour market is not the lads per se, but that they are typically less able, by virtue of their marital or parental status, to exploit the information they *do* receive about better jobs elsewhere (see Campbell, 1988).

Second, within Ireland, moving to a small high-tech firm does not necessarily mean that either the quality of the job, or its future prospects, go without saying. Many Irish software houses do not engage in extensive development work, and the possibilities for an individual to garner a broad range of software skills by moving to other Irish houses are limited. As indigenous Irish software companies are heavily grant-aided, these firms are highly vulnerable both to changing national technology policies and to competition in a small domestic market. The most attractive jobs in Irish software are in fact offered by firms such as the company in this case study. So long as the individual has a personal commitment to remaining in Ireland, the dotted-line job information grapevine runs towards – rather than away from – the multinational Irish branch offices. It was fear of redundancy which prompted both Ultan and Mary to want to leave their respective small companies for this one, with Ultan coming through the grapevine, and Mary through an employment agency.

Even with those two provisos, the basic point about the dynamics of the internal labour market remains: the insiders to the dominant job-related information network have better chances of hearing about job opportunities, and, equally important, of gaining a reputation amongst the managements (perhaps, especially, their own) who have the authority to promote staff.

The insiders are also better placed, as we have seen, to pick up the quiet 'tricks of the trade', which augment the skill range of the worker over time. Within this company, one of the most important tricks to pull off is to acquire direct experience of the necessary business know-how for the successful pricing, design and implementation of technical projects. The concluding section of this chapter looks at the differential chances of some of the staff in this company in acquiring just such a component to their skill base, and in being recognized and rewarded for having it.

Sponsorship and The Lads

Jack provides a nice example of a young lad who is being groomed by both Ultan and Fergus to become the latest 'key member' of the company's programming staff. When Fergus had first proposed the risks and benefits of pursuing the EPOS project to his senior management, his presentation had included that assigning 'somebody good' was essential if the project was to pay off. He had specifically asked for either Jack or Dave to work with him (Ultan decided that Jack was easier to release at the time). Jack, for his part, was 'really glad that Fergus managed it wangle it': 'When you learn to do business specifications and all that ... well, then, you're really a designer after that, and then you can go anywhere.'

Both Ultan and Fergus were explicit in praising Jack's work (he is 'speedy', 'inventive', 'hard-working', 'really on the ball on site visits'). Finding themselves in a position to reward him – to cultivate him in a way which can only enhance his career whether within or outside this particular company – they were happy to assign him to the EPOS project because he was 'a really good guy'. It was Jack's demonstrated worth which provided the first basis for his selection as Fergus' apprentice. However, we could equally argue that Mary demonstrates exactly the same verve and discipline which won Jack such favourable notice. But, Mary, for her part, feels a bit stuck.

She is an interesting instance of how a skilled and trusted staff member, working in a weak division of labour which encourages her to exercise her autonomy, is nevertheless thwarted in her career. Mary's job as Technical Support is only loosely specified and, like the lads, she has used her job to find opportunities for shaping it in the direction she wants her career to go (in her case, Sales). Yet unlike, say, Jack, the 'signals' she sends out to her colleagues and managers have not been picked up in a way which facilitates her transfer into a preferred job. She said:

> Technical Support can often be a good stepping stone into Sales. Within this area, and because I work very much on my own, I've cultivated a whole new angle. In my job as *I* do it, I do quite a deal of Sales Support as opposed to Technical Support. And that's very much my own choice, and very much the area I wish to work in. I've created a niche for myself, as people *do* use the channels, and the sales angle here is the most important function. But it's extremely difficult to transfer. You have to be, kind of, *sponsored* by someone like Gerard [a senior Sales manager]. And that's the problem. They tell you that you just don't have enough credibility with the

customers, but it's really that you don't have much credibility with them.

It would seem, then, that in Crompton and Sanderson's (1986) terms, Mary has greater difficulties than Jack, or other lads, in forming a careerist strategy within the company. If having the ability is the first prerequisite for moving up, being *sponsored* by someone higher comes a very close second. Here we find the crucial difference between Jack's and Mary's career chances: her ability to disseminate knowledge about her extra-curricular sales competences in an upward or lateral direction is thwarted by the absence of a listening patron. While her stature as a trusted worker gives her some autonomy over defining the terms of the work she will do, it does not follow that she will get credit for that work:

> I've done considerable selling, if you want to call it that, by making myself available as a Sales Support Person to the reps. And they use me. That's fine. I use them as well, to learn more about selling. But they get the credit on the sales. It goes into their bonuses, not mine. So, while I'm making sure I get the exposure to selling and the ups and downs that that involves, I still don't get the credit for it. It's as if I didn't have the exposure in the first place.

Ann is another person who could find herself being thwarted in her preferred career path. Like Mary, the issue of sponsorship is critical, though in Ann's case the patronage problem expresses itself in a different way. In her appraisal session she had asked to be moved from her *de facto* position as Trainer to specification work. Ultan, though, was only prepared to praise Ann's work in the following terms:

> Oh, Ann is a real gem. She has been wonderful on the training end of things. She's clear and coherent and she has a wonderful manner with people. She is probably the best trainer this company could hope to get. Who could replace her? I'd expect she'd stay training. That is certainly what I am recommending.

Ann's manager and patron – Ultan – will most likely sponsor Ann to stay put, because she is 'the best'. Like Mary, then, whatever other competences Ann may invent for herself in defining her job, she may not be able to translate those competences into a transfer out of training and into the 'action' areas. She may well find herself being highly-valued in the company but, lacking a sponsor, somewhat stuck in moving towards the core activities which underpin a successful commercial software career.

The three stories I have presented here are sufficient to make the point: providing a member of the lads can demonstrate that he has the necessary drive and ability to become 'one of the men', the chances are reasonable that he will receive positive sponsorship from his colleagues and managers to enable him to obtain an informal promotion into learning software's core skills. In contrast, non-lads (Ann, Mary and, indeed, men like Frank) may suffer either from an absence of sponsorship (Mary, Frank) or sponsorship of a detrimental kind (Ann).

Since the lads can rely on exploiting this career resource which is invisible in the sense that neither its power nor its practices find any formal expression in the structuring and management of software work, the lads 'just naturally' progress higher and faster through the skill hierarchy. Fergus, Michael, Declan, and even Jack are already more occupationally and organizationally mobile than the egalitarian job title of Programmer would suggest. Their designing skills, business flair and client contacts favour their gradual emergence as independent mobile professionals in the external occupational labour market (see Winstanley, 1986), and the key positions they occupy within the internal labour market suggest that they can more readily achieve the shift from 'being managed' to 'being manager' over the course of their organizational career within this company. In this informally-organized and collegiate workplace, it is, disproportionately, the lads who emerge as the occupational winners.

Note

An earlier draft of this chapter appeared as a working paper in the Edinburgh PICT (Programme on Information and Communications Technology) Working Paper series (No. 33).

References

ANDERSON, A. (1982) *Computing Skills Study*, London, IMS.

BAILYN, L. (1977) 'Involvement and Accommodation in Technical Careers: An Inquiry into the Relation to Work at Mid-Career', in VAN MAANEN, J. (Ed.) *Organisational Careers: Some New Perspectives*, New York, John Wiley.

BRUSCO, S. and SABEL, C. (1981) 'Artisan Production and Economic Growth', in WILKINSON, F. (Ed.) *The Dynamics of Labour Market Segmentation*, London, Academic Press.

CAMPBELL, K. (1988) 'Gender Differences in Job-Related Networks', *Work and Occupations*, vol. 15, no. 2, pp. 179–200.

CAUSER, G. and JONES, C. (1990) 'Technical Workers, Work Organisation and Career Structures in the Electronics Industry', paper presented to the Labour Process Conference, Aston University.

COLLINSON, D. and KNIGHTS, D. (1985) 'Jobs for the Boys: Recruitment into Life Insurance Sales', *EOC Research Bulletin*, 9 (Spring), Manchester, Equal Opportunities Commission.

CROMPTON, R. and SANDERSON, K. (1986) 'Credentials and Careers: Some Implications of the Increase in Professional Qualifications amongst Women', *Sociology*, vol. 20, no. 1.

DAVIES, J. (1985) 'Patterns and Paradoxes of Trainers' Careers: The Implications for the Influence of Training', *Journal of European Industrial Training*, vol. 9, no, 2.

FRIEDMAN, A. (1989) *Computer Systems Development: History, Organisation and Implementation*, John Wiley and Sons.

GABRIEL, J. and HOLZAPFL, F. (1981) 'Entrepreneurial Strategies of Adjustment and Internal Labour Markets', in WILKINSON, F. (Ed.) *The Dynamics of Labour Market Segmentation*, London, Academic Press.

GINZBERG, M. and BAROUDI, J. (1988) 'MIS Careers – A Theoretical Perspective', *Communications of the ACM*, vol. 31, no. 5.

GRANOVETTER, M. (1984) 'Small is Bountiful: Labor Markets and Establishment Size', *American Sociological Review*, 49, pp. 323–34.

GRIECO, M. (1985) 'Social Networks in Labour Migration', *Industrial Relations Journal*, vol. 16, no. 4.

GRIFFITHS, D. (1981) 'Job Evaluation, Technical Expertise and Dual Ladders in Research and Development', *Personnel Review*, vol. 10, no. 4.

HALL, P., MARKUSEN, A., OSBORN, R. and WACHSMAN, B. (1985) 'The American Computer Software Industry: Economic Development Prospects', in HALL, P. and MARKUSEN, A. (Eds) *Silicon Landscapes*, Allen and Unwin.

HEIMER, C. (1984) 'Organisational and Individual Control of Career Development in Engineering Project Work', *Acta Sociologica*, vol. 27, no. 4, p. 283–310.

KANTER, R.M. (1984) 'Variations in Managerial Career Structures in High-Technology Firms: The Impact of Organisational Characteristics on Internal Labour Market Structures', in OSTERMAN, P. (Ed.) *Internal Labour Markets*, MIT Press.

OAKEY, R. (1984) *High Technology Small Firms*, London, Frances Pinter.

PRESTON, A. (1986) 'Interactions and Arrangements in the Process of Informing', *Accounting, Organisations and Society*, vol. 11, no. 6.

RUBERY, J. (1978) 'Structured Labour Markets, Worker Organisation and Low Pay', *Cambridge Journal of Economics*, 2, pp. 17–36.

RUBERY, J. and WILKINSON, F. (1981) 'Outwork and Segmented Labour Markets', in WILKINSON, F. (Ed.) *The Dynamics of Labour Market Segmentation*, London, Academic Press.

STOREY, J. (1985) 'The Means of Management Control', *Sociology*, vol. 19, no. 2.

WINSTANLEY, D. (1986) 'Recruitment Strategies as a Means of Managerial Control of Technological Labour', paper presented to the Labour Process Conference, Aston University.

List of Contributors

Danielle Chabaud-Rychter is a researcher in sociology in the Group for Studies on the Social and Sexual Division of Work (GEDISST) in Paris, a laboratory of the French National Centre for Scientific Research (CNRS) and the Research Institute on Contemporary Societies (IRESCO). Her research has dealt with gender relations, domestic work and industrial work. She is currently researching the innovation, production, distribution and usage processes of everyday technical objects. Her publications include *Espace et temps du travail domestique* (with Dominique Fougeyrollas-Schwebel and Françoise Sonthonnax, Paris, Méridiens-Klincksieck, 1985), and 'Women Users in the Design Process of a Food Robot: Innovation in a French Domestic Appliance Company' in Cynthia Cockburn and Ruža Fürst-Dilić (Eds), *Bringing Technology Home: Gender and Technology in a Changing Europe* (Buckingham, Philadelphia, Open University Press, 1994).

Valerie Frissen is an assistant professor at the Department of Communication, University of Amsterdam. She teaches media studies, gender studies and research methodology at this department. Her research and publications focus on the uses of communication and information technologies in everyday life and on gender issues. She is also one of the coordinators of GRANITE, an international network on Gender and New Information Technologies.

Rosalind Gill is a Lecturer in the Sociology of Communications, and a Research Fellow at the Centre for Research into Innovation, Culture and Technology (CRICT), Brunel University. Her work is concerned with issues about gender and representation, and she is author of *Media, Gender and Culture* (Polity, forthcoming).

Keith Grint is a University Lecturer in Management Studies and Fellow in Organizational Behaviour at Templeton College, Oxford University. He has published papers on Women and Inequality, Japanization, Reengineering, Appraisal Systems, Black Workers, the Social Construction of Computer User Problems, Fatalism, Utopia and Social Theory. His *Sociology of Work* (1991) was published by Polity Press and he is currently completing a *Sociology of Management* and, with Steve Woolgar, *Deus ex Machina*.

Tove Håpnes is a Research Fellow at the Centre for Technology and Society at the University of Trondheim, Norway. She has worked on social studies of computer science, its historical development in Norway, and the present gender relations within different computer science studies at Norwegian universities. Currently she is studying the cultural integration of information and communication technology in Norwegian households.

Eric Hirsch is a Lecturer in Social Anthropology in the Department of Human Sciences at Brunel University. He has undertaken field research in Papua New Guinea and more recently in Southeast England. He is the co-editor of two books, *Consuming Technologies* (Routledge, 1992) and *The Anthropology of Landscape* (Oxford, forthcoming); a co-author of *Technologies of Procreation* (Manchester University Press, 1993); and is currently completing a monograph based on his research in Papua New Guinea.

Susan Ormrod has been a lecturer in the Department of Innovation Studies at the University of East London. Previously she was a researcher in the Centre for Research in Gender, Ethnicity and Social Change at City University, London, and in the Department of Psychology at the University of Manchester. Her research interests include social theory and feminism, and the social analysis of technology. She is co-author with Cynthia Cockburn of *Gender and Technology in the Making* (Sage, 1993).

Vicky Singleton worked as a Registered General Nurse before studying for a degree in psychology. She recently completed a PhD, *Science, Women and Ambivalence*, from which an article appeared in *Social Studies of Science* and a further article is to appear in a collection *Differences in Medicine*. Vicky works as a Lecturer in the School of Independent Studies and the Centre for Science Studies and Science Policy at Lancaster University, tutoring students' research on women, health and technology. Her interests include the public understanding of science and technology, the relation of feminist theorizing to social constructivism, and medical sociology. Her current research focus is public and professional responses to genetically engineered medical products.

Knut H. Sørensen is Professor in Sociology of Technology at the University of Trondheim and director of the Centre for Technology and Society. His main research interests are social studies of engineers and computer specialists, knowledge transfer, gender and technology, and technology and everyday life. He has published several papers and articles on gender and technology, in, for example, *Acta Sociologica* and *Social Studies of Science*. His most recent book is *Frankenstein's Dilemma* (Oslo, Ad Notam-Gyldendal, 1992, in Norwegian, together with Håkon and Andersen).

Margaret Tierney has been a Research Fellow at the Research Centre for Social Sciences, Edinburgh University, since 1990. Her research interests and publications are in the area of the evolution and management of the computing occupations; the management of strategic technical innovation in financial services; and the genesis and use of formal methods of software development.

Steve Woolgar is Professor of Sociology and Director of CRICT (Centre for Research into Innovation, Culture and Technology) at Brunel, the University of West London. He has published extensively in social studies of science and technology and is the author of *Laboratory Life: The Construction of Scientific Facts* (with Bruno Latour, Princeton, 1986); and editor of *Knowledge and Reflexivity* (Sage, 1988) and *Representation in Scientific Practice* (with Michael Lynch, MIT Press, 1990). He is currently researching the textual and reflexive dimensions of new technologies, and exploring the significance of social studies of science and technology for social theory.

Index